To the Memory

of

PIUS PARSCH

Augustinian Canon of Klosterneuburg
May 18, 1884–March 11, 1954

ABBREVIATIONS

CCL   *Corpus Christianorum, Series Latina*. Turnhout, 1953–
CL   Vatican II, Constitution on the Sacred Liturgy
DS   Henry Denzinger and Adolf Schönmetzer, *Enchiridion symbolorum*. 32nd ed. Freiburg, 1963.
DV   *Dei Verbum:* Dogmatic Constitution on Divine Revelation
Flannery   Austin Flannery, O.P., General Editor, *Vatican II: The Conciliar and Postconciliar Documents*. Collegeville, 1975.
GI   *General Instruction of the Roman Missal*
ICEL   International Committee on English in the Liturgy
LG   *Lumen Gentium:* Dogmatic Constitution on the Church
PC   *Perfectae Caritatis:* Decree on the Up-to-Date Renewal of Religious Life
PG   *Patrologia Graeca*, ed. J.-P. Migne. Paris, 1857–66
PL   *Patrologia Latina*, ed. J.-P. Migne, Paris, 1844–64
PO   *Presbyterorum Ordinis:* Decree on the Ministry and Life of Priests
SC   *Sources chrétiennes*. Paris, 1942–
TPS   *The Pope Speaks*. Washington, D.C., 1954–75; Huntington, Ind., 1975–

THE EUCHARIST

Essence, Form, Celebration

by

Johannes H. Emminghaus

Translated by

Matthew J. O'Connell

THE LITURGICAL PRESS

Collegeville   Minnesota

THE EUCHARIST: ESSENCE, FORM, CELEBRATION is the authorized English version of *Die Messe: Wesen-Gestalt-Vollzug* by Johannes H. Emminghaus; published by Verlag Osterreichisches Katholisches Bibelwerk, Klosterneuburg, Austria.

Nihil obstat: Rev. Joseph C. Kremer, S.T.L., *Censor deputatus*. *Imprimatur*: ✝ George H. Speltz, D.D., Bishop of St. Cloud. October 10, 1978.

ISBN 0-8146-1010-2

PREFACE

For almost fifty years now I have felt a deep sense of gratitude to Pius Parsch. The excellent parish priests at St. Meinolf in Bochum introduced me as a boy not only to service at the altar but to the liturgy itself. Even before my parents gave me my first Schott missal as a Christmas gift in 1928, I had been collecting Parsch's Sunday leaflets (*Lebe mit der Kirche*) that were then being used by the congregation. Later on I acquired his *Messerklärung* [1] and his *Liturgiekalendar*, which, in the form of *Das Jahr des Heiles*, [2] was my companion during my theological studies. When a happy dispensation brought me to the University of Vienna in 1967, and Klosterneuburg, beautifully situated between the Vienna Woods and the Danube, became my chosen home, in gratitude to Pius Parsch I planned to make *Das Jahr des Heiles* accessible to a new generation of my contemporaries (the most recent German edition, the third, had appeared in 1950).

After the Council, however, neither a new edition nor a revision was any longer possible, for reasons both of content and of language. But the basic principle that Parsch had followed was and continues to be valid: The *essence* of the Mass is intelligible only in the light of Christ's institution, as attested in the Scriptures, and of the Church's traditional teaching; the developed *form* or shape of the Mass is intelligible only in the light of Scripture and of the many changes that form has undergone in the

---

[1] *The Liturgy of the Mass*, translated by F. C. Eckhoff (St. Louis, 1936).
[2] *The Church's Year of Grace*, translated in five volumes by William G. Heidt, O.S.B., and others (Collegeville, Minn., 1953–58).

v

course of history, with its periods of flowering and decay; the celebration, finally, is intelligible only in the light of the form and especially of the living faith of men and women at any given time. Consequently, the dedication of this book to Pius Parsch is more than a sign of piety and gratitude; it also indicates the program and aim of the work.

The purpose of the book, then, is entirely practical: to help achieve an objectively true and responsible celebration of the community Mass. In this case, however, "practical" does not mean quickly and easily utilizable, like many of the aids and texts that are being offered to the public in great numbers. I do not intend to spare the reader the necessity of study and reflection, for I want him not only to participate actively but to participate in a way that is fruitful because of faith. This seems to me especially necessary at the present time, now that the texts and rituals have almost all been revised and a new Missal is available. The need now is to live with the new liturgy, to make it increasingly a part of our lives, to understand and celebrate it as both a sign of salvation and a self-expression of the Church. This is the sense in which the purpose of the book is a "practical" one.

As I wrote the book, I had in mind as its potential readers and users my fellow clergymen, along with teachers, catechists, and members of parish liturgical commissions, and not least my students at Vienna, to whom I feel deeply obliged. I have tried to make the book a readable one and have therefore included relatively few footnotes (all of them simple references to sources). I hope, nonetheless, that I have nowhere disillusioned the reader, who in picking up a book of supposedly objective information makes an act of trust in the author. I wish only to realize, in our time, Pius Parsch's wish that a living community should celebrate a living liturgy.

Johannes H. Emminghaus

Klosterneuburg, April 1976

CONTENTS

Introduction

Part One

BASIC STRUCTURE AND HISTORICAL CHANGE
IN THE CELEBRATION OF THE MASS   1

Chapter One

Chapter Two

Part Two

THE COMMUNITY MASS   99

Introduction   101

Chapter One

THE BEGINNING OF THE MASS   104

Chapter Four

THE CONCLUSION   208

INTRODUCTION

Nature and Celebration of the Mass
According to the General Instruction of the
Roman Missal
and the Constitution on the Sacred Liturgy
of Vatican II

I have written this book to help the reader understand and properly celebrate the Mass as reformed in accordance with the decrees of the Second Vatican Council. It is thus an "explanation of the Mass" in the tradition of Pius Parsch, to whom the book is dedicated. This means that the explanation looks both to the biblical foundations of the Mass and to its historical evolution through a tradition almost two thousand years old, with its high points and its low points, its developments that determined the future and its obvious dead ends that required reform and improvement.

We must inquire into both the will of Jesus in instituting the Mass and the long ecclesiastical tradition of its celebration if we are to discern clearly how the permanently valid form of the Mass is to take concrete shape today. Neither criterion alone and in isolation will provide the basis we need. A naïve return to the biblical data alone would amount to a rejection of the historical dimension, and thus of the ecclesial character of the liturgy. A simple historical development or transient adaptation to the demands of the moment, without constant reference to the will of Jesus in instituting the Eucharist, could easily overlook the sacramentality of the Mass and its efficacy for salvation. The Church is not free, however, to turn the Mass into something that would be considered edifying at the moment; she must carry out Christ's command to repeat what he had done.

Now that the liturgy has been reformed, this kind of book may seem to need a justification. Should we, can we, "explain the Mass" at all? If properly celebrated in accordance with the recent reform, should not the Mass be self-explanatory? And if some elements are unclear, should these not be regarded as part of that "mystery of faith" to which the celebrant refers immediately after the consecration?

Liturgy as Sign of Faith

Like all the sacramental signs, the Eucharistic liturgy is a sign of faith. Both sign and faith, however, are not static things but very much alive; and life immediately says "history," since living is a process. Faith is indeed first and foremost a grace given to man by God; from man's standpoint, however, it is at the same time a kind of learning process that depends upon preaching, experiences that are reflected on, all sorts of stimuli, and a whole "mystagogy"; the knowledge is not immediately given in full-blown form. Faith must be constantly nourished by Scripture and the preaching of the Church, especially the Church's teaching of her faith concerning the Mass.

The history of the Mass shows how this faith developed. History also means, however, that the elements of the liturgy that are subject to change may "have suffered from the intrusion of [something] out of harmony with the inner nature of the liturgy" (CL, no. 21; Flannery, p. 9). That this in fact happened is shown by the reforms that were judged necessary after the recent Council. For this reason, it will be profitable to begin by presenting and explaining the sound teaching of the Church in the context of the Bible (Part I, Chapter 1).

The sacramental signs of faith also need some explanation. When Christ instituted each of these signs, he undoubtedly instituted something that was in itself highly meaningful. We must remember, however, that even natural signs never derive their meaning solely from themselves; their vitality always depends in large measure on the experiences and conventions of a given group (for the signs of faith, the group is the Church). Liturgy is by its nature "liturgy that has evolved." A second purpose of this book, therefore, must be to make the meaning of the signs clearer and more intelligible (this was the pastoral aim of the whole Constitution on the Sacred Liturgy of Vatican II).

In the last ten years, a great deal of work has been done, and with notable success, to clarify the meaning of the sacramental signs. The work must, however, be constantly giving an account of itself; it must be accompanied by profound reflection. For example, we must not allow the removal of the language barriers to lead to a complete verbalization of the liturgy; the mystery must be respected even while we seek for intelligibility and rationality. The signs must not be improved solely for their own sake, but in order that they may be and remain signs of faith.

Another purpose of our explanation of the Mass must therefore be to explain the signs and, through interpretation, to make them more intelligible so that the faith expressed in the signs may bear fruit. A "second reform of the liturgy" will be needed for this purpose, now that the liturgical books and rituals have been improved. The aim of that future reform will be to support and nourish the faith through signs that are more easily understood and have a more vital impact.

The Mass as Center and Summit
of the Christian Sacramental Life

The first few articles of the General Instruction [henceforth *GI*] that accompanies the revised Roman Missal give a short summary of the Church's teaching on the Mass; the General Instruction is, in fact, a brief "explanation of the Mass." The first article provides a concise and pregnant description of the nature of the Mass:

> The celebration of the Mass, being the action of Christ and the hierarchically organized people of God, is the center of all Christian life for the Church, universal and local, and for each of the faithful. For the Mass is the climactic expression both of the action whereby God in Christ sanctifies the world, and of the worship that mankind offers to the Father as it adores him through Christ, the Son of God. In the Mass, moreover, the mysteries of redemption are recalled throughout the year, so that they become present in a certain way. All other sacred actions and all the works of Christian life are connected with the Mass, flow from it, and are ordered to it (*GI*, no. 1).

The Mass is thus the summit and center of the individual Christian's life. Through baptism in water and the Holy Spirit, the individual is reborn to faith and rescued from the state of sin and alienation from God into which he had been born in his first birth. He becomes a child of God, receives the forgiveness of his sins, enters into communion with Christ, and becomes a member of the people of God. Through confirmation he becomes even more like the Lord and receives the commission to bear witness to Christ before the world through a life of faith. In the Eucharistic meal he eats the body and drinks the blood of Christ under the signs of bread and wine; he thus gives experiential reality to the unity of God's people as expressed in fraternal love and communion. In the Eucharistic sacrifice of the Church, he shares in the real memorial of Christ's one, all-embracing sacrifice.

Baptism and confirmation initiate the Christian once and for all into the people of God; the Mass, on the other hand, is the ongoing, repeated sign of intimate communion with Christ and of the individual's dedication of his life to God. The Eucharist is thus the abiding proclamation and real application of the redemption that was given to mankind once and for all through the death and resurrection of Christ; it will have this function until he comes again in glory. In the Eucharist the Church and the individual Christian grow to the full stature of Christ. Thus the Mass is the center and summit of a Christian life that is based on faith.

The Mass is more than an act of worship; it is also, and even first, a sacramental application of redemption. In every sacrament God's action is prior to any action of man; he initiates the work of our sanctification, for apart from him we can do nothing (John 15:5). By faith, which seeks its complement in the sacraments, man lays hold of God's offer of salvation; only then, and thereby, can he worship God through Christ and in the Holy Spirit, and adhere to him as he lives his life.

The Mass is the privileged locus of God's saving action toward the baptized and at the same time of the worship of God "in spirit and truth" (John 4:24) by his believing people; in other words, the Mass brings man into a dialogue with God. This movement from God to man and then from man to God — the simultaneous "action of Christ and the . . . people of God" (*GI*, no. 1) — is characteristic of the Mass. Salvation is never simply handed to man on a platter. Even God takes him and his dignity as a person seriously and requires that he work at his own salvation. For this reason, not only in his life generally but even at Mass, he is not a mere recipient, but also, as part of a community, a conscious, active, devout, participating agent.

What is applied to us in the Mass is not simply salvation in its abstract validity and in its finished form, or as an effect of an earlier redemptive action by Christ (in his incarnation, death, resurrection, and ascension). No, the saving event itself, which happened once and for all in historical time, becomes present "sacramentally," or in sensible signs. By this means we are vitally related to the saving actions that Christ did "for us," so that the historically unique Christ-event is not only an objective reality for us, but is on each occasion really present to us.

Time, after all, is only a relational thing, measuring the succession of events that occur within our created world. God's action, on the other hand, transcends time. In the symbols of worship, therefore, Christ's saving action achieves a real presence; it is always "here and now." The active subject of this symbolic celebration of worship is the Church, and this means the Lord himself who continues to live and act in her. This is why the first article of the General Instruction, which we have already quoted, says of the mysteries of redemption that "they become present in a certain way," present, that is, in our space and time.

In addition, the whole series of the mysteries of our redemption unfolds sequentially during the liturgical year. The unfolding is something more than a simple pedagogical device geared to man's limited capacity for assimilation at any given moment. It is not the proclamation in the liturgy of the word alone that manifests the development; rather, the Eucharistic celebration as a whole is determined by the mystery being celebrated on each feast. For this reason, the Constitution on the Sacred Liturgy says:

> Holy Mother Church believes that it is for her to celebrate the saving work of her divine Spouse in a sacred commemoration on certain days throughout the course of the year. Once each week, on the day which she has called the Lord's Day, she keeps the memory of the Lord's resurrection. She also celebrates it once every year, together with his blessed passion, at Easter, that most solemn of all feasts.
>
> In the course of the year, moreover, she unfolds the whole mystery of Christ from the incarnation and nativity to the ascension, to Pentecost and the expectation of the blessed hope of the coming of the Lord.
>
> Thus recalling the mysteries of the redemption, she opens up to the faithful the riches of her Lord's powers and merits, so that these are in some way made present for all time; the faithful lay hold of them and are filled with saving grace (*CL*, no. 102; Flannery, pp. 28–29).

The Mass as Center of the Church's Self-Actuation in Proclamation, Service of the World, and Liturgy

The Mass is also the center of the Church's life; this is to say that it is part of a larger whole, and not itself the whole. The Dogmatic Constitution on the Church of the Second Vatican Council makes it clear that there are three essential elements in the nature and activity of the Church: proclamation that awakens faith and revitalizes it, service to the world, and liturgy (cf. *LG*, nos. 9–10). In this context, "liturgy" is equivalent to "application of salvation through the sacraments." The three elements — proclamation, loving service, and liturgy — form an indissoluble unity; no one of them can continue to exist without the other two. That is why from a very early date the Church linked her proclamation (liturgy of the word) and her caritative undertakings (fraternal meal; later, the collections for special needs of the poor) to the celebration of the Eucharist, at least in a symbolic way.

The preaching and missionary efforts of the Church in behalf of the Good News, as well as the Church's service of the world necessarily extend beyond the celebration of the Mass; they cannot be adequately carried out solely within the Eucharist. Yet the Eucharist remains the center and summit of the Church's entire activity. Even other liturgical celebrations (independent liturgies of the word, the catechesis of children and adults, participation in the Liturgy of the Hours, etc.) draw their vitality from the mystery of the Eucharist. The same is true when Christians meet, or live together, in the name of Jesus, and the Lord is consequently in their midst (Matthew 18:20). "All other sacred actions and all the works of Christian life are connected with the Mass, flow from it, and are ordered to it" (*GI*, no. 1).

Furthermore, meditation, the private reading of the Scriptures, personal prayer, veneration of the Eucharistic species apart from Mass, and other practices are necessary to support the liturgical celebration and to fill it with personal life. The isolated celebration of the Mass cannot by itself accomplish all their tasks, especially since time limits must often be placed upon the liturgical celebration. Only in this larger context and framework is the Mass truly the center of all piety and vital commitment to God.

The Hierarchically Ordered People of God
as Active Subject of the Liturgy

When the people of God gathers for the celebration of Mass, it is not an amorphous, undifferentiated mass of individuals, but is "hierarchically organized" (*GI*, no. 1). It is true enough that by reason of baptism and confirmation, the people as a whole possesses the dignity of being a chosen race, a royal priesthood, a holy nation, and a people belonging to God (1 Peter 2:9); it is a holy priesthood, set apart to offer spiritual sacrifices to God (1 Peter 2:5). In the Church, however, there is also the special *office* of servant of Christ and administrator of the mysteries of God (cf. 1 Cor. 4:1). For just as the Father had sent Christ as Shepherd, Teacher, and Priest, so he sent the apostles in the same role (John 20:21). The apostles in turn, by imposing hands, commissioned their successors to the same office of preaching, leadership, and administration of the sacraments (an office that contains the three grades of bishop, priest, and deacon).

In the last analysis, of course, it is always Christ himself who teaches, unites, and sanctifies. Those appointed to office do, however, represent him; that is, they body him forth, as it were, and act in his name. For this reason, it belongs to them to preside over the proclamation during the liturgy of the word and over the Eucharist proper. Moreover, because of the collegiality of all bishops and their respective presbyteries, the ordained local officials guarantee the unity of the local community with the entire one Church of Christ, in which the supreme office is the Petrine office of the Bishop of Rome.

All offices and special callings and talents (charisms) share the task of building up the Body of Christ. They are meant "for the equipment of the saints, for the work of ministry, for building up the body of Christ, until we all attain to the unity of the faith and of the knowledge of the Son of God, to mature manhood, to the measure of the stature of the fulness of Christ" (Eph. 4:12-13). In the community that is centered on the Eucharist, it is Christ himself, in the last analysis, who unites the whole Body of the Church and preserves it in unity (Eph. 4:16). He himself is present and active in the sacrifice of the Mass, being represented by the person who exercises the priestly office. He is present also (but not only) under the Eucharistic species and in all the sacraments. He is present in his word, which he himself speaks in the person of the proclaimer when the Sacred Scriptures are read in the Church. Finally, he is present in the praying and singing of God's priestly people, whenever two or three are gathered in his name (Matthew 18:20; see *CL*, no. 7a).

The organic structure of the Church and of the community that celebrates divine service requires an order and articulation that will assure unity (not uniformity!). "For as in one body we have many members, and all the members do not have the same function, so we, though many, are one body in Christ and individually members one of another. Having gifts that differ according to the grace given to us, let us use them" (Rom. 12:4-6). Equality in the Church, as in any society, does not consist in sameness or in having everyone on the same level; it means that all have the same dignity and calling. This is not to deny, of course, that privilege unmatched by readiness to serve would be an injustice to the whole Body. Offices exist in the Church only for the sake of the community of Christ, as services to and in it.

Those who hold office are not there to domineer over the faith of the community (2 Cor. 1:24) or over its liturgy. Laws governing public worship have developed out of the basic structure of the sacramental signs as experienced in the course of the two-thousand-year history of the liturgy; these laws resist the vagaries of subjectivity and attest the unity of the Church as a whole. There must be as much unity as is needed — but *only* as much as is needed. A community's worship requires a balance between order and spontaneity. Arbitrariness on the part of the president of the liturgy, over and above the quite variable norms given in the liturgical books, would be nothing but a reprehensible form of clericalism, for then the community would be a captive audience for the pet ideas and private opinions of the president.

The existence of law in the Church does not deny that the Church is a Church of love, since in the Church the order of law may not and must not become a tool for the exercise of power, but is meant as a benefit and a guarantee of the freedom proper to every Christian. Among the basic principles governing the communal life of modern societies is that those who are to be affected by any action should be heard. Only by the analogous application of this principle to the Church can the active, communal, and yet spontaneous participation of the entire people of God be assured. For this reason, the General Instruction says:

> It is extremely important that the celebration of the Mass, or Lord's Supper, be so ordered that the ministers and the faithful who participate in it, each exercising his proper role, may derive in fuller measure the fruits for which Christ the Lord instituted the Eucharistic sacrifice of his body and blood and entrusted it to his beloved spouse, the Church, as a memorial of his passion and resurrection.
>
> This order and purpose will be achieved if consideration is given to the nature and circumstances of each assembly and the whole celebration is so organized that it fosters a conscious, active, and full participation of the faithful, a participation of mind and body, inspired by fervent faith, hope, and love. That is the kind of participation the Church wants and the celebration calls for by its very nature. Moreover, the Christian people, by reason of their baptism, have a right and duty to celebrate the liturgy in this way (*GI*, nos. 2–3).

Article 1 of the General Instruction explained the significance of the Mass as center and summit of Christian life. Articles 2 and 3 look more closely at the form of the Mass.

Form of the Eucharistic Celebration: Meal and Sacrifice

The Mass is both the "Lord's Supper" and the "sacrifice of his body and blood" (*GI*, no. 2). There is good reason for mentioning the meal aspect of the Mass first, since in its basic structure, with which Articles 2 and 3 are concerned, the Mass is a rite derived from a meal, not from a sacrifice. As a memorial of his pasch, the Lord left his Church the Eucharist, that is, the prayer of thanksgiving over bread and wine as elements of a meal. It was precisely this that he bade her do in memory of him. He did not tell her to carry out a sacrificial rite, that is, something which in the history of religions involves the destruction, burning, or burial of some matter meant for sacrifice. He wanted to remain present with his community under the form of bread and wine as representing his body that was "given" and his blood that was "poured out" for us and "for the forgiveness of sins." It is important, then, that in celebrating the memorial of the Lord we give careful consideration to the meal aspect of the Eucharist.

Behind and above this meal form, however, lies the reality of the sacrifice of Christ and the Church. "Sacrifice" here is to be taken in its proper sense of self-giving; it does not refer primarily to the external accomplishment of a sacrificial ritual. In the history of religions and even under the old covenant, "sacrifice" means the surrender of things man needs for his life and by which he sets a great deal of store, but which he gives over to God by irreversibly removing them from his own use. In this sense, sacrifice is only a symbol of the giving of one's life, which is the true sacrifice. Were this not the case, sacrifice could easily degenerate into a "placating of the gods," in which the fulfillment of man's real religious duty would not be taken seriously; it could degenerate, in other words, into the hypocrisy and satisfaction with external works against which the Old Testament prophets had to be constantly on the alert.

Christ's death on the cross is thus the ultimate consequence of, and the symbol that brings to fulfillment, his lifelong obedient dedication to the Father's will; this lifelong self-giving is his real "sacrifice of his life." The Letter to the Hebrews, which interprets Christ's redemptive work as a priestly sacrifice of expiation, puts Psalm 40 on the lips of Jesus as he enters the world, and has him say: "Sacrifices and offerings thou hast not desired, but a body hast thou prepared for me; in burnt offerings and sin offerings thou hast taken no pleasure. Then I said, 'Lo, I have come to do thy will, O God,' as it is written of me in the roll of the book" (Heb. 10:5-7; Ps. 40:7-9).

In the Eucharist the Church enters into this total self-giving of Christ, and we individually attempt to enter into it as fully as we can. When we do this, the Mass becomes our sacrifice too, the expression of our complete surrender to God and his will. Merely to go through the motions of the Mass without this serious and complete dedication of our lives to God would simply be hypocrisy. Paul warns us: "Whoever, therefore, eats the bread or drinks the cup of the Lord in an unworthy manner will be guilty of profaning the body and blood of the Lord. Let a man examine himself, and so eat of the bread and drink of the cup" (1 Cor. 11:27-28).

The Mass a Communal Celebration

It is this interior dimension of self-giving that the General Instruction has in mind when it calls for the "conscious, active, and full participation of the faithful . . . inspired by fervent faith, hope, and love" (*GI*, no. 3).

Only secondarily does the participation involve the proper execution of rites, necessary though this is, since man is a totality composed of body and soul, and since the sacramental sign (the external action that appeals to the senses) should express and bring about the effect of the sacrament. A sacrament depends for its vitality on faith and repentance; otherwise it would be an empty rite as far as the recipient is concerned. The Church teaches not only that a sacrament is an objective and certain means of communicating grace, but also that the effectiveness of the sacrament depends on the disposition and attitude of the recipient, that is, on his faith, hope, and love.

A Christian's membership in the Church is not an abstract, "spiritual" belonging, nor does it mean merely that he feels himself to belong. Rather, being a member means that he is part of the community of the concrete local Church, which comprises a diocese united with its bishop. "In the local Church, the Mass at which the bishop presides with his presbytery and ministers, and in which the holy people of God participates fully and actively, should be regarded as the chief form of Mass, because it is such a richly meaningful sign. For in this form of Mass, the reality of the Church is best expressed" (*GI*, no. 74). But, in the parish Mass, too, the Church is present: "There should also be high regard for Mass celebrated with a community, and especially the parish community, since the latter repre- sents the universal Church in a given time and place, especially at the communal celebration on Sunday" (*GI*, no. 75).

While it is desirable these days that Mass be celebrated from time to time in connection with the pastoral care of specialized groups (children, youth, students, family groups, etc.), it remains true that the local Church becomes a visible and concretely experiential manifestation of the univer- sal Church especially in the parish liturgy attended by people from all age groups and every walk of life.

> The parish is the first organic and organized community in the diocesan Church, and therefore in communion, as the Council says, with the uni- versal Church.
>
> It is our first and normal spiritual family, resulting not so much from the homogeneity of its members, who are from all social classes, but from the dynamic virtue of a specific pastoral ministry, and from the cohesive effectivenss of the same faith and the same charity. . . . The parish is the school of the word of God, the meal of the Eucharistic Bread, the house of fraternal love, the temple of common prayer. And — says the Council — it is "in some manner the visible Church constituted throughout the world."[1]

[1] Paul VI, *È giorno di festa*: Remarks be- fore the Recitation of the *Angelus* (Sep- tember 7, 1969), in *Osservatore Romano*, September 8–9, 1969; translated in *TPS* 14 (1969–70) 258–59. [One word in this transla- tion has been changed as here quoted.] The quotation at the end of the excerpt is from Vatican II's Constitution on the Sacred Liturgy, no. 42.

A principal mark of the Mass liturgy, then, is its community character. It brings Christians together in the name of Jesus and involves the active participation of God's people in the Eucharist. A fundamental principle governing this participation is that each person should do that, and only that, which is in keeping with "his proper role" (*GI*, no. 2).

The same Article goes on to speak of a fruitful participation: The faithful should derive the fruits of salvation in rich measure from the memorial celebration of Christ's death and resurrection. That, after all, is the meaning and intended effect of every sacrament, but especially of the Eucharist. The other sacraments are geared to specific situations in which the human being finds himself: his once-and-for-all initiation into the Church through baptism and confirmation; his healing, if required, through penance and the anointing of the sick; his choice of a state of life through marriage and orders. The Eucharist, however, is the Christian's "daily bread" and the sacrament he most frequently receives; as such, it is the center and summit of his life (*GI*, no. 1).

For the reason just indicated, the "sacramental practice" of a Christian can in large measure be judged by the way he participates in the Sunday Eucharist. This "going to Church" is in fact, and has at all times been regarded as, a good yardstick for measuring his overall attitudes toward the Church. This is why Article 3 calls for a "conscious" participation. In the past there has been a good deal of emphasis on the objective efficacy of the sacraments, especially in medieval Scholasticism and in post-Tridentine theology. It was necessary to oppose those who denied this efficacy, but the polemics led to a somewhat excessive emphasis. The result has perhaps been a onesidedness in Catholic preaching on the sacraments, as though the sacraments had their effect without man's cooperation and were thus a kind of magic.

In a similar way, a one-sided view of the liturgy as an "objective" action of the Church, to be performed in accordance with strictly binding instructions and rubrics as found in the authoritative books and rituals, could easily give the impression that the subjective involvement of minister and recipient was quite secondary and played no decisive role. This impression was deepened by the fact that the ceremonies were performed in a language unintelligible to most people. And yet the sacraments are meant for man as a rational being, that is, a conscious person who is capable of understanding. The liturgy, especially nowadays, requires an intelligent participation.

The new use of the vernacular languages is a valuable help to this end; the linguistic barrier that had so many unfortunate effects has now happily been removed. Liturgy draws its vitality, however, not from words alone, but even more from the signs used. These must be adapted to modern man and his life; he must be able to understand them and put them into practice. Many signs have become part of the liturgy in the course of time. The signs are therefore subject to change and replacement; they may even have to be invented anew, depending on the social and cultural situation (in mission countries, for example, or due to the transition from an agricultural to an industrial civilization). According to Article 3 of the General Instruction, the celebration must take into account "the nature and circumstances of each assembly." This is because signs, even liturgical signs, should be a proclamation, and not a mysterious veil over the reality intended.

It is a notable fact, and one helpful to us moderns, that the basic signs used in the seven sacraments are few in number, and are such that men today can still make intelligent use of them: water and oil, bread and wine, the laying on and extending of hands. Moreover, despite many claims to the contrary, modern man is still familiar with symbols; he meets them in business and advertising, in the area of prestige and social status, in celebrations and gatherings, in abstract painting and technical formulas, though our everyday life and work is frequently more rationalized and verbalized than in earlier cultures.

Even for the sake of humanization and a more humane life, the vital influence of the world of symbols on our age is something very desirable. To bring that world alive should certainly be the aim of our educational efforts, in view of the way in which social relations and the lives of individuals have evidently become diminished, sapless, and impoverished. Fifty years ago, in books that are still valuable,[2] Romano Guardini argued that man needs to experience symbols, not just for the sake of participating in the liturgy, but even for the sake of preserving his humanity.

Against this background the conciliar Constitution on the Sacred Liturgy says:

> With zeal and patience pastors of souls must promote the liturgical instruction of the faithful and also their active participation, both internal and external, taking into account their age, condition, way of life and standard of religious culture. By so doing pastors will be fulfilling one of the chief duties of a faithful dispenser of the mysteries of God, and in this matter they must lead their flock not only by word but also by example (*CL*, no. 19; Flannery, p. 9).

It must be one of our most important tasks today to celebrate the liturgy in a truly human manner. The aim is that no explanation of the Mass should be necessary during the Mass, because the liturgy has become the intelligent, conscious self-expression of the community.

---

[2] *Liturgische Bildung* (Rothenfels, 1923); *Von heiligen Zeichen* (Rothenfels, 1922, 1923; 3rd ed., Mainz, 1927). The second of these books has been translated by G. C. H. Pollen: *Sacred Signs* (London, 1930).

Inasmuch as the Mass is the coordinate, dialogical action of God and men, its very nature requires active participation. We cannot simply accuse people in the past of a purely passive attendance at Sunday Mass; even then, after all, personal prayer sustained the Sunday service (there were exceptions, of course). Usually, however, people did not "pray the Mass"; they rather "prayed during Mass." The Mass, though, is not a sum total of numerous personal prayers; it is a totality, a well-structured whole made up of action, praying, and singing, with individuals carrying out their varied roles in an ordered way. No one person may do everything; neither may all collectively do everything. Like every other community, the community that celebrates the Eucharist is made up of differentiated parts. The first distinction is between president and congregation.

These two active subjects each execute their own part, or delegate it to someone. The president (bishop or priest) acts as leader of the gathering. He acts in the name of Christ when he speaks the prayers that belong to him by his office. He is also a member of the people of God, however, and he prays in their name when he articulates the thanksgiving and petitions of the community (which the community makes its own and acknowledges as its own by its "Amen"). The president is also the official proclaimer and interpreter of God's word. According to circumstances, he can be aided by concelebrants, a deacon, and, usually, a reader.

The community, for its part, may act as a body in word and song, response and acclamation. It may also, especially for actions that a crowd finds it difficult to perform properly, allow itself to be represented by members of the community that are delegated for these actions. Thus, for the more difficult kinds of singing, which require somewhat lengthy training and practice, the community may be represented by the choir or schola with its cantor (the Greek word *scholē* means "leisure" and the school in which the leisure is spent). For the procession with the gifts or such services as the bringing of the liturgical vessels, it is represented by the servers; for help in the singing, by a choirmaster or an organist. Even homely services such as cleaning and polishing the church, laying out the hymnals and other aids, bringing those ill of body or mind to their places for Mass, taking up the collection, and many other tasks, are in the last analysis liturgical tasks, making it possible for a communal celebration to proceed successfully and without hitches.

We speak, therefore, of a distribution of liturgical roles. Each person contributes to the celebration what his office calls for or his abilities allow. Lest the various services be left to chance, so that stopgaps become necessary, assignments must be made and practices held; this is a matter best left to a responsible group, usually the community's liturgical committee. It will also be the task of the committee to organize the education of the community's liturgical consciousness. It must be borne in mind here that the same ideas and methods will not be equally useful everywhere. It is always a concrete community, with its peculiar abilities and limitations, that gathers for its Eucharist.

Also required is a full participation, involving the whole human being. Man is a creature of the senses; only by means of the sensible can he grasp spiritual realities. There is no such thing as a conversation directly between two souls, but only through perceptible words, gestures, or communications mediated by the senses. It is characteristic of every sacrament and all liturgy that to the external there corresponds something internal, to the visible sign the appropriation of God's gifts which are usually invisible. The human body is expressive: attitude and gesture, word and facial expression, attest what is in the mind and heart; conversely, expressive bodily actions such as standing and kneeling, sitting and walking, are helpful in intellectual and spiritual movement or meditation.

Shared outward attitudes (but without anything of the military drill about them) always help the individual experience the oneness of the community.

Finally, and above all, the participation must be marked by piety. The characteristics of participation that we have thus far been discussing had already been mentioned by the Constitution on the Sacred Liturgy (no. 14) before being repeated in the General Instruction. The latter, however, deliberately adds, "inspired by fervent faith, hope, and love" (no. 3). The three virtues are the essence of a Christian life and its fulfillment, and of all piety, whether personal or liturgical. The whole realm of external signs exists for the sake of the really important thing, and liturgical reform means not only a reform of the signs, but first and foremost the deepening of faith. Just as any symbol draws its vitality from the dynamic understanding of existence which the group already shares, but becomes empty and dead when that understanding gradually disappears, so the liturgy depends for its vitality on faith, hope, and love. Without these it is dead.

After ten years of liturgical reform, much has been accomplished as far as externals go. There has been a good deal of adaptation and improvement. If, however, we confuse the means (reform of the signs; a more comprehensive proclamation of the redemptive message) with the end (the renewal of God's people, which was the Council's aim), then we may achieve a greater expertise in the Church's life, but we shall have accomplished nothing that really counts. What we need now is a "second liturgical reform," by which we will interiorly appropriate the purified and improved means of expression in the sacramental life, and thus make of them an authentic self-expression of the Church in her liturgical celebrations.

Part One

Basic Structure and Historical Change in the Celebration of the Mass

1 BASIC STRUCTURE OF THE MASS

A. The Celebration of the Eucharist

The Church celebrates a Eucharist because the Lord at the Last Supper bade her do so: "Do this in remembrance of me" (Luke 22:19; 1 Cor. 11:24). The commission contains two elements: a doing and a remembering, or, more accurately, a remembering in and through the doing. The remembrance, then, is not something static, without relation to action, but rather something dynamic. It is an action — and an action done in union with others, in community. In addition, the doing or acting is not purely spiritual but involves sensible things, so that we may speak of it as an expressive action that manifests and bodies forth its properly spiritual meaning in sensible ways. Herewith we already have the characteristics of the sacramental order and thus of liturgy, even before we say anything at all about the laws governing the construction and structure of the commemorative action the Lord has bidden us repeat.

The action consists in the imitation of a model which the Lord himself provided as a permanent institution. The model was a meal, or, more exactly, an action within a meal: namely, the blessing spoken over bread and wine. It was thus an action that was relatively independent of its context; it could be, and in fact soon was, abstracted from the more extensive action of the total meal. This happened once the larger meal, which provided a framework for this specific action, became the occasion for improprieties and abuses that disturbed and even negated the very meaning of the Eucharistic action (lack of moderation; drunkenness; partisanship).

The blessing over bread and cup in praise of God (*eucharistia* in Greek; *gratiarum actio* or *benedictio* in Latin) included words of Christ which interpreted the gifts of bread and wine that he was giving his disciples to eat. The bread and wine were said to be not only his body and blood, but (in sacrificial language familiar to his Jewish fellows at table) his body "given" and his blood "poured out" as an expiatory offering "for you" and "for all."

1. ESSENCE OF THE EUCHARIST ACCORDING TO THE ACCOUNTS OF INSTITUTION

The action in which Christ established the Eucharist has been recorded for us in the "accounts of institution," which are almost identical in the first three evangelists (Mark 14:22-24; Matthew 26:26-28; Luke 22:19-20). Closely related to these is 1 Corinthians 11:23-25, where Paul reminds his readers of the Lord's legacy. The account is most detailed in Luke, where it reads as follows: "And he took bread, and when he had given thanks he broke it and gave it to them, saying, 'This is my body which is given for you. Do this in remembrance of me.' And likewise the cup after supper, saying, 'This cup which is poured out for you is the new covenant in my blood.'"

Matthew and Mark do not have the interpretative clause "which is given for you" in the blessing of the bread; Paul does have it, however (1 Cor. 11:24). The words over the cup show greater variation in the four accounts. Luke and Paul (in 1 Corinthians) seem to lay special emphasis on the cup, the container holding the wine, as a symbol of the new covenant, while Mark and Matthew speak directly of "the blood of the covenant, to be poured out on behalf of many."

In the four Eucharistic prayers of the Mass, we have a text that conflates all four accounts:

> He took bread, said the blessing, broke the bread
> and gave it to his disciples, saying:
> Take this, all of you, and eat it:
> this is my body which will be given up for you.
> In the same way, he took the cup, filled with wine.
> He gave you thanks, and giving the cup to his disciples, said:
> Take this, all of you, and drink from it:
> this is the cup of my blood,
> the blood of the new and everlasting covenant.
> It will be shed for you and for all men
> so that sins may be forgiven.
> Do this in memory of me (ICEL).

The four traditional texts, now reflected in the Eucharistic prayers, that we call "the accounts of institution" are not a stenographer's report of what Jesus said. By the time they were written down (1 Corinthians around 55 A.D., the three Gospels in the seventies of the first century), people had already been celebrating the Eucharist for a generation or more. The accounts thus give us a picture of the Eucharist as celebrated in the apostolic community; we shall have to discuss this Eucharist and its development later on. At the same time, however, the accounts are intended to be true to the inherited tradition, and the authors are convinced that they are transmitting Jesus' institution with complete fidelity to its form and intention, even while, as we know today, they already reflect a stage in the later development of the celebration, in which the blessings over the bread and over the cup have been made to parallel each other more closely.

At the same time, it is likely that explicative or interpretive phrases have crept into the accounts. These phrases are not really novelties, however, but flow effortlessly from what Jesus said and intended. What had simply been presupposed when he spoke at the Last Supper is now made explicit and brought to the mind's attention. It is thus possible to say that the text has been "theologized" by the addition of interpretive language that clarifies what the community had been doing for some time in a more or less straightforward and unreflective way. The celebration of what the Lord had instituted and ordered to be repeated is older than any theological insight into it.

We must bear in mind, however, that the theological reflection goes back to men who were present at the institution. Most important, it depends on a world of images that is nourished by the Old Testament and is by no means outmoded even today, a world in which Christ and the apostles lived and were fully at home. A further point not to be overlooked is that the biblical authors intended their account to serve as a norm for their contemporaries and for posterity: Thus and not otherwise was the memorial of the Lord to be celebrated, as Paul explicitly says in 1 Corinthians 11:23. This is to say that the accounts of institution were more than simple reports; they were redacted with theological and liturgical purposes in mind.

Careful study of the accounts has enabled us to recognize and clearly distinguish three lines of tradition: (1) a very old text in Mark that reflects the thought world of a community made up chiefly of Jewish Christians, and that influenced the later redactions of Matthew and Luke; (2) a tradition based on a paschal theology that led Luke especially (22:7-23) to combine older texts in accordance with this scheme; similar bits of tradition are clearly present in the other accounts as well; and (3) the Johannine account (13:1–17:26, which complements the promise of the

Eucharist in 6:51-58). We do not possess an original account in Aramaic that would be the common basis for all the accounts in Greek, but such an original can be glimpsed behind the Markan text.

The best place for us to begin is with Luke's account, since his is the most detailed and since, in addition, he repeats the Markan tradition with its Old Testament atmosphere and combines it with a paschal theology.

a) The New Covenant in the Atoning Blood of Christ

The reliance on Old Testament conceptions is especially clear in Jesus' words over the cup: "This cup which is poured out for you is the new covenant in my blood" (Luke 22:20). In this verse, Luke repeats what we have in Mark 14:24, but varies it slightly: "This is my blood of the covenant, which is poured out for many." The covenant idea is one that has lost much of its vitality for us, though we frequently speak of the "new covenant" or "new testament"; but it was at the heart of the Jew's entire religious thought and action. Because of God's covenant with his people, the Jew knew himself to have been chosen by God and to live in a covenant relationship with him. Fidelity to the covenant was the basic theme of his entire religious, social, and national existence.

The enacting of the covenant between God and Israel is recounted in chapter 24 of the Book of Exodus. It was a story very much alive for every religious Jew, and therefore for Christ and his apostles. In the account we are told:

> Moses wrote all the words of the Lord. And he rose early in the morning, and built an altar at the foot of the mountain, and twelve pillars, according to the twelve tribes of Israel. And he sent young men of the people of Israel, who offered burnt offerings and sacrificed peace offerings of oxen to the Lord. And Moses took half of the blood and put it in basins, and half of the blood he threw against the altar. Then he took the book of the covenant, and read it in the hearing of the people, and they said, "All that the Lord has spoken we will do, and we will be obedient." And Moses took the blood and threw it upon the people, and said, "Behold the blood of the covenant which the Lord has made with you in accordance with all these words" (Exod. 24:4-8).

Moses' words about the covenant blood (v. 8) are taken over verbatim into the account of the supper. Evidently, then, there is a parallelism between the old covenant and the new covenant now mediated by Christ. As Moses mediated the old covenant, so Christ mediates a new covenant. To the former people of God with its twelve tribes, there corresponds the new people of God, here represented by the twelve apostles, to whom Christ (in close connection with his action of institution) gives the power proper to the kingdom of God: "You are those who have continued with me in my trials; as my Father appointed a kingdom for me, so do I appoint for you'' (Luke 22:28–29).

The old covenant and the new alike are concluded and sealed by covenant blood that is poured out: the old covenant by the blood of sacrificial animals, the new by the blood of Christ himself. Christ's mediatorial role and his covenant blood are ideas that later will run through the entire Letter to the Hebrews. His mediatorship infinitely surpasses in effectiveness the mediation exercised in the old covenant: "When Christ appeared as a high priest . . . he entered once for all into the Holy Place, taking not the blood of goats and calves but his own blood, thus securing an eternal redemption'' (Heb. 9:11-12).

It is further to be noted that in connection with, or as a conclusion of, the sealing of the old covenant, there was a festive meal: "They [the chief men of the people of Israel] beheld God, and ate and drank'' (Exod. 24:11). The idea that covenant blood had expiatory power was taken for granted by the Jews, and it runs through the Old Testament. It was the vital conception that accounted for the regular bloody sacrifices in the Temple, since these were intended as the fulfillment of a duty imposed by the covenant.

There is a mention of covenant blood in the prophet Zechariah (9:9-11), and it is important in our present context, since all four evangelists incorporate part of the passage into their passion narratives, which begin with the entry of Jesus into Jerusalem on Palm Sunday. Matthew (21:5) and John (12:15) quote Zechariah's prophecy with regard to the entry: "Rejoice greatly, O daughter of Zion! Shout aloud, O daughter of Jerusalem! Lo, your king comes to you; triumphant and victorious is he, humble and riding on an ass, on a colt the foal of an ass'' (Zech. 9:9). Mark (11:2-8) and Luke (19:29-36) allude to the prophecy without directly quoting it. Now, immediately after the promise of the king of peace entering Jerusalem, Zechariah has these words of consolation: "As for you, because of the blood of my covenant with you, I will set your captives free from the waterless pit'' (Zech. 9:11).

For those who lived in a world shaped by the Old Testament promises, the establishment of a new covenant was part of the expectations concerning salvation that Christ fulfilled. Jeremiah had promised such a new covenant in the eschatological time of salvation:

> Behold, the days are coming, says the Lord, when I will make a new covenant with the house of Israel and the house of Judah, not like the covenant which I made with their fathers when I took them by the hand to bring them out of the land of Egypt, my covenant which they broke, though I was their husband, says the Lord. But this is the covenant which I will make with the house of Israel after those days, says the Lord: I will put my law within them, and I will write it upon their hearts;

> and I will be their God, and they shall be my people. And no longer shall
> each man teach his neighbor and each his brother, saying, "Know the
> Lord," for they shall all know me, from the least of them to the greatest,
> says the Lord; for I will forgive their iniquity, and I will remember their
> sin no more (Jer. 31:31-34).

The new covenant was to be one that touched the very core of man's
person, for it would not be written on stone, as the old law had been, but
upon man's heart (Jer. 31:33). Christ fulfilled this promise as a teacher
moving among his brothers (Matthew 23:8) and revealing himself directly
to the little ones and the children (Matthew 11:25). The abiding real presence of Christ in the Eucharist fulfilled completely the promise of the
Emmanuel ("God with us") who would dwell among his people (Jer.
31:33). In consequence of Christ's redemptive work, men receive through
the sacraments of baptism and penance a complete freedom from sin and
guilt (Jer. 31:34).

The atoning power of the rite that establishes the new covenant is
further emphasized and brought to the fore in the "for you" that accompanies the "body given" and the "blood poured out." Behind the phrase
lies the theology of witnessing and martyrdom of contemporary Judaism,
the central idea of which was that one person represents and makes
atonement for the others. It is the theology of the fourth of the Servant
(*Ebed Yahweh*) Songs (Is. 52:13–53:12), and Jesus relates his own redemptive action to it when he says: "The Son of Man also came not to be
served but to serve, and to give his life as a ransom for many" (Mark
10:45). The preposition "for" in this context has the force of "as a substitute for" or "as representative of"; in other words, one man replaces and
represents the others or the many (or: "for all," since "many" and "all"
are simply alternative ways of translating the Hebrew *rabim*), and the
others are thereby liberated.

A readily comprehensible example of what is meant would be Maximil-
ian Kolbe. For the sake of — and in place of — a fellow prisoner who
had been selected by lot for a terrible death, he entered the starvation cell
and died, while the other went free and survived. Kolbe was a "martyr"
in the Jewish sense, for he suffered as representative of another. Such is
the role of the Servant of God according to Isaiah 53: he dies *for* his
people. From this viewpoint, it makes no difference whom the inspired
writer understood the Servant to be: a collective figure (Israel in its entirety or an ideal Israel that would constitute a "holy remnant") or an
individual (a concrete person such as a historical king or Moses returned
to earth or an ideal prophet who would come in the final age). The essential point here is that the personage is one who makes atonement as a
representative and whose death is understood as a cultic sacrifice.

We are familiar with the passage from Isaiah, since it is read in the Good Friday liturgy. It is worth reproducing here, however, so that the context of Jesus' action at the Last Supper may be clear:

Who has believed what we have heard?
 And to whom has the arm of the Lord been revealed?
For he grew up before him like a young plant,
 and like a root out of dry ground;
he had no form or comeliness that we should look at him,
 and no beauty that we should desire him.
He was despised and rejected by men;
 a man of sorrows, and acquainted with grief;
and as one from whom men hide their faces
 he was despised, and we esteemed him not.

Surely he has borne our griefs
 and carried our sorrows;
yet we esteemed him stricken,
 smitten by God, and afflicted.
But he was wounded for our transgressions,
 he was bruised for our iniquities;
upon him was the chastisement that made us whole,
 and with his stripes we are healed.
All we like sheep have gone astray;
 we have turned everyone to his own way;
and the Lord has laid on him the iniquity of us all.

He was oppressed, and he was afflicted,
 yet he opened not his mouth;
like a lamb that is led to the slaughter,
 and like a sheep that before its shearers is dumb,
 so he opened not his mouth.
By oppression and judgment he was taken away;
 and as for his generation, who considered
that he was cut off out of the land of the living,
 stricken for the transgression of my people?
And they made his grave with the wicked
 and with a rich man in his death,
although he had done no violence,
 and there was no deceit in his mouth.

Yet it was the will of the Lord to bruise him;
 he has put him to grief;
when he makes himself an offering for sin,
 he shall see his offspring, he shall prolong his days;
the will of the Lord shall prosper in his hand;
 he shall see the fruit of the travail of his soul
  and be satisfied;
by his knowledge shall the righteous one, my servant,
 make many to be accounted righteous;
 and he shall bear their iniquities.

Therefore I will divide him a portion with the great,
  and he shall divide the spoil with the strong;
because he poured out his soul to death,
  and was numbered with the transgressors;
yet he bore the sin of many,
  and made intercession for the transgressors (Is. 53:1-12).

Jesus is this servant of God in Isaiah. He suffers *for* his people as their representative: "The Lord laid on him the iniquity of us all" (Is. 53:6); "He was wounded for our transgressions, he was bruised for our iniquities" (Is. 53:5; etc.). But the representative makes atonement: "Upon him was the chastisement that made us whole, and with his stripes we are healed" (53:5); "He bore the sin of many, and made intercession for the transgressors" (53:12). The atonement is accomplished, moreover, by a cultic expiatory sacrifice: Jesus suffers "like a lamb that is led to the slaughter" (53:7) and "makes himself an offering for sin" (53:10).

The idea, then, that Jesus gives his life as a real sacrificial victim in his "body given for many" and his "blood poured out for many" is by no means a later interpretation read into the text, but is clearly present in the account of the institution of the Eucharist, where it points to the reality underlying Jesus' action and act of institution: "The Son of Man also came not to be served but to serve, and to give his life as a ransom for many" (Mark 10:45).

In the context of an expiatory sacrifice, the "giving" of the body and the "pouring out" of the blood acquire their full meaning. Jesus is the true servant of God; he is "like a lamb that is led to the slaughter" (Is. 53:7) and "makes himself an offering for sin" (53:10). It was by the "giving" of a sacrificial victim that the non-Levite in the old covenant performed his sacrificial action; the Levite accepted the victim, slaughtered it, and "poured out" its blood at the foot of the altar. The two actions — the giving of a sacrificial victim and the pouring of the blood — together constituted a sacrifice.

Jesus, then, is the expiatory victim of the new covenant: "Christ, our paschal lamb, has been sacrificed" (1 Cor. 5:7). The salvific and expiatory power of the Lord's death is applied to the disciples at the Supper, even before the physical death occurs; the community experiences that power in the Eucharist.

Jesus fully accepts the Father's commission to suffer in expiation and goes to his death with full knowledge of what is at stake. He consciously, and indeed expressly, celebrates this meal as his last on earth. Just before the institution of the memorial of the Lord, Luke tells us how Jesus foretold his death in two statements:

And when the hour came, he sat at table, and the apostles with him.
And he said to them, "I have earnestly desired to eat this passover with

you before I suffer; for I tell you I shall not eat it until it is fulfilled in the kingdom of God. And he took a cup, and when he had given thanks he said, "Take this, and divide it among yourselves; for I tell you that from now on I shall not drink of the fruit of the vine until the kingdom of God comes" (Luke 22:15-18; cf. Mark 14:25; Matthew 26:29).

This twofold prophecy of Jesus' death "is steeped in purest hope," [1] for his death is his very own act and will bring not an end but the beginning of something new: the dawning reign of God. In other words, Jesus' death is already an anticipation of his resurrection. It is against that background of awareness that his command to repeat the Eucharist must be seen: "Do this in remembrance of me" (Luke 22:19; 1 Cor. 11:24). The commission looks to the future, to the time of the Church and the activity of Christ's eschatological community. Jesus is instituting the ecclesial sacrament of the Eucharist.

Let us sum up this first set of theological statements that the accounts of institution make concerning the meaning and nature of the Ecuharistic meal — a set of statements based on Jewish thinking and a Jewish understanding of the realities involved. The Lord who is present under the elements of bread and wine that make up a meal is the new Moses, the mediator of the new covenant that brings the new Israel into being. This new covenant, which Jeremiah had foretold for the final age, Jesus seals, not with the blood of sacrificial animals, but with his own blood. In the giving of his body and the shedding of his blood, he acts as the true servant of God and offers an expiatory sacrifice for the sins of the many. He knowingly accepts his death as the unconditional offering of his life to the Father, but he is also sure, in hope, that he will eat and drink again in the kingdom of God. His command to repeat what he has done looks to the time after his death and resurrection, the age of the Church and the sacraments.

b) The Eucharist as Passover of the New Covenant

A second line of interpretation, likewise based on Jewish ideas and liturgical actions, explains the Eucharist as a "new Passover" or, more accurately, as "an alteration of the meaning and form of Passover." This interpretation is consciously present, especially in Luke (22:7-20), who presents the data of tradition as an account of a Passover. Matthew (26:17-19) and Mark (14:12-16) are also aware of the connection with Passover. In addition, the explanatory words over the bread and the wine reflect the Passover custom of referring to the familiar foods and liquids only when they had some special meaning that transcended the moment.

The composition and redaction of the Lukan text is entirely determined

[1] Heinz Schürmann, *Der Abend-* *tesdienstordnung, Gemeindeordnung,* *mahlsbericht Lucas 22, 7-38 als Got-* *Lebensordnung* (Paderborn, 1955), p. 21.

by the Passover concept. In 22:7-13 he gives, to begin with, a detailed account of the preparation for the Passover meal (the account is very close to that in Mark 14:12-16). Then he makes use of an ancient bit of tradition (22:15-18)[2] so that he may introduce the "first cup" of the Passover meal, with its blessing of "the fruit of the vine" (22:18), and make the explanatory words concerning Passover parallel with those Jesus uses in his new act of institution. Luke thus describes the Passover in the manner prescribed by the *haggadah*, or liturgical ritual for Passover. Nothing is said of the slaying and eating of a Passover lamb, and consequently we may envisage a Passover meal without a lamb; if so, then Christ himself was the Passover lamb (cf. 1 Cor. 5:7) even at the Last Supper.

The date of this Passover meal raises some difficulties. According to the first three evangelists, it seems clear, and is taken for granted, that Christ celebrated the meal with the disciples on the day observed by the Jews generally. According to John, however, Jesus dies at the hour when the Passover lambs are being slain, for the Jews were unwilling to enter the praetorium, the governor's official residence, "so that they might not be defiled, but might eat the passover" (18:28). Pilate was therefore forced to come out to them. The date of the Passover thus differs by a day in John and in the Synoptics.

At the same time, John is evidently cognizant of the tradition based on the theology of Passover. In the fact that Jesus does not have his legs broken after death (John 19:36), John probably sees the fulfillment of the instruction that "you shall not break a bone of it [the Passover lamb]" (Exod. 12:46). For John, then, as for Paul, Jesus himself would be the new Passover lamb, the fulfillment of the old. However, we cannot exclude the possibility that John is simply quoting part of Psalm 34:20: "He [the Lord] keeps all his [the just man's] bones; not one of them is broken," especially since he interprets the piercing of Jesus' side (John 19:34) as the fulfillment of a prophecy of Zechariah (12:10). In both cases John would see God rescuing the suffering just man.

It will be worth our while here to sketch briefly the significance and sequence of a Jewish Passover meal. It will enable us to understand better the New Testament Passover theology that is especially prominent in Luke.

The Jewish Passover was a memorial meal, a feast with a deeply religious and at the same time political meaning. Each year, at the first full moon of the spring season, people celebrated, that is, gave conscious

---

[2] Schürmann, *op. cit.*, p. 18, sees in the verses a "very old account of the Supper in the form of a highly symmetrical double logion, which, however, because of the in- adequate account of the action with the bread, was not found acceptable as a valid report of the Supper."

presence to, the great deeds God had done for his people at the exodus from Egypt. These great deeds began with God's merciful "passing over" (*pascha, pesah*) the homes of the Israelites on the night when he slew all the first-born of the Egyptians (Exod. 12:29). They included the rescue of the people with the help of the Sea of Reeds, the sealing of the covenant on Sinai in the blood of the peace offering and in the covenant meal (Exod. 24:4-11), and the conquest of Canaan, the promised land. These various events were all involved in the making of the covenant and in the existence of Israel as God's covenanted people.

The Passover, described in Exodus 12:1-14, 21-28, was regarded as commanded and indeed instituted by God himself. The passage in Exodus originates in the Deuteronomistic and Priestly tradition. The pericope has this further point in common with the account of the institution of the Lord's Supper, that it not only recounts the institution but already reflects the celebration as practiced after the Settlement. For example, the procuring of the lamb four days before the meal itself (Exod. 12:3) is evidently a prescription for the repetition of the original Passover. Original and repetition are here fused.

Let us read the text in the Book of Exodus that recounts the institution of the Passover.

> The Lord said to Moses and Aaron in the land of Egypt, "This month shall be for you the beginning of months; it shall be the first month of the year for you. Tell all the congregation of Israel that on the tenth day of this month they shall take every man a lamb according to their fathers' houses, a lamb for a household; and if the household is too small for a lamb, then a man and his neighbor next to his house shall take according to the number of persons; according to what each can eat you shall make your count for the lamb. Your lamb shall be without blemish, a male a year old; you shall take it from the sheep or from the goats; and you shall keep it until the fourteenth day of this month, when the whole assembly of the congregation of Israel shall kill their lambs in the evening. Then they shall take some of the blood, and put it on the two doorposts and the lintel of the houses in which they eat them. They shall eat the flesh that night, roasted; with unleavened bread and bitter herbs they shall eat it. Do not eat any of it raw or boiled with water, but roasted, its head with its legs and its inner parts. And you shall let none of it remain until the morning, anything that remains until the morning you shall burn. In this manner you shall eat it: your loins girded, your sandals on your feet, and your staff in your hand; and you shall eat it in haste. It is the Lord's passover. For I will pass through the land of Egypt that night, and I will smite all the first-born in the land of Egypt, both man and beast; and on all the gods of Egypt I will execute judgments: I am the Lord. The blood shall be a sign for you, upon the houses where you are; and when I see the blood, I will pass over you, and no plague shall fall upon you to destroy you, when I smite the land of Egypt. This day shall be for you a memorial day, and you shall keep it as a feast to the Lord; throughout your generations you shall observe it as an ordinance for ever". . . .

> Then Moses called all the elders of Israel, and said to them, "Select lambs for yourselves according to your families, and kill the passover lamb. Take a bunch of hyssop and dip it in the blood which is in the basin, and touch the lintel and the two doorposts with the blood which is in the basin; and none of you shall go out of the door of his house until the morning. For the Lord will pass through to slay the Egyptians; and when he sees the blood on the lintel and on the two doorposts, the Lord will pass over the door, and will not allow the destroyer to enter your houses to slay you. You shall observe this rite as an ordinance for you and for your sons for ever. And when you come to the land which the Lord will give you, as he has promised, you shall keep this service. And when your children say to you, 'What do you mean by this service?' you shall say, 'It is the sacrifice of the Lord's passover, for he passed over the houses of the people of Israel in Egypt, when he slew the Egyptians but spared our houses.'" And the people bowed their heads and worshiped.
>
> Then the people of Israel went and did so; as the Lord has commanded Moses and Aaron, so they did (Exod. 12:1-14, 21-28).

Verses 43-50 of this chapter expressly limit participation in the Passover meal to Israelites. Verse 46c prescribes that no bone of the Passover lamb is to be broken (cf. above, and see John 19:36).

The Jews celebrated, and still celebrate, the Passover on the fourteenth day of the month Nisan, which is the first month of spring (equivalent to March-April). Since a lunar month always begins at the new moon, the full moon will occur on the fourteenth. The fact that Nisan is accounted the first month of the year (earlier the year had been thought of as beginning in the fall) is here attributed to a command of God (or Moses), but also corresponds to the Babylonian calendar in use since the time of Hammurabi. Even prior to the legislation of Moses, the feast had already existed as a feast celebrated by nomads at the time of changing pastures; the herders celebrated a cultic meal at which a first-born lamb was sacrificed, roasted over the fire, and eaten.

There is a clear reference back to this earlier stage in the prohibition against eating the lamb raw or boiled (v. 9); such a prescription marks a conscious effort to preserve the original character of the feast as a meal of nomads (by contrast with the customs of hunting tribes or farmers). The same remark applies to the unleavened bread (*mazzah*; pl., *mazzoth*). The *mazzoth* were flat cakes of unleavened bread, baked on flat, heated stones. From the viewpoint of the development of civilization, the *mazzoth* represented an advance over the eating of uncooked kernels (see the plucking of the heads of grain on the Sabbath: Matthew 12:1; Mark 2:23; Luke 6:1) or the roasting of kernels and ears over a fire (Lev. 23:14; Josh. 5:11; etc.), since in baked bread the starch content of the grain was already eliminated by the pounding or milling, the wetting and the heating, and the bread was thus better prepared for human enjoyment; the work done by teeth and saliva had been anticipated, as it were.

On the other hand, the flat, unleavened bread of the nomads was much older, more primitive, and plainer than the usual bread which the peasant leavened and baked in an oven. It was a "bread of affliction," as the Passover ritual calls it. In the time of Jesus, apart from Passover week people usually ate bread of the kind eaten by the peasants (see the parable of the leaven that begins: "The kingdom of heaven is like leaven which a woman took and hid in three measures of meal, till it was all leavened" — Matthew 13:33). Meat roasted over a fire and nomads' bread were a striking sign to the Israelite peasant, a reference back to the period when Israel was still a wandering nomadic people and strangers in Canaan.

The place where the Passover was eaten, when the feast was celebrated for the first time in Egypt, was, of course, the homes of the Israelite families. After the centralization of the cultus and the reform of Josiah, it had to be celebrated at Jerusalem. The instruction concerning Passover in the Book of Deuteronomy reflects this development (16:5), but projects this much later custom back into the wilderness period: "You may not offer the passover sacrifice within any of your towns which the Lord your God gives you; but at the place which the Lord your God will choose [=Jerusalem], to make his name dwell in it, there you shall offer the passover sacrifice, in the evening at the going down of the sun, at the time you came out of Egypt."

After the return from exile, then, the Passover was celebrated only in Jerusalem (Ezra 6:20; cf. also the practice of Jesus' parents in Luke 2:41). Christ himself and his apostles are careful to follow the custom. That is why he sends the disciples into Jerusalem to prepare for the meal (Matthew 26:18; Mark 14:13; Luke 22:8), then comes himself into the city at evening, takes his place at table (Matthew 26:20; Mark 14:17-18; Luke 22:14), and leaves the city again when the meal is ended (Matthew 26:30; Mark 14:26; Luke 22:39; John 18:1). After the final destruction of the Herodian Temple, the Passover once again became a meal taken in the homes of the Diaspora Jews; that is the custom that has prevailed down to the present time.

The course of the Passover meal was precisely regulated, in Jesus' time, not only by the passage cited above from the Book of Exodus (ch. 12) but also by custom.[3] The complete Passover celebration comprised both the preparatory rites and the meal itself. The preparation began with the selection of the lamb four days before the feast (tenth day of Nisan), the baking of the unleavened loaves, and the ceremonial removal, or even burning, of all leavened bread before the noon prior to the feast (cf. 1 Cor. 5:7: "Cleanse out the old leaven that you may be a new lump, as you

[3] Mishnah, Seder Moed, Tractate Pesahim ("Feast of Passover"), in The *Mishnah*, translated by H. Danby (Oxford, 1933), pp. 136–51.

really are unleavened. For Christ, our paschal lamb, has been sacrificed"). Just before sundown on the fourteenth of Nisan (first day of
Passover), the lambs were slaughtered in the Temple in accordance with
the sacrificial ritual. This meant that the lamb "given" was killed by the
head of the household and that the priests took the blood and "poured it
out" at the foot of the altar of sacrifice. The head of the household then
took the lamb home, where it was roasted on a spit and prepared for the
family meal.

Pilgrims were invited to share the meal with relatives or friends. If they
were too many for such an invitation, they formed "brotherhoods"
(*haburoth*; sing., *haburah*), with the oldest or highest ranking member
taking the part of the head of the household. Such a situation is evidently
presupposed in Luke 22:7-13 (Matthew 26:17; Mark 14:12-16), with Jesus
acting as master of the household for his community of disciples.

The meal was eaten, if possible, in a room that was adorned and illumi-
nated in a festive manner. According to Luke 22:12 (Mark 14:15), the
room was an upper room and provided with couches for reclining at table.
In earlier times, the prescription of Exodus (12:11) was obeyed and the
meal was eaten while the participants stood, dressed in the garb of travel-
ers; it was also eaten hastily, as it had been the first time, before the flight
from Egypt. By the time of Christ, however, it had long become the
custom to recline at table, as at a Hellenistic banquet, even though this
practice detracted greatly from the symbolic and commemorative character of the meal. The guests on their couches faced the low central table, or
even simply a mat spread on the floor, where the food was placed, leaning
on their left elbow, with the right hand free for eating. The guests did not,
however, form a fully closed circle; one side of the table was unoccupied
so that the dishes might more easily be brought and placed down. The
head of the house had the place of honor, which was either at the center or
at one end of the three-quarter circle of guests. The place at his right
(since the person reclining there would be "close to his breast"; cf. John
13:25; 21:20) was the second place of honor; the head of the house could
converse more easily with him than with the other guests.

The course of the meal was as follows. The host uttered a prayer of
thanksgiving to bless a first cup containing "the fruit of the vine" (Luke
22:18), and everyone drank from it. Then the unleavened bread and "bitter herbs" were served, the "bitter herbs," or *maror*, being a kind of leek
that was dipped in salted water and vinegar. It was unusual to begin a
meal with such a dish; under normal circumstances a Jewish meal had to
begin with the ritual breaking of bread over which a prayer of thanksgiving, a kind of grace before meals, was spoken.

After this, the meal proper was put on the table, and the memorial rite
began with the narration and praise of God's saving works in his people's

behalf. This act of *anamnesis* or commemoration turned the whole banquet into a Passover meal. The post-Talmudic forms of celebration customary today have introduced a number of ritual actions that are probably of relatively late origin: the covering of the bread, the washing of hands, the transformation of part of the Passover narrative into an epic hymn (the *Dayyenū*), and probably the words spoken over the "bread of affliction," words that certainly represent the outlook of a later time: "Now we are here; next year may we be in the land of Israel. Now we are slaves; next year may we be free men"[4] (in other modern versions of the Passover rite, the words are recited only at the end of the meal or are repeated there).

Despite these later insertions, the basic structure (especially according to Exodus 12 and the Tractate Pesahim of the Mishnah) still stands out clearly. The narrative (*haggadah*) of the host, which gave the whole meal its character, was elicited from him by a question from the son: "Why is this night different from all other nights?" (cf. Exod. 12:26). In response the father said: "We were slaves of Pharaoh in Egypt and the Eternal our God brought us out from there with a strong hand and an outstretched arm. Now if God had not brought out our forefathers from Egypt, then even we, our children, and our children's children might still have been enslaved to Pharaoh in Egypt."[5]

The host then continued the story down to the occupation of the country. Especially striking in this account were the interpretive words spoken over the foods that were characteristic of this meal rarely eaten at any other time. Thus, over the Passover lamb itself the host said: "It is the sacrifice of the Lord's passover, for he passed over the houses of the people of Israel in Egypt, when he slew the Egyptians but spared our houses" (Exod. 12:27). He spoke of the unleavened bread, which the Israelites snatched up in haste before they had a chance to leaven it (Exod. 12:34), as "the bread of affliction which our forefathers ate in the land of Egypt."[6] And he said that bitter herbs were being eaten "to recall that the Egyptians embittered the lives of our forefathers in Egypt."[7] Throughout the narrative, words and gestures complemented each other to make the whole very impressive. Thus, as he spoke the words over the unleavened bread, the host lifted the bread a bit from the table.

A second cup of wine was poured, and the host continued the story of the Exodus, along with the praise of God's actions in rescuing his people. This section of the narrative culminated in the first part of the Great Hallel (Psalms 114 and 115:1-8). The first part of the Haggadah had focused on the bitter sufferings of the people; the praise of God over the second cup was far more joyous in character and emphasized the ongoing protective

[4] Nathan Goldberg, *Passover Haggadah* (New York, 1966), p. 8.   [5] *Ibid.*, p. 9.   [6] *Ibid.*, p. 8.   [7] *Ibid.*, p. 23.

care of God which was such a source of gladness for his people. At this point the second cup was drunk and the *mazzoth* were eaten. With these actions the commemorative rite was essentially complete, and the meal, insofar as it looked to the allaying of hunger, was closed with the eating of the lamb.

After the meal the third cup was poured, again with a blessing. This blessing was an expanded form of the usual prayer after a meal, and included specifically Passover elements. Finally, the second part of the Hallel (Psalms 115:9-18, 116, and 117) was sung. This probably marked the end of the banquet in its original form.

It seems that in the time of Christ, the fourth cup, which later became customary as a kind of transition to conversation at table after the joyous meal, had not yet been introduced, since "when they had sung a hymn," the Lord immediately went out to the Mount of Olives (Mark 14:26; Matthew 26:30; Luke 22:39). The Passover meal must usually have ended around midnight.

It is clear that the Passover meal consisted of two basically independent parts: a festive meal that allayed hunger and a commemorative rite (anamnesis). The festive meal contained all the elements that people generally, even today, think of as part of a normal meal: meat (the Passover lamb), carbohydrates (bread, in this case, unleavened, instead of potatoes or products with yeast), vegetables (leeks, "bitter herbs"), a side dish (stewed fruit), and wine.

The anamnesis aimed at as impressive as possible a presentation of the whole course of liberation, from the Exodus to the occupation or settlement. The primitive gestural elements — standing clad for a journey or flight, and eating in haste — had indeed been replaced by reclining on couches. Nonetheless, there was still the striking contrast between the bread of affliction and bitter herbs, on the one hand, and the cup of wine, on the other, as the symbol of the covenant and its fulfillment by God in giving his people fruitful land for crops, where wine was the symbol of joy and festivity; this contrast functioned as a sign that gave the participants an insight into the original events. The contrast between forced labor and freedom, bitterness and joy, suffering and deliverance, ran through the whole rite. This anamnesis, as we said, was the specific, formative factor in the festive meal and gave it its name; at the same time, it was also a sign in its own right and could thus be separated from the meal proper.

This Passover rite in the narrower sense was a commemorative meal for the Jew. "Commemorative" did not mean, however, that he was simply reminded of the past events; it meant rather that the abiding fidelity of God to the covenant became present. Exodus 13:3-4 already speaks of "this day," and the Mishnah, Tractate Pesahim, expressly says: "In every generation a man must so regard himself as he came forth himself out of Egypt.''[8] The saving act which God performed in the historical past thus became in the Passover feast an abidingly present, gracious reality. When the Jew of today ends his Passover feast with the words, ''Speedily lead your redeemed people to Zion in joy. Next year in Jerusalem!''[9] his intention corresponds to Paul's when the latter tells the Christian that in the Eucharist ''you proclaim the Lord's death until he comes'' (1 Cor. 11:26), words that have been incorporated into one of the acclamations in the new Eucharistic Prayers.

The correlation between sign and saving event (or expectation of salvation) gave the Jewish Passover a ''sacramental structure.''[10] The Hebrew term *zikkaron* (which corresponds to *anamnesis* or ''memorial'') gave clear and conscious expression to this theology of a presence that was based on the fact that God in his eternity transcends the temporal sequence proper to the created order. As a matter of fact, our Christian theology of the sacraments is likewise grounded in the last analysis on this conception that was already familiar to Judaism.

Against this background of the sacramental conception of the Passover which Jesus' Jewish contemporaries had, and of the symbolic character of the lamb, the bread, and the wine, Christ's action at the Supper becomes clear and intelligible. He is establishing a new covenant and giving to his disciples the symbols of the new Passover: no longer the bread of affliction and the cup of the covenant, but his very self under the forms of bread and wine.

This is the place to recall that his self-surrender to death occurred on the same day as the Passover supper (since, according to Jewish reckoning, the old day ended and the new one began at sundown; Holy Thursday evening and Good Friday afternoon were parts of the same day). This brings home to us even more tellingly the fact that Christ is ''our paschal lamb'' (1 Cor. 5:7). The slaying of Christ as paschal lamb before sunset on the day of Passover was his real ''historical'' self-surrender in expiation ''for us,'' while the Supper was an anticipation of it that rendered it already present in signs and symbols. Our later Eucharist is a real memorial that renders it present, under the identical food-symbols, during the subsequent period, until the Lord comes again. Supper and Mass derive their substance from the same sacrificial reality and render it present under the same signs.

It is not easy to determine today whether Jesus' farewell meal was in fact a Passover, or whether the first three evangelists simply used the Passover framework in order to bring out the sacramental character of

---

[8] Pesahim 10, 5, in Danby, *op. cit.*, p. 151.
[9] Goldberg, *op. cit.*, p. 43.
[10] Cf. St. Thomas Aquinas, *Summa theologiae*, III, q. 60, a. 2 ad 2: the immola- tion of the paschal lamb was one of the ''sacraments of the old law.'' So was the eating of it (I-II, q. 102, a. 5c).

Jesus' action. Paul simply says that Jesus' action took place "on the night when he was betrayed" (1 Cor. 11:23). John, as we noted earlier, has Jesus die at the time when the Passover lambs were being slaughtered in the Temple; he thus locates the Last Supper on the day before the Passover meal. And yet the accounts of the Supper, the background provided by the memorial celebration, and the otherwise abnormal explanatory words over the bread and wine makes clearest sense if we suppose that the Last Supper was in fact a Passover meal.

The facts to be considered are these: The meal took place in Jerusalem (cf. Deut. 16:5-6), although at this time the Lord was usually spending his evenings in Bethany (Mark 11:11) or on Mount Olivet (Luke 22:39), and in fact returned to the latter on this night too, once the meal was over (Mark 14:26; John 18:1), although he could just as well have eaten his evening meal there to begin with; there was the ritual number of participants required for a Passover; the celebration began in the evening after sunset, as was prescribed in the Book of Exodus (12:8); the breaking of bread "as they were eating" (Mark 14:22; Matthew 26:26) was a practice specific to the Passover meal, while on other occasions bread was broken to the accompaniment of the prayer before meals; the hymn of praise at the end of the meal (Mark 14:26; Matthew 26:30) replaced the usual prayer after meals that was spoken over a cup of wine; above all, there were the unusual words of explanation or interpretation over the bread and the wine.

One point deserves our special attention: The form of the "Lord's Supper" as established by Christ for his future Church determines the basic form of the Mass. Every meal is the basis for communion, belonging, brotherhood, community. This spirit was especially evident in the Supper room, inasmuch as all ate from the one loaf that was broken, and all drank from the one cup that was passed around; all ate some food from a single dish (John 13:26) and reclined at the same table (Luke 22:21). Paul emphasizes the unitive aspect of the meal: "The cup of blessing which we bless, is it not a participation in the blood of Christ? The bread which we break, is it not a participation in the body of Christ? Because there is one bread, we who are many are one body, for we all partake of the one bread" (1 Cor. 10:16-17).

Christ, too, emphasizes the spirit proper to this table-community, for, though he presides, he is also there as one who serves (Luke 22:27), he washes the feet of the others (John 13:1-7), and he settles the quarrel about rank that breaks out even at table (Luke 22:24-27) by drawing their attention to the way he himself has acted: "I have given you an example, that you also should do as I have done to you" (John 13:15).

The rediscovery of the meal context is undoubtedly extremely important for giving a vital shape and form to the Mass. It is no accident when the General Instruction of the Roman Missal speaks of the Mass as the Lord's Supper (no. 2), before going on to stress its character as Eucharistic sacrifice.

c) *The Bread of Life*

The Gospel of John, the last of the four to be written (*ca.* 100 A.D.) contains no account of institution. Clearly, the interest of this Gospel in the Lord's Supper is theological rather than liturgical, since the Eucharistic celebration in the various communities had already received a more or less fixed form. John does tell us of a farewell meal (13:1–17:26), but he mentions the meal as such only in passing (13:2) or tells us of the washing of feet that took place during the meal (13:4) and of sharing food with the betrayer (13:26). The atoning power of the covenant blood that was so important for the understanding of the Eucharist in the first three Gospels plays hardly any role in John. The Passover context is mentioned (in 18:28 the Jews do not enter the procurator's hall, lest they be defiled and be unable to eat the Passover), but is not regarded by John as essential to the Eucharist.

The decades have passed; other problems and theological concerns are more important in preaching, especially in Hellenistic Asia Minor, where Jews are fewer in number. Gnosticism is winning attention with its denigration of the "flesh" and thus, in the last analysis, its denial of the genuine "incarnation of the Word" and the reality of our redemption by Jesus. It is this new situation that accounts for the lapidary statement at the beginning of the fourth Gospel: "The Word became flesh and dwelt among us" (1:14).

Here we must be careful to note that "flesh" and "body" are simply English-language variants (reflecting a single Hebrew word, *basar*) and mean the same thing. The Synoptics and Paul report the words of institution as "This is my body" (Matthew 26:26; Mark 14:22; Luke 22:19; 1 Cor. 11:24), while John always speaks of Jesus' "flesh," because he adopts the language of the Gnostics in his conflict with them, although he means in fact exactly what the Synoptics mean. Preaching is never situated outside of time and space, but always looks to the concrete conditions of a given sociocultural context. There is a variety of such contexts even within the relatively short period it took for the redaction of the New Testament writings.

John's teaching on the Eucharist, then, is not to be found in an "account of institution," but in his sixth chapter, which recounts Jesus' promise of the bread from heaven. Verses 48-58 are the most important:

> I am the bread of life. Your fathers ate the manna in the wilderness, and they died. This is the bread which comes down from heaven, that a man may eat of it and not die. *I am the living bread* which came down from

heaven; if anyone eats of this bread, he will live for ever; and *the bread which I shall give for the life of the world is my flesh*. The Jews then disputed among themselves, saying, "How can this man give us his flesh to eat?" So Jesus said to them, "Truly, truly, I say to you, unless you eat the flesh of the Son of man and drink his blood, *you have no life in you*; he who eats my flesh and drinks my blood has eternal life, and I will raise him up at the last day. For *my flesh is food indeed*, and *my blood is drink indeed*. He who eats my flesh and drinks my blood abides in me, and I in him. As the living Father sent me, and I live because of the Father, so he who eats me will live because of me. This is *the bread which came down from heaven*, not such as the fathers ate and died; he who eats this bread will live *for ever*.

The thing that is most important to John as a theologian is the real identity of the bread and wine with the flesh and blood of Jesus: he is really and truly present under these forms. Our attention is caught by the frequent use of the auxiliary verb "to be": "I *am* the living bread" (6:35, 48, 51); "the bread . . . *is* my flesh" (6:51); etc. In the Aramaic which lies behind the words of institution as reported in the New Testament, the auxiliary "is" would not appear; literally translated, the Aramaic words of institution would read: "This here, my body" and "This here, my blood." Evidently, even with the verb "is" omitted, the identity of subject and predicate is being asserted, so that the canonical Greek text of the New Testament is fully justified in introducing the "is." In any event, John for his part is strongly emphasizing the identity of bread and flesh. Watering down the "is" to mean "means," "represents," "symbolizes," or something similar is unjustified — the bread *is* the flesh of Jesus, and the wine is his blood.

A further point that is important to John is the food character of the Eucharist. The very fact that the discourse on the bread of heaven is linked to the immediately preceding feeding of the five thousand (John 6:1-15) is already significant: "For my flesh is food indeed, and my blood is drink indeed. He who eats my flesh and drinks my blood abides in me, and I in him" (6:55-56). Even when his hearers openly reject what he says (6:52), he insists on the eating and drinking of his flesh and blood, and in no way softens his demand. The same is true when he turns to the Twelve (6:67), who end by confessing their faith in him (6:68).

This bread, then, is bread for believers. One and the same faith embraces both him and the bread; both he and the bread have "come down from heaven."

The significance of this bread is that it is given "for the life of the world" (6:51c), so that "if anyone eats" of it, "he will live for ever" (6:51b). "Life" is a key word in John, and means that the life of Jesus, his wholly special existence as God-man, is communicated to the believer

through the sacraments of the Church. "Life" is almost identical with
what we now speak of as "grace."

A final point that is important for John is the eschatological significance
of the Eucharist: "he will live for ever" (6:51b, 58) and "I will raise him
up at the last day" (6:54). The Eucharist is the community's food during
the whole period while the Church lasts, until the Lord comes.

2. THE BASIC FORM OF THE EUCHARIST

People like to talk today of the Mass being a meal in form, but that is an
oversimplification. The Mass involves a meal, but it is not simply a meal.
In its basic form the Mass is a *eucharist*, that is, a blessing or prayer of
praise over bread and wine, which are the elements of a meal, though in
this case a meal in which the eating is symbolic and sacramental. A meal
to allay hunger *can* be linked to this Eucharistic meal, as was done in the
early days of the Church, when it was called an "agapē," and as is done
occasionally today when the Eucharist is celebrated in someone's home.
Most of the time, however, a liturgy of the word, rather than a regular
meal, was connected with the Eucharist; also connected could be the
administration of other sacraments, as is our practice today with baptism,
confirmation, orders, and marriage, and, occasionally, even the anointing
of the sick. When other sacraments are thus linked to the Eucharist, they
determine the readings and prayers, and thus the overall character, of the
liturgy of the word, and are related to the Eucharist as to the source,
summit, and center of Christian life.

This linking of other sacraments to the Eucharist is an ancient and
legitimate tradition. As early as the second and third centuries we find the
administration of baptism (instead of the usual liturgy of the word) being
joined to the celebration of the Eucharist, according to Justin and Hippolytus; the latter also tells us of episcopal consecration taking place in
connection with the Eucharist. A Mass of ordination provided the normal
context for the ordaining of priests.

When Paul speaks of the Eucharist as "the Lord's supper" (1 Cor.
11:2), he clearly distinguishes it from the other meal. For what the Corinthians do in an unloving manner at their gatherings (11:21-22) cannot be
called the celebration of the Lord's supper; rather, each one "eats the
bread or drinks the cup of the Lord in an unworthy manner" and therefore
is "guilty of profaning the body and blood of the Lord" (11:27). The Mass
is not simply a sharing of food and drink, a meal the disciples of Jesus take
together; it is the repetition of his Eucharist, a very specific prayer of
thanksgiving over bread and wine as elements of a meal.

As we saw above, in the Passover feast the commemorative rite was enclosed within a regular meal; the latter, however, was not in itself the Passover, but became the Passover because of the special commemorative rite. Similarly, when the first Christians continued to celebrate the memorial of Christ in connection with a regular meal (the "agapē"), the agapē itself was not the memorial of the Lord, however much brotherly affection and concern for the suffering members of the community the agapē might embody. The memorial of the Lord was the prayer of praise in which man thanked God and "consecrated" the bread and wine. The early history of the Mass makes it clear that the regular meal and the sacramental Eucharistic rite were soon separated, because the connection was the occasion for many unbecoming actions.

If Christ's last meal with his disciples was indeed a Passover meal (this is possible, even probable, but not certain), then it is a striking fact that the interpretive rites with their new meaning were separated from any new "Christian Passover" at a very early date. There is no evidence that in the meals they did take for some time in connection with the Eucharist, the early communities preserved any form of Jewish Passover meal, or even that they celebrated the memorial of the Lord only once a year, on the date of the Jewish Passover. It is not certain that the Acts of the Apostles is referring to the celebration of the Eucharist when it reports that "day by day, attending the temple together and breaking bread in their homes, they partook of food with glad and generous hearts" (2:46). At least it can be said, however, that the reference to the breaking of bread, which was a Jewish ritual at ordinary meals, is an important hint to us of the form the earliest Eucharist must have taken.

Every Jewish meal, especially one with a special cultic orientation, as, for example, the meal on the eve of the Sabbath, characteristically began and ended with a thanksgiving (*berakah*), that is, with a prayer of praise over the bread at the beginning of the meal and over the wine at the end. Of the two blessings, the one over the bread was much the shorter and simpler: "Blessed are you, Lord, our God, King of the world, who has brought forth bread from the earth." The blessing spoken over the cup at the end of the meal was more extensive and solemn. It begins with a dialogue that calls for attention from the participants, shifting the focus of their thoughts from the meal to prayer:

> *Host:* Let us praise the Lord.
>   *All*: The name of the Lord be praised now and for ever!
> *Host*: Praised be our God, because we eat of his gifts and live by his
>   favor.
>   *All*: Praised be he and praised be his name.

This short dialogue is followed by the prayer of thanksgiving, which has four parts: (1) thanksgiving to the Creator and Sustainer, who gives (2) the land, (3) the sanctuary, and (4) everything that is good.

> Praised be you, Lord our God, King of the world, because you nourish all things in goodness, kindness, and mercy. Praised be you, O God, who nourish all things.
>
> We thank you, Lord our God, because you have given us a goodly land for our inheritance that we might eat of its fruits and be filled through your kindness. Praised be you, Lord our God, for the land and our food.
>
> Have mercy, Lord our God, on your people Israel, on your city Jerusalem, and on Zion, the place where your glory dwells and your altar and sanctuary stand. Praise be you, O God, who build Jerusalem.
>
> Praised be you, Lord our God, King of the world, for you are good and show kindness to us.

This blessing after the meal praises the goodness of God as Lord and Creator of the universe, but also as the covenant God who proves his fidelity by giving his people possession of the land and dwelling among them there. In other words, God is praised as both Creator of all things and as Author of the history of salvation. The emphasis on petition in the third paragraph, evidently reflecting the time after the destruction of the Temple, is not a discordant note in the prayer of praise, since God is the all-powerful One who can turn even disaster into a means of salvation.

There are many more recent versions of the prayer after meals. They frequently introduce new elements but do not change the structure. Such an expansion may be seen, for example, in the blessing spoken by the host over the "third cup" at the Passover meal. The expansion in no way alters the basic scheme of the prayer, for the third cup really marked the end of the Passover meal proper. What followed was part of the religious (second part of the Hallel) and domestic festive celebration centering around the "fourth cup." It seems quite certain today that from the form-historical point of view, the blessing after the meal, whether the meal was a Passover meal or some other cultically oriented meal, was the point of origin for the Eucharist of the Christian communities.

We have no accurate knowledge of the precise concrete form of the earliest Christian "blessing of bread" (before a meal). We can assert, however, that it must have been a specifically Christian expansion of the Jewish form, and one that possibly originated with Jesus himself. The disciples at Emmaus, after all, recognized Jesus on the evening of the first Easter Sunday by the manner in which he "broke bread" (cf. Luke 24:30-31, 35), that is, not by the way he divided the bread and gave it to them, but by his personal way of praising God in the blessing before the meal. The "breaking of bread" referred, among the Jews, not so much to the physical act of dividing the bread as to the words of thanksgiving spoken during the physical act.

In my opinion, it is certain, or at least highly probable, that from the very beginning, Christians in breaking bread did not simply praise God as the one who "brings forth bread from the earth." They must have given their prayer a specifically Christological coloring, including perhaps the very words Christ himself had used.

We have an example of such Christian expansions of the Jewish blessings of bread and wine in the *Didache*, or "Teaching of the Twelve Apostles," a document from the first half of the second century, originating probably in Syria. It was a popular piece of writing in antiquity, but then it disappeared and was found again only a hundred years ago at Constantinople by Philotheos Bryennios, who later became metropolitan of Nicomedia. In addition to catechetical sections, the *Didache* contains instructions for administering the sacraments and, in chapters nine and ten, for the "thanksgiving" (the Eucharist?). The document appears to have originated at a very early date, since there is little differentiation between blessing at table and Eucharistic prayer. The important point, however, is that the Jewish models of thanksgiving for God's creative and redemptive activity have been thoroughly reworked to make them Christological. Though there is still no agreement on whether or not the prayers were meant for the Eucharist, they are nonetheless an interesting reflection of the early period and are therefore given here:

> IX. With regard to the prayer of thanksgiving [*eucharistia*], offer it in this fashion. First, for the cup: "We thank you, our Father, for the holy vine of David your servant, which you have revealed to us through Jesus your servant. Glory be yours through all ages! Amen." Then for the bread broken: "We thank you, our Father, for the life and knowledge you have revealed to us through Jesus your servant. Glory be yours through all ages! Amen. Just as the bread broken was first scattered on the hills, then was gathered and became one, so let your Church be gathered from the ends of the earth into your kingdom, for yours is glory and power through all ages! Amen." Let no one eat or drink of your eucharist, except those baptized in the name of the Lord. For it is of this the Lord was speaking when he said: "Do not give what is holy to dogs."
>
> X. When your hunger has been satisfied, give thanks thus: "We thank you, holy Father, for your holy name which you have made to dwell in our hearts, and for the knowledge and faith and immortality you have revealed to us through Jesus your servant. Glory be yours through all ages! Amen. All-powerful Master, you created all things for your name's sake, and you have given food and drink to the children of men for their enjoyment, so that they may thank you. On us, moreover, you have bestowed a spiritual food and drink that leads to eternal life, through Jesus your servant. Above all, we thank you because you are mighty. Glory be yours through all ages! Amen. Lord, remember your Church and deliver it from all evil; make it perfect in your love and gather it from

the four winds, this sanctified Church, into your kingdom which you have prepared for it, for power and glory are yours through all ages! Amen. May grace come and the world pass away! Amen. Hosannah to the house of David! If anyone is holy, let him come; if anyone is not, let him repent. *Maran atha!* Amen.'' Allow the prophets to give thanks as much as they wish.[11]

Chapter fourteen of the *Didache* certainly speaks of the Sunday Eucharist. The text of the prayer of thanksgiving is not given, but perhaps it is intended to be the same as the one in chapters nine and ten. The emphasis in chapter fourteen is chiefly on the spirit of brotherhood and forgiveness as a condition for the celebration, and on the Eucharist as the fulfillment of the pure eschatological sacrifice foretold by the prophet Malachi (1:11):

> XIV. Come together on the Lord's day, break bread and give thanks, having first confessed your sins so that your sacrifice may be pure. Anyone who has a quarrel with his fellow Christian should not gather with you until the two are reconciled, lest your sacrifice be profaned. For this sacrifice is the one of which the Lord says: "In every place and at every time offer me a pure sacrifice, for I am a great king, says the Lord, and my name is marvelous among the nations" (Mal. 1:11, 14).[12]

We must assume that in the very first period of the Church's life, the "blessings" of bread and wine which made up the celebration of the Eucharist were separated from one another by the eating of a regular meal. This situation was soon felt to be less than ideal, and the two blessings were brought together to form a single action with two parts.

In the process, the parallelism of the two blessings was accentuated, far more than it had been in the Jewish prayers. It is likely that since the blessing over the cup was much longer, more solemn, and richer in content, it attracted the blessing over the bread to itself, that is, both were placed at the end of the regular meal. It is likely that the linking of the two occurred very early, perhaps in the forties of the first century, since Paul's account in 1 Corinthians, which is to be dated around 55 A.D., presents the union of the two blessings as something taken for granted (this, even though he mentions that the blessing of the cup originally took place "after supper" and not directly following upon the blessing of the bread — cf. Luke 22:20). As we have already seen, this manner of celebrating the Eucharist, that is, with the two blessings not separated by a meal, is taken as normal by the first three evangelists (in the seventies of the first century) and must have been already practiced by the apostles.

---

[11] Greek text in Anton Hänggi and Irmgard Pahl (eds.), *Prex Eucharistica: Textus e variis liturgiis antiquioribus selecti* (Spicilegium Friburgense 12; Fribourg, 1968), pp. 66–68; and in J.-P. Audet, *La Di-* *dachè: Instructions des apótres* (Paris, 1958), pp. 234–36.

[12] Text in Hänggi-Pahl, *op. cit.*, p. 68; Audet, *op. cit.*, p. 240.

We can say, then, that the celebration of the Eucharist in the apostolic communities, as distinguished from the Last Supper which Jesus celebrated, was characterized by the linking of the two blessings and the placing of them at the end of the regular meal. The next step was to separate the Eucharist entirely from the community meal; this took place in the post-apostolic period. The connection with a community meal was abandoned, and the place this meal had occupied was taken over by a liturgy of the word consisting of reading, sermon, and prayer. This step begins a new stage in the elaboration of the definitive form of our Eucharistic celebration; the liturgy of the word and the liturgy of the Eucharist were united to make a single communal celebration.

B. The Liturgy of the Word

1. REASONS FOR ITS INTRODUCTION

The linking of a regular meal with the Eucharist must have caused disagreements from the very beginning. The early Christians undoubtedly soon felt the truth of the old saying that no one likes to pray when his belly is full. As a result, quite early in the apostolic period the blessings over the bread and the cup were brought together and placed at the end of the meal instead of being separated, as they had initially been, by the whole length of the meal. By bringing the two blessings together, the Church made it easier for the participants to "discern the body of the Lord" (cf. 1 Cor. 11:29). But even this move was evidently insufficient, since the regular meal with all its potential negative aspects still preceded the memorial of the Lord and caused problems for the celebration of the Lord's Supper.
Paul, for example, criticizes the celebration at Corinth:

> But in the following instructions I do not commend you, because when you come together it is not for the better but for the worse. For, in the first place, when you assemble as a church, I hear that there are divisions among you; and I partly believe it, for there must be factions among you in order that those who are genuine among you may be recognized. When you meet together, it is not the Lord's supper that you eat. For in eating, each one goes ahead with his own meal, and one is hungry and another is drunk. What! Do you not have houses to eat and drink in? Or do you despise the church of God and humiliate those who have nothing? What shall I say to you? Shall I commend you in this? No, I will not (1 Cor. 11:17-22).

This picture of a community gathered for worship is rather depressing. Corinth was, of course, a seaport, and therefore hardly the most moral of towns; we need only recall Paul's warning that an incestuous man must be

expelled from the community. But we would not expect that even at the
Eucharist he would have to be criticizing Christians for uncharitableness,
antisocial behavior, factionalism, gluttony, and drunkenness. Unrest due
to discrimination on ethnic grounds is something we hear of in Jerusalem
at an early date: "Now in these days when the disciples were increasing in
number, the Hellenists murmured against the Hebrews because their
widows were neglected in the daily distribution" (Acts 6:1). The answer
in this situation had been to appoint deacons who would serve table and
prevent partisanship in the community. The meals, despite their name of
"agapē," evidently elicited not only selfless love of neighbor but selfish-
ness as well.

In any event, the factions at Corinth can easily be explained by the
custom in antiquity of eating at a common table. By "common table" here
I mean that people usually ate from the same plate and often even drank
from the same cup. We frequently find this custom still alive today among
peasants, for example, when they are working in the fields. Now when
people are all eating from the same dish, it is in the nature of things that
the group gathered around the table cannot well number more than about
a dozen; if there are more than a dozen, some will be too far away to reach
the plate. When the numbers grow, then, the number of groups must
likewise increase. In the refectories of Egyptian monks — for example, in
the monastery of St. Simeon at Aswan — I saw a number of low circular
benches built of brick; the common dish was probably set in the center,
and ten or twelve diners sat on the circular bench and reached into the
dish. So too, when the Corinthian community met for meals, it probably
broke up into several groups, perhaps five or six if the total number of
participants was fifty or sixty.

We should not be surprised that the groups were soon differentiated
according to social class or some other shared interest, and that they
regularly consisted of the same members. There were several rich man-
ufacturers at Corinth (for example, the married couple Aquila and Pris-
cilla, tentmakers with whom Paul worked while there — Acts 18:2-3), but
there were certainly slaves and poor people as well. With rich and poor
sitting in separate groups, the difference in the quality and quantity of
their respective meals must have been very quickly felt. If the rich did not
find the "agapē soup" rich enough, they probably made sure to eat at
home first; but that only gave more time and cause to drink heavily at the
community meal. "One is hungry and another is drunk" (1 Cor. 11:21).
Unrest and factions in the community were the inevitable result.

The obvious solution was to separate the meal entirely from the
Eucharist. Since in the Mediterranean world the main meal of the day was
taken in the evening (and still is; in Spain, for example, you cannot get a

menu in a restaurant before 8 p.m.), the communal meal continued to be eaten at that time, whether it was a meal to succor the poor or a fraternal gathering of the community. The Eucharist, however, was transferred to the morning, when it was much more likely that people would not yet have broken their fast, especially from intoxicating liquors. Thus Peter on Pentecost could easily turn aside the accusation of drunkenness: "It is only the third hour of the day" (Acts 2:15).

The separation of the Eucharist from the communal meal entailed significant changes. To begin with, the available space was divided up in quite a different way. At the communal meal, the participants were divided into groups of seated or squatting diners in various parts of the room, each circle focused on a low table or even a simple mat on which the common dish stood. In the new situation of the Eucharist, there was but a single table on which the Eucharistic gifts were laid. More than this, the many tables and the one table were quite different in character. The many were simple tabletops set close to the ground, or were even just mats on the floor; the new table was higher and served a further practical purpose, since the president of the assembly stood at it.

The former separate groups of diners now became a single large group, and the president faced the rest of his fellow celebrants as they stood before him in a half- or three-quarter circle, with the table as not only the central point but also the focus of attention, though the table soon was shifted from the center of the space to a wall. We assume that the participants now stood instead of reclining or squatting as previously, since standing was felt by people of that period to be more appropriate in this situation.

With the elimination of the regular meal, the proper form and shape of the Eucharist emerged more clearly. It evidently consisted now in the eating and drinking of the "signs," the bread and wine that had been transformed by the prayer of thanksgiving into Christ's body and blood. And yet this reduction to essentials must also have been felt as something of an impoverishment. A symbolic meal involving only the preparation of the gifts, the prayer of thanksgiving, and the eating of the gifts could not but be fairly brief, and probably seemed too short to satisfy the religious feelings of the community. What had been eliminated was not simply the sociableness of the agapē, but the leisure for proclamation, reading, exhortation, explanation, song, etc., as well.

It is likely that at the community meals, letters, communications, and greetings from neighboring communities were read, and especially from the founders of the community (the apostles or other missionaries). The letters of Paul usually end with prayers of praise that sound very much like a transition from a meal to a Eucharist. We should recall here that the new formulas for greeting the community at the beginning of Mass are, for the most part, concluding formulas from Paul's letters. An example of instruction given during a fraternal meal is given in the Acts of the Apostles: "On the first day of the week, when we [Paul and his companions] were gathered together to break bread, Paul talked with them, intending to depart on the morrow; and he prolonged his speech until midnight. There were many lights in the upper chamber where we were gathered . . ." (Acts 20:7-8). Luke goes on to say that a young man named Eutychus, who was sitting in a window, fell asleep while Paul was talking, and fell from the third story — surely an encouraging episode for preachers less gifted than Paul!

In order to restore such basic elements of a Christian liturgy as reading, singing, preaching, and praying, a liturgy of the word was added to the Eucharist. A model for this was ready at hand in the liturgy of the synagogue. The community did not unthinkingly follow this synagogue model, but it did take the model into account in shaping into an organized whole the elements of word and prayer that were already present in the communal meals.

In John's account of the Last Supper, he tells us more about such a liturgy of the word than he does about the Eucharist proper. And we may understand Paul's exhortation in the Letter to the Ephesians (5:18-20) as a warning to use the time at the community gatherings not wastefully but for mutual edification: "Do not get drunk with wine, for that is debauchery; but be filled with the Spirit, addressing one another in psalms and hymns and spiritual songs, singing and making melody to the Lord with all your heart, always and for everything giving thanks in the name of our Lord Jesus Christ to God the Father." That kind of exhortation is a better introduction to a liturgy of the word than to the earlier communal meal.

2. The Example of the Synagogal Liturgy

The liturgy of the word in the synagogue was the result of careful thought on the part of prudent Jews in the Babylonian diaspora, after the first Temple had been destroyed and the people had been deprived of their central sanctuary and sacrifices. It is difficult for us to realize how great a cultural shock the destruction of Jerusalem caused the Israelite people. Had God proved unfaithful to his covenanted people? Were the gods of the heathen stronger than Yahweh? In addition, how incomparably more splendid was the culture and civilization of the conquerors than that of the tiny populace of Palestine, composed mainly of peasants! The magnificent religious feasts of the new rulers were likewise an abiding temptation.

Was it not better simply to acknowledge the real situation and follow the new and clearly more powerful gods, to seek assimilation and through marriage be absorbed into this alien people as quickly as possible?

The intellectual and spiritual leaders of the Jews — the "scribes," the "intellectuals" — quickly realized the need of the hour. Now that the Temple was gone, Israel must establish itself on a new basis, and center its life on the word of "instruction" (the later "Torah" of the five books of Moses, that is, "the law" in the Pentateuch) and on the "expectation" of the salvation that had been and still was being promised by the prophets.

The current division of the Old Testament writings into "Moses and the prophets" (see, for example, Luke 16:29; or "Moses and Elijah" in Matthew 17:3, Mark 9:3, and Luke 9:30, 33) reflected synagogal usage; the dyad summed up tradition and the history of salvation, down to its future ending. Down to our own day, the history of Judaism, apart from relatively short periods when the people had a central sanctuary, has been the history of the synagogue. Israel survived by means of the synagogue; that is why we now think of Judaism and synagogue as practically synonymous, and we have every justification for this.

The word perdures, while worship in the temple, even according to Jewish belief, is in abeyance until we see "the holy city, the new Jerusalem, coming down out of heaven from God, prepared as a bride adorned for her husband" (Apoc. 21:2). That new liturgy that will mark the coming of the Messiah in glory is the object of a hope that both the old and the new Israel share; even Christian liturgy is only a preparation for it (cf. *CL*, no. 8). It is also worth noting that the Greek words *synagoga* (gathering of the covenanted people by God) and *ekklesia* (calling of men from among the nations to form the new people of God) are almost identical in meaning; both derive from the same original Hebrew idea. Here again, the Church is heir to the synagogue.

The components of a synagogal liturgy are determined by the nature of the occasion and the course followed by a religious gathering. There are a greeting and a reflection on what is about to take place; a first reading from "God's instruction" (from the Torah; this reading was called the *parasche*); singing, then reflection on what had been heard, while the new scroll was being brought forward; a second reading (from the prophets; a look into the future and the fulfillment of the promises; this reading was called the *haftarah*); a sermon, in which God's word, spoken "in those days," was made concrete and actual for "today"; prayer, blessing, and dismissal.

The first Christian community was thoroughly familiar with the synagogal service. Jesus himself regularly attended the synagogue on the Sabbath: "And he came to Nazareth, where he had been brought up; and he went to the synagogue, as his custom was, on the sabbath'' (Luke 4: 16). On that occasion he also let it be known that he was the Messiah whom Isaiah had promised (61: 1-2). According to Luke's account, Jesus, as one who was familiar with the Scriptures, came forward to do the second reading, the *haftarah* or reading from the prophets, and then to comment on it:

> He stood up to read; and there was given to him the book of the prophet Isaiah. He opened the book and found the place where it was written, ''The Spirit of the Lord is upon me, because he has anointed me to preach good news to the poor. He has sent me to proclaim release to the captives and recovery of sight to the blind, to set at liberty those who are oppressed, to proclaim the acceptable year of the Lord.'' And he closed the book, and gave it back to the attendant, and sat down; and the eyes of all in the synagogue were fixed on him. And he began to say to them, ''Today this scripture has been fulfilled in your hearing.'' And all spoke well of him, and wondered at the gracious words which proceeded out of his mouth (Luke 4: 16-22).

In his missionary work, Paul, and probably other missionaries as well, liked to take advantage of the synagogal liturgy of the Diaspora Jews. It was a perfectly logical step, after all, to follow up the reading of the prophetic promises with the proclamation that the Messiah had in fact already come. That is how Paul proceeded at Antioch in Pisidia (Acts 13: 14-41), at Iconium (Acts 14: 1), at Philippi (Acts 16: 12), at Thessalonica (Acts 17: 1), and elsewhere. He was eager to preach to his fellow Jews, and the opportunity was there because of the synagogal practice of inviting traveling visitors, if they were scribes, to speak to the assembled community: ''Brethren, if you have any word of exhortation for the people, say it'' (Acts 13: 15).

Preaching in the synagogue was not reserved to priests but could, in principle, be done by anyone capable of it, if the president of the synagogue, who was in charge of the assembly, issued the invitation. Paul was not a Levite, but belonged to the tribe of Benjamin (Rom. 11: 1; Phil. 3: 5). According to Old Testament law, Jesus himself was not a ''priest'' but a ''layman'' from the house of David and the tribe of Judah (Matthew 1: 3). The synagogal liturgy was essentially a liturgy conducted by laymen, even though Levites were given preference for certain actions, such as the final blessing.

By the time of Jesus, long tradition had created a variety of functions in the Jewish liturgy of the word and had also produced a definite arrangement of the assembly hall. The president of the synagogue (*archisynagogos*) had his set place on ''Moses' seat'' (Matthew 23: 2), amid the group of leaders (*archisynagogoi*) and facing the congregation. He appointed the readers and preachers on the occasions when he chose not to fill these roles himself. At times a master of ceremonies (*hazzan*) assisted him. The officiant's chair and the pulpit were usually elevated, as archeologists have discovered in excavated synagogues. The congregation sat on three sides of the hall in a three-quarter circle around the reading desk and the president. It is uncertain, but not improbable, that there was some sort of choral group to handle responsorial or antiphonal psalmody. Notable, too, was the "hierarchic opposition" of president and congregation. The very earliest church buildings — for example, the mid-third century church at Dura Europos on the Euphrates — were very much like contemporary synagogues; evidently, a similarly structured liturgy led to a similar use of space.

3. The Basic Shape of the Liturgy of the Word

The earliest Christian liturgies of the word resembled those of the Jewish communities. The earliest accounts, for example that of Justin Martyr (middle of second century) tell us that there were two readings, a sermon, and a closing prayer. Justin does not mention singing, but on this point we receive unexpected help from a pagan witness, Pliny the Younger, governor of Bithynia in Asia Minor. In a letter to his friend Emperor Trajan, he reports that he had sent an observer to attend the Christian assembly. The observer told him that the Christians were accustomed to meet on a set day before dawn (*stato die ante lucem*) and sing an antiphonal hymn to Christ as their God; at the meeting they bound themselves to commit no violations of the law; then they departed and gathered again at a later hour for an inoffensive meal.[13] This report, written soon after 100 A.D., also attests the transfer of the liturgy to the morning hours and its separation from the regular community meal.

The shape of both the Jewish and the Christian liturgies of the word shows the dialogical structure proper to all liturgy. God initiates the process of salvation and addresses himself to men. His word reaches men and summons them to faith; through listening, silence, or hymnic reflection on the great deeds of God, the word that is heard creates a place for itself in the hearer, and the proclamation by the preacher, as he actualizes the word or gives it relevance here and now, makes it easier for the word to make its way into the soul. Finally, man can turn back to God in faith, confession, and shared prayer. Isaiah depicts this descending and ascending movement of the word in an impressive and beautiful comparison:

> For my thoughts are not your thoughts, neither are your ways my ways, says the Lord. For as the heavens are higher than the earth, so are my ways higher than your ways and my thoughts than your thoughts. For as

---

[13] *Epistulae*, Bk. 10, no. 96; text in K. Kirch, *Enchiridion fontium historiae* *ecclesiasticae* (5th ed.; Freiburg, 1941), pp. 22–23.

the rain and the snow come down from heaven, and return not thither but
water the earth, making it bring forth and sprout, giving seed to the sower
and bread to the eater, so shall my word be that goes forth from my
mouth; it shall not return to me empty, but it shall accomplish that which
I purpose, and prosper in the thing for which I sent it (Is. 55:8-11).

C. The Liturgy of the Word and the Eucharist as a Single Celebration

It was probably in the post-apostolic period, before the end of the first
century, that the Mass acquired the basic shape it has retained down to
the present time. The development did not take place everywhere at the
same time and in the same way. Yet, despite a multiplicity of religious
customs, there was an evident tendency in the Church, from the very
beginning, to assimilate the essential rites and the forms of organization of
the various communities.

Paul's account of the Last Supper is just as much a witness to this as are
the accounts in the Gospels. The evangelists clearly want the celebrations
in the communities to resemble one another, with the actions and words
of Christ as the model, while Paul gives explicit instructions to the same
effect. The celebration of the Lord's Supper was not simply to take any
form the moment might suggest, but was to be done in accordance with
Christ's last wishes. To preserve the link between liturgical action and its
historical origins, though not in a purist and unhistorical way, is a permanent obligation of the liturgy.

The relative uniformity in the celebration of the Mass in East and West
is attested at the end of the *First Apology* of Justin Martyr. Justin was
born in Flavia Neapolis (ancient Shechem) in Palestine and, in the reign of
Emperor Antoninus Pius, came by way of Ephesus to Rome (after 138),
where he was active as a professor of philosophy; in about 165 he was
beheaded along with six companions. Being a widely traveled man, he
knew the liturgical customs of a number of communities; consequently his
account of the liturgy is extremely important. In chapters 65–67 of his
First Apology, Justin gives two descriptions of the celebration of Mass. In
chapter 65 he describes the Eucharistic liturgy that accompanies the sacrament of baptism and in which the administration of the sacrament
replaces the liturgy of the word; then, after some dogmatic statements on
the nature of the Eucharist (chapter 66), in chapter 67 he gives a summary
description of the Sunday liturgy.

> *Chapter 65.* After we have thus cleansed the person who believes and
> has joined our ranks, we lead him in to where those we call "brothers"
> are assembled to offer prayers in common for ourselves, for him who has
> just been enlightened, and for all men everywhere. It is our desire, now

that we have come to know the truth, to be found worthy of doing good deeds and obeying the commandments, and thus to attain eternal salvation. When we finish praying, we greet one another with a kiss. Then bread and a cup containing water and wine mixed with water are brought to him who presides over the brethren; he takes them and offers prayer, glorifying the Father of all things through the name of the Son and the Holy Spirit; and he utters a lengthy thanksgiving because the Father has judged us worthy of these gifts. When the prayer of thanksgiving is ended, all the people present give their assent with an "Amen!" ("Amen" in Hebrew means "So be it.") When the president has given thanks and the people have all signified their assent, those whom we call "deacons" distribute the bread and the wine and water, over which the thanksgiving has been spoken, to each of those present; they also carry them to those who are absent.

Chapter 66. This food we call "eucharist," and no one may share it unless he believes that our teaching is true, and has been cleansed in the bath of forgiveness for sin and of rebirth, and lives as Christ taught. For we do not receive these things as though they were ordinary food and drink. Just as Jesus Christ our Savior was made flesh through the word of God and took on flesh and blood for our salvation, so too (we have been taught), through the word of prayer that comes from him, the food over which the thanksgiving has been spoken becomes the flesh and blood of the incarnate Jesus, in order to nourish and transform our flesh and blood. For in the memoirs which the apostles composed and which we call "gospels," they have told us that they were commissioned thus: Jesus took bread and, having given thanks, said: "Do this in memory of me; this is my body"; and in a like manner he took the cup and, having given thanks, said: "This is my blood," and he gave it to the apostles alone. . . .

Chapter 67. . . . And on the day named after the sun, all who live in city or countryside assemble, and the memoirs of the apostles or the writings of the prophets are read for as long as time allows. When the lector has finished, the president addresses us, admonishing us and exhorting us to imitate the splendid things we have heard. Then we all stand and pray, and, as we said earlier, when we have finished praying, bread, wine, and water are brought up. The president offers prayers of thanksgiving, according to his ability, and the people give their assent with an "Amen!" Next, the gifts over which the thanksgiving has been spoken are distributed, and each one shares in them, while they are also sent via the deacons to the absent brethren.

The wealthy who are willing make contributions, each as he pleases, and the collection is deposited with the president who aids orphans and widows, those who are in want because of sickness or other cause, those in prison, and visiting strangers; in short, he takes care of all in need.

The reason why we all assemble on Sunday is that it is the first day: the day on which God transformed darkness and matter and created the world, and the day on which Jesus Christ our Savior rose from the dead. On the day before Saturn's day they crucified him, and on the day after Saturn's day, that is, on Sunday, he appeared to his apostles and disciples and taught them what we have presented for your consideration.[14]

[14] *Apologia I*, 65–67; text in Hänggi-Pahl, *op. cit.*, pp. 68–73.

The account is exceptionally informative for us, for it tells us that by 150 A.D., at the latest, the basic outline of the Mass was already as we know it today. We are told that in the liturgy of the word on Sunday, the basic elements were at least these: two readings by a lector, a sermon by the president, and prayer in common at the end (ch. 67). The prayer in common was kept even when the administration of baptism replaced the liturgy of the word (65); presumably the mystagogic rites of the sacrament were regarded as a substitute for the readings. The celebration of the Eucharist proper, which is described twice in almost identical terms (65 and 67), follows the three-stage rhythm of Jesus' own action (66). He took bread and wine; gave thanks, explaining the new meaning of the bread and wine; and he distributed them; so in the Christian Eucharist there is a bringing of the gifts, a Eucharistic prayer, and a distribution.

The true presence of the Lord in the bread and wine is affirmed in a straightforward manner, as though it were self-evident. The communal meal, in connection with which the Eucharist had been celebrated in the apostolic period, has meanwhile been separated from the liturgy. The feeding of the poor by means of the gifts made at Mass by the better-off members of the community took place at its own time, probably in the evening according to Mediterranean custom.

Special emphasis is laid on the participation of the community. The president is to the fore as the active agent, but the assenting "Amen" of the congregation is twice explicitly mentioned.

The designation of Sunday as the day for the community assembly was long since accepted, as the New Testament shows us for the apostolic period. The Lord arose on the first day of the week (Matthew 28:1; Mark 16:2; Luke 24:1; John 20:1) and appeared that same day to the apostles in the upper room (John 20:19; Luke 24:36) and to the disciples at Emmaus (Luke 24:31). The fact of the community's assembling on the first day of the week is explicitly attested for Troas (Acts 20:7) and for Corinth (1 Cor. 16:2; here, as in Galatia, the liturgy was the occasion for collecting money for the Jerusalem community). In the Apocalypse of John (1:10), Sunday is already called "the Lord's day," as it is in the *Didache* (14:1) and in St. Ignatius of Antioch's letter to the community of Magnesia in Asia Minor (9:1).

Let us summarize briefly. The origin of the celebration of Mass was the farewell meal — probably a Passover meal — which Jesus took with his disciples and in which he spoke the new interpretive words over the elements of a meal, namely bread and wine. These elements, as his "body given" and his "blood poured out," represent, that is, make present, his death and expiatory sacrifice. The disciples are to imitate what he did and thus celebrate a memorial of him by speaking a blessing (*berakah, eucharistia*) over the bread and wine, as was the Jewish custom at the blessing that began the meal and at the blessing over the third Passover cup.

In the apostolic period, the two blessings, previously divided by the regular meal, were brought together, formulated as parallels, and placed as a single rite at the end of the meal. In the post-apostolic period, once the communal meal with its divisive abuses had been separated from the Eucharist entirely, the latter was connected with a liturgy of the word that was structured like the synagogal liturgy. This development began in the first century and was already completed by the middle of the second century (around 150, according to the testimony of Justin Martyr). This basic structure of the Mass has remained normative for the Church down to the present time and is manifest in all the Eucharistic rites to be found in the history of the Church.

2 HISTORICAL CHANGE IN THE CELEBRATION OF THE MASS

A. The Creative Early Period

As our look at the basic structure of the Mass has already shown us, the apostolic and post-apostolic communities gave genuine but not slavish obedience to Christ's commission that they celebrate his memorial using the elements and prayers proper to a festive meal. The concrete circumstances of each period, however, forced the communities to develop suitable forms. As is usual with beginnings, the early history of the Mass was marked by the exercise of extensive creativity until a form was found that best suited the needs of the moment, even though it would have to undergo new changes as time brought new situations; the one proviso was that the basic structure remain unchanged. Over and over again, ceremonies supplied or suggested by the sociocultural context would be tested and then, when adopted, fused with what was unique and specifically Christian in the Mass.

In this chapter we shall endeavor to provide a brief sketch of the historical forces that influenced and shaped the celebration of the Mass. We have no intention, however, of offering a complete history of the liturgy. A limited number of historical facts will be presented that are, or could be, of some value for understanding the liturgy as we now have it and possibly for shaping it further. Such facts as had but passing significance or ceased to operate at some earlier time have gone unmentioned. Frequently, however, the real contemporary meaning that shapes and forms had when first introduced were later forgotten, yet the forms have been preserved to the present time. In such cases, historical explanation can still be helpful in the attempt to gain an objectively valid and more profound understanding of these forms, or even to infuse new life into them.

1. THE JEWISH AND HELLENISTIC HERITAGE

Christ, his apostles, and the first communities lived in a world that was formed by Jewish thinking and Jewish liturgical practice.

This is enough to tell us that the Christian liturgy derived its initial forms from Judaism. Research, especially during the last fifty years, has made it clear that Christian worship has its roots in Judaism, especially in the latter's intertestamental form — that is, the Judaism of the period that saw the redaction of the final writings of the Old Testament and the first writings of the New — much more than in Hellenism and its mystery religions, in which the nineteenth century preferred to see the origins of Christianity and its liturgy.

As we noted earlier in some detail, the idea of a real memorial, which is basic to an understanding of the Mass, is a Jewish idea. In Jewish theology, God is graciously, "sacramentally" present, as the faithful covenant-God of the community, whenever the memorial of his saving deeds is celebrated. Similarly, the Mass is always the "new Passover." whether or not the Last Supper of Jesus was truly a Passover meal, that is, whether in sheer historical fact it was such a meal or whether the Synoptics — Luke in particular — simply imposed on it a theological interpretation relating it to Passover. This is so because the Eucharist derives its vital power from the *today* of God's saving action.

The Eucharistic prayer, which is the central component of the entire Eucharistic worship, derives from the blessings or praises (*berakoth*, *eucharistiai*) of domestic Jewish liturgical celebrations. In addition, the material elements used in the celebration of the Eucharist already had a cultic dimension because of the role they played in the Passover meal. While bread was basic in man's nourishment, wine was that which "cheers gods and men" (Judg. 9:13) and "gladdens the heart of man" (Ps. 104:15), and was characteristic of a Jewish festive meal as contrasted with the usual simple evening meal of the Palestinian peasant, at which water was drunk. In the Passover *haggadah* of the master of the household, the bitter experiences in Egypt were to the fore as he explained the *mazzah* or "bread of affliction"; when it came to the cup of wine, however, attention turned to the great deeds of God, up to and including the occupation of Palestine under Joshua. Even prior to the occupation, Isaac, in his blessing of his first-born, sums up a good land as one that supplies "plenty of grain and wine" (Gen. 27:28). We should also bear in mind the high cultic dignity that bread had in the *minhah*, or cereal offering (Lev. 2; etc.) and wine in the libation (Exod. 29:38-41; Num. 15:2-15; Lev. 23:13), and both gifts in the sacrifice of Melchizedek (Gen. 14:18).

As we have already seen, the Christian liturgy of the word was also largely taken over from the synagogue, where we find forms of common prayer and psalmody, liturgical proclamation and preaching. There can be no mistaking the basic similarity between the "Eighteen Blessings" (the *Shemoneh 'Esreh*, a prayer with eighteen stanzas) at the end of the synagogal liturgy and the prayers of the Christian community (see St. Justin).

The signs used in the other sacraments were also all to be found in the world of Jesus and the apostles; the ritual baths, the anointings, and the laying on of hands (as a ritual of blessing and of reconciliation, but also as the sign by which rabbis and official teachers in Israel were initiated into their office). Even the furniture later used in Christian places of worship was familiar to Judaism; for example, the presidential chair and the benches for the collegial priesthood. The synagogue inspired the early Christian Syro-Aramaic basilicas (fourth to seventh centuries) that were built in the region beyond Antioch on the Orontes; these too had an elevated bema or podium for the reader in the middle of the nave and curtains hiding the altar (like the curtain in front of the chest containing the Torah scrolls).

The seven-day week was also an inheritance from Judaism, even though the first day of the week, being the day of Christ's resurrection, soon became more important than the Sabbath; the principle applied in dividing time was the same. For a long time Easter was celebrated on the same day as the Jewish Passover. This custom held on longer in the East, among the Quartodecimans, who initially kept the fourteenth of Nisan as the date, than in the West, where Easter was moved to Sunday, thus manifesting the new understanding of what Passover meant for the Christian. The feast of Pentecost was already known in Judaism as the Feast of Weeks (the feast held after seven weeks; cf. Deut. 16:9) and as the feast of the fiftieth day (*pentekostē* is the Greek word for "fiftieth"; cf. Tob. 2:1; 2 Macc. 12:32), the point of reference being Passover (cf. Lev. 23:15-16).

Another inheritance from Judaism was the duty of praying morning and evening and at the third, sixth, and ninth hours; these times of prayer live on as Lauds, and Vespers, Terce, Sext, and None in the Breviary. Many of our prayer formulas are Jewish in origin: for example, the summons to prayer ("Let us pray"; "Let us give thanks to the Lord our God"); the endings of prayers (the "forever and ever" formulas); acclamations and interjections (*Amen*, "So it is; so be it"; *Hosannah*, "Save!"; Halleluja,

"Praise Yahweh!''); and the pleonastic response "And with your spirit" (= "And with you"). The style of the priest's presidential prayers likewise reflects Jewish practice, for in both the "paradigm" pattern is followed; that is, after God has been invoked, his past saving deeds are recalled and become the basis for confident petition through Christ our Lord.

Judaism was also familiar with the cult of the martyrs, which would later become very important in the Church, especially in connection with the Mass and the altar. The Pharisees decorated the tombs of the prophets and just men who had been slain for their adherence to the truth (cf. Matthew 23:29-30; Luke 11:48). According to Roman law, a tomb, generally speaking, was to be left untouched, but the Jewish custom was to place the dead in a rock chamber where the flesh would decay, and later on to transfer the bones to small sarcophaguses (ossuaries, *osteothekai*). Recent archeological excavations at Jerusalem have brought countless such "reliquaries" to light. We are told that the dead Christ was laid in a "new tomb where no one had ever been laid" (John 19:41; cf. Matthew 27:60; Luke 23:53). In other words, tombs could be used a number of times.

The Christian practice of gathering and preserving the relics of the martyrs for future veneration is mentioned for the first time in the Acts of the martyrdom of St. Polycarp of Smyrna. It is there reported that after the Saint's body had been cremated, "we collected the bones that were more precious to us than costly gems and more valuable than gold, and we buried them in a suitable place. There, as far as possible, we will gather in joy and gladness, and the Lord will let us celebrate the anniversary day of his martyrdom."[1]

Some of the early forms inherited from Judaism were later enriched with Hellenistic elements, and at times even transformed by them. Thus the celebration of Easter rid itself almost entirely of the customs and motifs that marked the Jewish feast, and instead laid a heavy emphasis on the symbolism of light and especially on the transition from darkness to the coming of light. The emphasis was very likely conditioned by the fact that the celebration took place during the night and lasted until morning. In any case, Christ was celebrated as the Light of the world (cf. Matthew 4:16; Luke 2:32; John 1:5, 9; 8:12; etc.).

This rich symbolism carried over to baptism. The administration of the sacrament to sunrise — especially at Easter — made it appropriate to utter the renunciation of Satan while facing the west, and the commitment to Christ while facing the east and the rising sun. In imitation of secular

[1] *Martyrdom of Polycarp*, 18; Greek text in Herbert Musurillo, *The Acts of the Chris-* *tian Martyrs* (Oxford, 1972).

customs connected with bathing, the sacrament of baptism was enriched by a subsequent anointing. The anointing became one of the rites leading into confirmation and even became more important than the imposition of hands by which originally the sacrament had been administered (cf. Acts 8:17).

The expressions of assent that had been used in the Jewish blessing after a meal were transformed under the influence of the typically Hellenistic *axios* (= worthy, right) acclamations, and the result is still to be seen in the dialogue before the preface of the Mass.

It seems we must look solely to the Hellenistic world for the origin of the "discipline of the *arcanum* (secrecy)" that was maintained for a time in the early Church. This was an obligation to maintain secrecy concerning the religious rites, and had been typical of the Hellenistic mystery religions.

It was above all in the area of vocabulary that the liturgy, in the Roman Empire, laid aside its Jewish garb (except for a few words like "Amen") and donned a Hellenistic garb. This latter shows through today, despite all the linguistic changes since that time, in the basic vocabulary we still use in connection with the public worship of the Church: Eucharist and liturgy, hymn and anamnesis, mystery and epiclesis, Epiphany and Pentecost, etc.

2. FREEDOM AND ORDER IN THE FORMULAS OF PRAYER

When the *Didache* (10:6) allows the prophets "to give thanks as much as they wish," and when Justin in his *First Apology* (67:5) reports that at the Eucharist the president offers prayers of thanksgiving "according to his ability," these notices amount to particular applications of a general principle, namely, that in the early Church the celebrant exercised freedom in formulating the liturgical texts. A charism attached to the office enabled the bishop and presbyter to formulate and lead the public prayer of the community. (Since the Latin verb *orare* means both to speak and to pray, an *oratio* amounted to a "prayer-speech.") The early Church took seriously St. Paul's warning, "Do not quench the Spirit" (1 Thess. 5:19). In consequence, we must reckon with a wide variety of formulas in the early period. There must very soon have been written texts or at least prayers inherited and learned by heart, but there were no prescribed and binding formulas.

Freedom did not mean caprice. In the First Letter to the Corinthians (11:23-26), Paul expressly speaks of what he had "received from the Lord" and "delivered" to the community; he evidently intended that this tradition not be changed. We have already noted that the intention of the Synoptic evangelists in their accounts of institution was to pass on something meant to be normative.

The most important element in the fidelity of liturgical texts to tradition was that these texts should embody the common faith; they must have the "dogmatic accuracy" which Pope St. Celestine I (422–432) was to demand, in keeping with the principle that the "law of belief" and the "law of prayer" must be in harmony.[2] Both the will to unity among all who confessed the name of Jesus, and inherited custom were from the beginning important factors leading to unity in liturgical matters. Justin Martyr, for example, had been raised in Palestine, had known the customs of Asia Minor, and had lived in Rome before describing the course of the Mass, which was evidently everywhere the same. When St. Polycarp of Smyrna visited Pope Anicetus in Rome in 154, he accepted the invitation to preside over the Eucharist; clearly, the rite celebrated in Asia Minor hardly differed from that celebrated in Rome, at least in the basic structure of the liturgy of the word and of the Eucharist proper.

One factor that led to unity was the role of examplar which the liturgy in the administrative centers or capital cities of the various Roman provinces (dioceses at a later date) played in relation to the hinterland. Another factor making for approximation and even assimilation was the principle of collegiality in the episcopal and presbyteral orders; in addition, the bishops of the large cities kept in close touch with one another. From a very early date, the ground was already being prepared for the later system of patriarchates (see below). In fact, the model and forerunner of this system is to be found in the civil government of the Roman Empire, which cultivated a respect for the fact that regions and states had in the course of time developed their own traditions.

The early third century (*ca.* 225) has left us a precious witness to the liturgy as celebrated in the age of the martyrs. We refer to the *Apostolic Tradition*, a liturgical book written by the Roman priest Hippolytus, which is especially interesting with regard to the question of freedom and obligation in the liturgy. Hippolytus was a man of very conservative views, and quite unsympathetic to the evidently more "progressive" circle around the man who had once been a slave and then became Pope Callistus I (217–222). Hippolytus even went into schism for a while, but was reconciled to the Roman Church through martyrdom and was later venerated as a saint.

Hippolytus, a learned and prolific writer, composed, among other books, a Church order which he pointedly entitled *Apostolic Tradition*.

---

[2] Cf. the *Indiculus*, c. 8 (attributed to Pope Celestine I), in Henry Denzinger and Adolf Schönmetzer (eds.), *Enchiridion symbolorum* (32nd ed.; Freiburg, 1963), no. 246 [henceforth *DS* with number of text, e.g., *DS* 246].

His aim was to establish definitively the rite he knew as traditional, though it did not, as he thought, go back to apostolic times. In any case, he describes the same kind of liturgy we have already seen reported by Justin Martyr sixty or seventy years before. There is this difference, that Justin had simply given an outline of the rite, while Hippolytus gives us liturgical texts that were intended to serve as models and have in fact done so, especially for baptism and episcopal ordination.

Of great interest to us is the Canon, or Eucharistic prayer, which Hippolytus offers. It has been rewritten to become the Second Eucharistic Prayer of the recently reformed Roman liturgy. Here is a translation of Hippolytus's text:

Bishop: The Lord be with you.
    All: And with your spirit.
Bishop: Lift up your hearts.
    All: We have lifted them up to the Lord.
Bishop: Let us give thanks to the Lord.
    All: It is right and just.
Bishop: We thank you, O God, through your beloved child Jesus Christ,
    whom you have sent to us in the final age as Savior and Redeemer and messenger of your will;
    who is your Word, inseparable from you, through whom you created all things and who was pleasing to you;
    whom you sent from heaven into the womb of a Virgin and who, having been conceived, took flesh and was manifested as your Son, being born of the Holy Spirit and the Virgin;
    who carried out your will and won for you a holy people;
    who extended his arms in suffering, in order to free from suffering those who trust in you;
    who, when he was about to hand himself over to his passion, in order to destroy death and break the devil's chains, to tread hell under foot and lead the just to the light, to fix the term and reveal the resurrection, took bread, gave you thanks, and said, "Take and eat: this is my body which will be broken for you";
    who in like manner took the cup and said, "This is my blood that is poured out for you. When you do this, do it in memory of me."
    Therefore, remembering his death and resurrection, we offer you the bread and the cup, and we thank you for deeming us worthy to stand before you and serve you.
    We ask you to send your Holy Spirit upon the offering of your holy Church, and to grant that all your saints who share in it may be filled with the Holy Spirit and strengthened in their belief in the truth, so that we may praise and glorify you through your child Jesus Christ, through whom be glory and honor given to you, the Father, and to the Son with the Holy Spirit in your holy Church, now and for all ages.
    All: Amen.[3]

[3] *Traditio apostolica*, 4; text in Bernard Botte, *La Tradition Apostolique de saint Hippolyte: Essai de reconstitution* (Liturgiewissenschaftliche Quellen und Forschungen 39; Münster, 1963), pp. 10–16; also in Hänggi-Pahl, *op. cit.*, pp. 80–81.

This text is extremely important because it is the earliest surviving Eucharistic prayer and shows the continuity in the formulation of the Eucharistic prayer over a period of almost two thousand years. The Jewish prayer at the end of a meal clearly provides the pattern: an introductory dialogue, followed by the praise of God for his work in creation and redemption. There is this difference, of course, that the work of redemption, when specified in Hippolytus's prayer, does not refer to the old covenant but directly to God's action in Christ: the incarnation, the "winning of a holy people," the redemptive suffering, death, and resurrection of Christ, and his final gift at the Last Supper.

In Hippolytus's view, the celebration of the memorial is unmistakably the Church's sacrifice that is effected by the Holy Spirit (through the "epiclesis"), who also makes communion a saving sacrament. The final doxology is almost the same as ours today, except that in Hippolytus praise is given to the Father *and* the Son rather than to the Father *through* the Son.

Characteristic of the style of this Eucharistic prayer is the unbroken flow which is created by the series of relative clauses attached to "your beloved child Jesus Christ," and which has been deliberately preserved in the translation, awkward though it is for our modern ear. (In the official translation of the new Eucharistic prayers and other presidential prayers, relative clauses have usually been recast as independent clauses: "O God, you have . . ." instead of "O God, who . . . .") But whatever the style, the element of praise is very prominent in Hippolytus's prayer, with the Father, through the Son and in the Spirit, being the source of all blessings and therefore deserving all praise.

This type of Eucharistic prayer is what Hippolytus tells us is traditional, even "apostolic," and therefore to be taken as normative. We may well believe that in such Eucharistic prayers other saving acts of God were also mentioned; the text as Hippolytus gives it sounds like a brief summary. (We may think, too, that the words "worthy to stand before you and serve you" are occasioned by the episcopal ordination that has just preceded this Eucharistic prayer.) We must also note what Hippolytus says about his Eucharistic prayer: "Let the bishop give thanks in the manner we have described. It is by no means necessary, however, that in giving thanks the bishop use the same words we have, learning them by heart as it were; rather, let each one pray according to his ability."[4] Later editors crossed out the words "by no means," and had Hippolytus ordering everyone to use the formulary he had set down!

Despite the fact that the author of the text had been leader of a schismatic community at Rome, the text itself was seen to be entirely orthodox, and it came into general use throughout the Church. It has been preserved

[4] Chapter 4, in Botte, *op. cit.*, p. 28; Hänggi-Pahl, *op. cit.*, p. 80.

for us in Latin and especially in Egyptian (Sahidic, Bohairic, Arabic, Old Ethiopic) translations, and was known in fact for centuries as the "Egyptian Church Order," until scholars of our century (Schwartz, Connolly, Elfers) recognized its Roman origin. Hippolytus's text also became the basis for what is probably an Antiochene liturgy in the *Apostolic Constitutions* (fourth century). Clearly, Hippolytus's prayer must have met a generally felt need; the age of the charismatics was over.

3. Facing the East at Prayer

"Orientation" at prayer, that is, the physical turning toward the east while praying, seems rather meaningless to us today, but it exercised a very important influence on the Christian liturgy from an early date. In particular, it determined the layout of church buildings from the third century on, and, later, the position taken by the celebrant during the Eucharistic liturgy. Until quite recently, it was almost a fixed rule that a church should face east, that is, that the separate choir area should be at the east end of the building; only serious reasons having to do with the layout of the city itself or the nature of the terrain made a departure from this principle acceptable. In antiquity, people regarded the principle as very important; thus, even in everyday life, it was thought essential that the main streets of a city should run north-south and east-west, and thus reproduce the axle-trees formed by the four cardinal points. In this way the order of the heavens was reflected in the plan of the city; only then was the city "in order." Much more, then, were sacred buildings obliged to follow this pattern and observe the proper direction in worship.

It is obvious that when people pray inside a temple, they should turn to the image of the god and thus to the Holy of Holies. After all, even in ordinary conversation we turn face and body to the other. That is why the Old Testament frequently uses phrases like "Turn your face" or "Lift up your hands to the holy place" (Ps. 134:2; etc.) with reference to individuals praying, while God in turn is said to "send you help from the sanctuary" (Ps. 20:3). Logically, then, when the believer found himself far from the sanctuary, or sojourning in a foreign country where all was bitterness to him, or living in the Diaspora, he turned, when praying, to the sanctuary, and did so not only with the interior desire of the heart but even in the exterior position and posture he adopted. In prisoner of war camps, for example, men knew in precisely which direction their homeland lay.

We find a record of this custom in Judaism, along with the reason for it, in Solomon's prayer at the dedication of the Temple, as set down in the postexilic redaction of 1 Kings 8:44-45: "If thy people go out to battle against their enemy, by whatever way thou shalt send them, and they pray to the Lord toward the city which thou hast chosen and the house which I have built for thy name, then hear thou in heaven their prayer and their supplication, and maintain their cause." And again, in verses 48-49: "If they repent with all their mind and with all their heart in the land of their enemies, who carried them captive, and pray to thee toward their land, which thou gavest to their fathers, the city which thou hast chosen, and the house which I have built for thy name; then hear thou in heaven thy dwelling place their prayer and their supplication, and maintain their cause."

As a matter of fact, the ancient synagogues that have been excavated face toward Jerusalem. Thus, in Dura Europos on the Euphrates the synagogue faces west; in Ostia near Rome and on the island of Delos, southeast; in Galilee, south; in Gaza, northeast; etc. As indicated, in these cases we have what is called a "centralization" rather than an orientation in the strict sense of a "facing eastward." We ourselves now use the phrase "to orient oneself" in a similar way: not only to turn to the east, but to get one's bearings, to adjust to a situation.

In the beginning, the doors or windows of Jewish houses of prayer faced Jerusalem and were opened during prayer, in order, as it were, to allow the prayer to move freely in the direction of the sanctuary. There is an allusion to this custom in the Book of Daniel: "When Daniel knew that the document [ordering his death] had been signed, he went to his house where he had windows in his upper chamber open toward Jerusalem; and he got down upon his knees three times a day and prayed and gave thanks before his God, as he had done previously" (6:10). Later on, beginning in the second/third centuries after Christ, synagogues contained a holy of holies, set against the wall that looked toward Jerusalem. Here a chest containing the Torah scrolls (*Aron Kodesh*) stood behind an obligatory curtain (*parokhet*); here too was the seven-branched candelabrum (*menorah*). All of these the synagogue took over from the temple. It must be remembered, however, that the Jew in the synagogue looked beyond the shrine with the Torah, where God dwelt among his people by means of the word; the Jew was oriented to the last day and the coming Messiah.

The Mishnah and the Talmud take the physical orientation for granted.[5] Even today the Jew says his obligatory prayers while facing in the direction of the Temple, which, though destroyed long ago, will be rebuilt again in the days of the Messiah or will descend from heaven, really or symbolically. In this respect, we share the expectation of our Jewish brothers, for St. John, in his vision of the messianic age at the end, sees "the holy city

[5] Mishnah, Seder Zeraim, Tractate Berakoth 4, 5 (Danby, *op. cit.*, p. 5); and in the Talmud, Tractate Yebamoth 105b, in *The Babylonian Talmud: Seder Nashim: Yebamoth*, translated by I. W. Slotki (1959), 3:726–27.

Jerusalem coming down out of heaven from God, having the glory of God, its radiance like a most rare jewel, like a jasper, clear as crystal'' (Apoc. 21:10-11).

After the middle of the second century A.D., by 200 at the latest, when the last great Jewish uprisings had been crushed and the Jewish people were forced to lay aside, for the time being at least, their hopes for a central sanctuary, the practice of turning to the east took on a primarily messianic meaning. But in Judaism and Christianity the meaning differed, reflecting confessional divergences. Jews naturally looked for a Messiah who *would come* in Jerusalem, while Christians awaited a Messiah who *would return* from the east (cf. Matthew 24:27: "For as lightning comes from the east . . . , so will be the coming of the Son of Man''; cf. Apoc. 7:2). Prayers said while facing eastward became, for the Christian, an eschatological confession of the divinity of Jesus. If the Christian, like the Jew, were to face toward the former Temple, he would be denying the divinity of Christ, since the Jew thought the promised Messiah had not yet come; by praying toward the east, the Christian showed that he was awaiting Christ as the Son of God "who will come again in glory."

A favorite theme of the paintings and mosaics in the sanctuaries and, later, the apses of churches came to be the cross, regarded as the herald and "sign of the Son of Man" who will be "coming on the clouds of heaven" (Matthew 24:30) in order to judge the world and bring the kingdom to its completion. To pray toward the east, therefore, was to pray with a correct faith to the Father through Christ in the Holy Spirit. Not only the faith but even the bodily attitude of the Christian was a profession of faith. What could be more natural, then, than to structure the church building in such a way that the eastward position for prayer was rendered easy and suggested to the devotee by the arrangement of the physical space?

The oldest extant church, in Dura Europos on the Euphrates and dating from the mid-third century, faces east, and this was not accidental, since the church was part of a larger complex, and rooms that faced in other directions were also available. The churches of the Eastern empire usually had the apse at the east end from the beginning; Roman churches (Lateran, St. Peter's, St. Paul's Outside the Walls on the road to Ostia, etc.) originally had apses at the west end, but after 420 the altar was regularly placed at the east end. In either case, the principle that the length of the church should be on an east-west axis was everywhere the same.

The law of orientation was to have important consequences. It had hardly any application when it came to the liturgy of the word (included under the term here are the Office and the general intercessions of the faithful), but it did come into play in the official prayers of the Eucharist.

The practice of having the celebrant face the congregation at prayer changed rather early into the practice of having the celebrant and congregation face in the same direction — the east. In the long run, this in turn influenced the position of the celebrant at the altar; now he always kept his back to the people. It also led to the transfer of the bishop's chair from the back wall of the apse to the side of the sanctuary, and to the transfer of the altar from the center of the sanctuary to the rear side of it, where in the course of time the altar became a kind of console table. Through these changes our churches came to resemble long passageways, and they have kept this appearance down to the present.

The principle of orientation admittedly disappeared from the popular consciousness in the Middle Ages and in modern times; yet on grounds of tradition, though frequently with no grasp of the real point, it continued to be observed in the construction of churches and the location of altars. In our day, the logical conclusion has been drawn from the change of consciousness, and the altar is again being placed in the center between priest and people. In other words, the "ideological" law of orientation, by which the original and natural relationship between celebrant and congregation had been distorted and become unfamiliar, has now been given up in favor of the older and, from the functional viewpoint, certainly more correct face-to-face position of priest and people. It is to be noted that even in the past the change of position for the celebrant at the altar was never carried through with logical consistency; for example, the so-called papal altars in the Roman basilicas, as well as the pontifical Mass itself, represent a different line of tradition.

B. The Inclusive Church

Throughout the entire third century, the Church was already changing from a collection of "communities of brothers" into an inclusive Church (*Volkskirche*, or "Church of the people," that is a Church to which the entire population, and not just committed believers, belonged). Contrary to what is often said, the shift did not begin only with the "Constantinian Turning Point," that is, with the official recognition of the Church by the State and with the consequent realization on the part of people that it was no longer dangerous but, on the contrary, advantageous to be a Christian.

It is a waste of time regretting or approving the historical fact. If the Church is to be obedient to the Lord's command, "Go therefore and make disciples of all nations, baptizing them in the name of the Father and of the Son and of the Holy Spirit, teaching them to observe all that I have commanded you" (Matthew 28:19-20), she must be a missionary Church. She must expand and inevitably become an inclusive Church, for that is a logical conclusion from the premise. Otherwise we would have to suppose that God's will for man's salvation is not really universal and that what he really wants is a small Church of the "chosen" and the "pure" (Greek *katharoi*, from which the German word for "heretic," *Ketzer*, is derived). Such, however, is not the mind of the Church.

There is no doubt, of course, that an inclusive Church will look a lot different from a small persecuted community of confessing Christians. A tree builds up ring after ring of wood, out to the outermost bark-covered layer that gets barely enough of the sap. Analogously, an inclusive Church must turn what used to be a relatively short catechumenate for adults preparing for baptism into a lifelong catechumenate for those baptized as children; otherwise she will be corrupted by what we might call "Christianity without personal decision." Even in our day, the community that gathers around the altar must, in all modesty, accept the mission of being the leaven in the mass of the inclusive Church (see Matthew 13:33).

1. THE PROBLEM OF LANGUAGE

If we prescind from the very early Jewish-Christian communities of Jerusalem and Judea, the language of the early Church was Greek. Even the Jews of the Diaspora spoke Greek in their everyday life; they had even translated the Bible into Greek for their own use (the Septuagint). The New Testament writings of the first century were written in the form of Greek known as *koinē* ("common [language]," that is, the Greek commonly spoken and written in the eastern Mediterranean world). Even Christian circles in Rome spoke Greek, as did the middle class and the simpler people generally. Only the African provinces continued to use Latin, with the result that African Christian writers like Tertullian and Cyprian in the third century composed their works in that language. On the whole, however, language barriers within the Church were almost non-existent.

In the Roman Empire, especially from the late third century on, a process of disintegration can be observed that was doubtless hastened by the great political and military crises. The self-assertive tendencies of the various provinces acted as centrifugal forces within the more or less uniform imperial culture and led to radical changes on the cultural scene. Aspirations that had always been at work beneath the surface but had been scorned as barbarian suddenly acquired new vitality; frequently these aspirations were very much favored by Christians, as for example among the fellahin of Egypt or the population in the Syrian hinterland.

Despite the thoroughly cosmopolitan outlook of Christianity and its deep-seated tendency to regard all cultures as equal, during this period it often fostered an awareness of the old ethnic traditions and helped in the development of new national cultures. In this respect, it was especially important that Christianity had, on the whole, reached and evangelized the lower strata of the population rather than the influential upper level of the culture, for this meant that the self-assertive thrust in the provinces came from below rather than from the top.

It can be taken as axiomatic for the early period of Church history that the colloquial language of everyday life was always and unquestioningly used in common worship. This meant that for a long time Greek was the most widely used language. Now the situation changed, and the problem of translation suddenly became pressing, increasingly so as the Church advanced from the Hellenistic world of the Mediterranean coast into the hinterland. Alexandria, for example, was a Hellenistic city, but down the lengthy oasis formed by the Nile the people generally spoke Coptic, Sahidic, or Bohairic. The situation was the same for Antioch on the Orontes, a city that soon became "a Hellenistic island in an Aramaic sea." [6]

At Rome, too, by the early fourth century at the latest, people were becoming aware once again of their native Latin language. It had been taken for granted that the Roman liturgy of Hippolytus in the third century should be in Greek, but under Pope Damasus, in the mid-fourth century, the problem of language or translation had become urgent. Around 370, Marius Victorinus, in his commentary (in Latin) on St. Paul, could still quote liturgical texts in Greek. Around 380/390, however, that is, only ten years or so later, Amrbrosiaster, in his exegesis of the Pauline letters (exegesis which Erasmus mistakenly attributed to St. Ambrose), was quoting a section of the Roman Canon in Latin; he also pointed out a mistake in translation that has not been corrected even in our day, namely, that Melchizedech should be characterized not as "high priest" (*summus sacerdos*) but as "priest of the Most High God" (*sacerdos summi Dei*) in accordance with Genesis 14:18.

There is good reason, then, for thinking that the beginning of an official Latin liturgy at Rome is to be dated around 380, during the pontificate of Pope Damasus. This judgment is supported by the fact that at this same period and by commission from the same Pope, Jerome was producing the official Latin translation of the Bible, known as the Vulgate, which was meant to supply a single text for universal use and which, in fact, quickly supplanted the early private translations.

The beginnings of the Latin Roman liturgy are rather obscure. The oldest manuscripts date only from the seventh/eighth century and, frequently, from Frankish scriptoria. They contain, of course, much older

---

[6] The words are those of Viktor Schultze.   *ten* 3: *Antiocheia* (1930).
See his *Altchristliche Städte und Landschaf-*

liturgical material that goes back in part (the Canon, for example) to the fourth century and derives, or claims to derive, from popes such as Leo the Great (440–461), Gelasius I (492–496), and Gregory the Great (590–604). A great deal of research — philological, theological, and liturgico-historical — has been done on these texts, and we now have a much clearer picture of the development, though we have not reached certainty on all points.

The Latin liturgy, as we have it from the fourth/fifth century, is not simply a translation of Greek models, but a restatement in a new idiom. There was no attempt at a word-for-word transposition, no attempt to dye the old coat a new color, as it were. Rather, the whole liturgy was given an authentically Latin shape and form, a truly Latin embodiment. This becomes especially clear when we compare the Canon of Hippolytus (translated some pages back) with the Roman Canon (see Part II, Chapter 3 B 2, below), or when we analyze the style of the Latin collects.

Hippolytus's Eucharistic prayer was characterized by an even flow that was achieved by attaching a series of relative clauses to the opening address, with each clause directly or indirectly illustrating the creative and redemptive action God alone could accomplish. The Roman Canon, on the other hand, is a highly artificial but also thoroughly artistic structure. Its center is the words of consecration and the formula of sacrificial offering; around these, and grouped in strictly symmetrical fashion, are the expressions of sacrificial intention, the petitions, the lists of intercessors, and the epicleses for consecration and communion (though the meaning of these was obscured).

Not only is the structure of the Roman Canon new and independent, but the style of speech is that of the jurists and rhetoricians of late antiquity. We may note especially the doubling or tripling of adjectives, and, in general, what strikes our ear as a rather punctiliously dignified manner of expression. The sacrificial aspect of the Mass is so emphasized that the Canon speaks of almost nothing else, and the element of praise finds expression, for practical purposes, only in the prefaces. The distinction between the variable prefaces and the almost completely unvarying Canon is made especially evident by the interposition of the Sanctus. The latter was originally spoken by the celebrant alone, but it very early became a kind of acclamation by the people and then bulked disproportionately large by reason of its being sung in a manner that eventually became quite artistic.

The various presidential prayers, or orations, of the Mass are specifically Roman in their impressive clarity, pregnant succinctness, conciseness, and lapidary form. They are often artistic productions of high literary quality, attractive and elegant, but their brevity and polish must at times have made excessive demands on the simple Christian.

The new incarnation of the liturgy in Latin in the fourth/fifth century stands as a paradigm for all future time. A liturgy takes root fully only when it has been not simply translated but so reworked that the concrete praying community can experience and acknowledge it as its own and find itself expressed therein. Such a transformation, however, can hardly be accomplished once and for all. Rather, it must be continually improved and adapted to a constantly changing culture, especially if it is to be celebrated in the living language of a people or country. In addition, there must very likely be the possibility of varying it according to the age, social condition, and intellectual background of the particular celebrating community. That is why this early period of "translations" is instructive even for us today.

2. LITURGICAL CENTERS

In the course of the fourth, fifth, and sixth centuries, the patriarchates came into existence within the Great Church, another name the historians give to the "inclusive Church." These were to play an extremely important part in the development of the liturgy, so much so that a "Rite" came to be characteristic of, and indeed almost synonymous with, each "union of Churches" or patriarchate.

Christianity was a religion of the cities, and it was from the major cities of the ancient world — Antioch, Alexandria, Rome, Ephesus, Corinth, and Carthage, to give but a few examples — that the missionaries carried Christianity into the surrounding countryside. In consequence, the bishop or archbishop of the major city soon acquired a pre-eminence in the diocese, the latter itself having been formed as a result of the relations of reciprocal dependence that had naturally grown up in the course of time between major city and surrounding area.

If the see in question had had an apostle or a disciple of the apostles as its founder, it was regarded as a preserver and defender of authentic apostolic tradition. Thus Antioch represented an ancient Petrine tradition, while Rome represented the traditions of both Peter and Paul. Alexandria boasted that it had been founded by Mark, a disciple of Peter. The bishops of such sees enjoyed a special pre-eminence from a very early period; they presided over regional synods, ordained (and, if need be, deposed) the bishops of their province, arbitrated in disputes, etc.

The cultural and economic infrastructures of the empire undoubtedly favored this development of the patriarchal sees, inasmuch as the large cities were crossroads for the trade routes, ports through which grain or oil were exported, and seats of provincial government; they enjoyed cultural eminence, the splendor peculiar to a planned community, and so forth. A further point that favored these cities was that they were focal points in the network of ecclesiastical communication and could serve as venues for conferences and synods. These structures of local interrelations were the foundation on which the larger ecclesiastical units were built, and they were instrumental in integrating the various early Churches into a single united Church.

The several imperial reforms of late antiquity led to the formation of "dioceses" (administrative units), each with a metropolis as its capital. These changes were reflected, during the post-Constantinian period, in the departmental structure of the Church, but the old ethnic and cultural units continued to be respected. The pre-eminence of the older large cities was of course unaffected, but the bishops (now called "metropolitans") of the new metropolises generally acquired, through assimilation, the same rights as the old archbishops; in fact, in many cases the old archbishop became the new metropolitan, as at Alexandria or Antioch. In other cases, however, the future proved, in the long run, to be with the new system of metropolitans rather than with the old system.

This shift is most evident in the position Constantinople acquired as the New Rome. Constantinople first had to gain its release from an older complex, whose center was Heraclea in Thrace, and achieve a certain degree of ecclesiastical independence. It quickly did so, for its metropolitan, bishop to the imperial court, was listed by the First Council of Constantinople (canon 6; 381 A.D.) immediately after the bishop of the Old Rome. Now that the old province of Asia had been subordinated to him, the metropolitan of Constantinople could claim for himself the importance that had attached to the old apostolic sees such as Ephesus and the other early foundations in Asia Minor, the "seven stars" of the Apocalypse (Apoc. 1:20). As a matter of fact, the newly founded Constantinople came in time to be far more important than the older sees and patriarchates of Alexandria and Antioch, which in the meanwhile had lost much of their influence. As a result, from the sixth century on, the metropolitan of Constantinople enjoyed the title of "Ecumenical Patriarch."

During the same period, the bishop of Jerusalem, whose inherited position of honor had been confirmed by the Council of Nicaea in 325 (canon 7), became a patriarch. In the West, however, the bishop of Rome claimed to be sole patriarch, and his more assertive exercise of papal primatial power prevented any other archbishop or metropolitan from attaining patriarchal rank. This was true even of Carthage, a city that in Cyprian's time had been as important as any Eastern diocese, but had gone into a sharp decline ever since the barbarian invasions. Under the Vandals the Arians controlled the city; in Justinian's time the city became subordinate to Constantinople; and, finally, in the seventh century it fell to the Arabs. The once flourishing Christianity of the ancient province of Africa was almost wiped out.

During the Christological controversies of the fifth century (Council of Ephesus in 431 and of Chalcedon in 451), the Nestorian and Monophysitic-Jacobite Churches went into schism and were soon thereafter lost to the empire in the Persian and Arabic onslaughts of the seventh century. Even in these areas, however, the patriarchal system developed in a similar manner, though persecutions created great difficulties. Thus in West Syria, Edessa acquired pre-eminence, while in East Syria and Persia great unions of Churches were established that even in the Middle Ages were expending astonishing energy on missions to the east as far as China. These Churches were rendered powerless, however, by the Tartar invasions. Events followed a similar course in Armenia, which was the center of so much conflict.

As we mentioned earlier, the new patriarchal sees of the great ecclesiastical units naturally proved to be liturgical no less than administrative centers, and the various episcopal sees attached to each patriarch followed his lead. The result was various liturgical families, within each of which only unimportant local differences were to be found. We must bear in mind, however, that before the divergence between liturgical groups, there had existed a general unity and notable similarity in the liturgy everywhere. We had occasion to observe how the liturgy of Hippolytus took hold in Rome and Italy, in Egypt and Antioch. Consequently, the basic components of the liturgy were almost everywhere identical, and the differences that arose concerned only secondary rites. In the early Church, moreover, the influence of Jerusalem was felt throughout all the liturgical provinces; the Holy City was, in Anton Baumstark's well-known phrase, the "devotional center" of all liturgy.[7]

A comprehensive listing and description of all these ancient liturgies would undoubtedly be very interesting, and valuable from the ecumenical viewpoint as well, but would take us beyond the limits of this book, which is concerned primarily with the Latin Mass. We shall therefore give a very brief and highly simplified rundown. (1) The Alexandrian Liturgy of St. Mark, along with the Coptic Liturgies of St. Cyril, St. Basil, and St. Gregory, and the Anaphora of the Apostles used in Ethiopia. (2) The Antiochene Liturgy of St. James, originally taken over from Jerusalem; other forms attached themselves to this (e.g., the "Clementine Liturgy" in the *Apostolic Constitutions*, which can ultimately be traced back to Hippolytus) or, as in the eastern hinterland, departed from it (e.g., the Liturgy of West Syrian Edessa or the Liturgy of the Apostles Addai and Mari in East Syria). (3) The Liturgy that became most widespread, especially through the later mission among the Slavs in the Balkans and in

---

[7] On the importance of Jerusalem as a liturgical center, see Baumstark's *Comparative Liturgy*, 3rd ed. by B. Botte, translated by F. L. Cross (Westminster, Md., 1958), *passim*.

Russia, was the Liturgy of Constantinople, which is named, with only limited justification, after St. John Chrysostom (354–*ca*. 407), the Church Doctor from Antioch who was patriarch of Constantinople from 398 to 404. This Liturgy of St. John Chrysostom, which is Antiochene-Cappadocian in origin, gradually pushed into the background the Liturgy of St. Basil, which was likewise used in early Constantinople, and also influenced practice at Alexandria and in Armenia. In the West, people often think of the Liturgy of St. John Chrysostom as being *the* Liturgy of the Eastern Church.

The number of different Latin liturgies in the West was greater in antiquity than is generally realized; most of the non-Roman liturgies disappeared from use only with the post-Tridentine unification of the liturgy. We can get a good idea of the relation between common substance and local variation if we recall, for example, that the oldest witness to parts of the Roman Canon is to be found, not at Rome, but in the *De sacramentis* of St. Ambrose, bishop of Milan, author of the liturgy proper to Milan, though this liturgy was heavily Romanized in the Carolingian period.

Closely related to the Ambrosian Liturgy was the Liturgy of Aquileia, which was suppressed only in 1594. In Benevento (southern Italy), too, the local Liturgy resisted the trend to unification that had been felt especially since Gregory the Great, and kept its own character for a long time. The Old Spanish Liturgy was in its prime under the Visigothic bishops of the seventh century; it survived the Arab conquest (711) and is therefore usually called the "Mozarabic" Liturgy (*musta' rib* = arabicized). Its use was already sharply curtailed under Pope Gregory VII (Synod of Burgos, 1081); once the Missal of Pope Pius V had been introduced in 1570, the Spanish Rite was, and still is, used only in a chapel of the Cathedral of Toledo.

The extensive Frankish realm especially had its own liturgy, the Old Gaulish (occasionally but erroneously called the "Gallican"), which at a very early date underwent strong Eastern influences. The particular liturgical customs of the Celtic-speaking populations, especially in Ireland and its sphere of influence, were closely related to those of the Old Gaulish and Old Spanish Liturgies, but they gradually disappeared under the Romanizing influence of the Anglo-Saxon Benedictines — in England from the seventh century on, in Brittany in the ninth century, and in Ireland itself only in the twelfth century (Synod of Cashel, 1172).

According to the Council of Trent itself, local traditions that were at least two hundred years old were not to be abolished by the new Missal and Breviary, though this frequently enough is just what happened, often as late as the nineteenth century. The Liturgies of Braga, Lyons, Milan, and Toledo have survived, as have individual components of Liturgies proper to some of the Latin religious Orders (Carthusians, Cistercians,

Premonstratensians, Carmelites, and Dominicans). Only time will tell how long these variants will continue to be used. Certainly it is desirable that in many cases they should survive, after any needed reforms.

Today, at any rate, as a result of all these developments in the course of history, we are able to recognize and justify the relativity of each specific form of liturgy and the legitimate coexistence of a plurality of liturgies.

3. COLLECTION AND CODIFICATION

When individuals or groups are unable to formulate a celebration independently, they readily borrow from other times or places or persons. Collections of material come into existence. An inclusive Church will be soonest driven to this expedient, and the Church of the post-Constantinian period willingly adopted it.

The more extensive and the more accepted such collections of material were, the more ready people were to make them their own. Material thus appropriated was, however, more highly regarded, the more authoritative it was or claimed to be. If necessary, the material was attributed to important individuals: apostles, doctors of the Church, or popes. Thus many collections of texts that were originally for private use became widely used in the course of time because they went under borrowed names. In the East, the names of Mark, Chrysostom, Basil, and the Roman bishop Clement, and in the West the names of Ambrose, Leo, Gelasius, and Gregory were especially favored, and helped texts and even whole liturgies to win widespread acceptance.

What has long been customary or what carries the authority of a great name easily comes to be regarded, especially in worship, as definitively valid, and people are loath to make changes in it. The modern sociology and psychology of worship have been able to bring to light laws that we today cannot and should not easily ignore. In certain circumstances, it is on the basis of such laws that "codification" takes place, rather than through the deliberate action of a legislator. Many phenomena in the contemporary liturgical reform have made us aware of this.

Hippolytus is a highly significant example of such laws at work. He made a collection of traditional texts, gave them authority by entitling the collection (in good faith) *Apostolic Tradition*, and could count on it being immediately accepted because what he was presenting was in fact material that had long been in use. Even so, the success of his collection was amazing: it determined the future in northern Italy and at Rome no less than in Egypt, at Antioch, and (from Antioch) at Constantinople. That the texts were so readily accepted shows that they met a felt need of celebrants whose creative powers had waned, and that these individuals liked to use formularies they could assume were "the right kind."

The earliest collections of presidential prayers were not compiled under the Church's authority but were for private use. A celebrant collected them into booklets (*libelli*) and then added whatever he found useful. He might pass them on to a successor or lend them to a brother celebrant, and these men in turn would make their own additions. Since the parishes within a diocese were not clearly defined in the early centuries, and since the members of the bishop's presbyterium were conscious of being a college, we must assume that as a general rule the bishop's celebrations served as a model and were adapted to local situations. The relatively extensive similarity, in basics, of the liturgy from province to province meant that texts which had proved useful could readily travel to other areas. Pilgrimages, especially to the Holy Land and to the tomb of Peter at Rome, to "the bearer of the keys of the kingdom of heaven," were very important for liturgical exchanges throughout the entire Church.

Important contributions to the prayer formularies of the later Roman Missal came from the "sacramentaries," which were collections of prayers for the use of the presiding celebrant in the liturgy. The oldest of these collections may date from as far back as the sixth century, but they have come down to us only in much later, usually Frankish manuscripts. It is typical of them that they were passed on under the names of popes who had in fact relatively little to do with them: Leo the Great (440–461), Gelasius I (492–496), and Gregory the Great (590–604). We do know, however, that these popes were very much concerned with the liturgy; in addition, it is possible, even probable, that prayers they composed were preserved in archives and became part of the later collections.

One very old sacramentary purportedly has Leo the Great for its author — the Leonine Sacramentary or, as it is usually called today, the Verona Sacramentary (Verona being the place where the manuscript was preserved). It contains presidential prayers for the feasts of the saints and is divided according to the months of the year. Its material is purely Roman in character, although the book was not compiled by a Roman nor intended for use at Rome.

Precisely because of this last-named fact, the Verona Sacramentary never acquired the importance, even for a limited liturgical area, of the comprehensive and pluriform group of manuscripts that bear the name Gelasian Sacramentary. Of this book there are two basic versions or types: an older and a more recent. There is disagreement about the original compiler and the place of origin of the older type, but it can at least be said that Pope Gelasius I was certainly not the editor of it. The collection came into existence in the sixth century, possibly at Rome or perhaps in Campania. It follows the Church year and contains formularies for Sundays and feastdays, for the feasts of the saints, and for numerous votive Masses for special occasions.

The collection quickly acquired high standing at Rome, but not for very long — a few decades at most. Then, in its entirety or in excerpts (*libelli*), the book passed over into the Frankish kingdom in the seventh/eighth century. On the way it picked up non-Roman (e.g., Milanese) additions; this can be seen especially from the formularies for the saints, each of whom was venerated in a certain locale, and in many cases not at Rome. This expanded collection almost completely supplanted the Old Gaulish liturgical material. Here too, in eighth-century France, there arose in rich abundance the "Later Gelasians"; the latter, especially once the popes became dependent on Frankish power, underwent new Roman, specifically "Gregorian," influences, of which we shall be speaking in the next section of this book.

In Rome, meanwhile, the Gelasian Sacramentary was displaced after a few decades by the Gregorian Sacramentary. Pope Gregory the Great was not himself, however, the author or even the editor of this collection, although a number of formularies may well be from his pen. The manuscripts of this group preserve a large amount of liturgical material from earlier centuries, but because of the high esteem Gregory enjoyed in all matters liturgical, everything that bore his name (rightly or wrongly) was gladly accepted, even outside Rome and even in France, as we shall see. We may note here that our present-day Missal is heavily indebted to the ancient tradition of the sacramentaries; many of the prayers we use go back almost fifteen hundred years.

The Roman liturgical sphere was not the only one to have its sacramentaries. We know of some from the Old Gaulish Liturgy (e.g., the Gothic Missal [*Missale Gothicum*], the Old Gaulish Missal [*Missale Gallicanum Vetus*], the Bobbio Missal), and from the Mozarabic, the Ambrosian Milanese, and the Celtic (Stowe Missal) Liturgies. Some prayers were recently taken over from these non-Roman sacramentaries into the new Missal of Pope Paul VI.

As the sacramentary was meant for the presiding celebrant, so the lectionary (book of readings) was meant for the reader, whether he was, as far as the sacrament of orders went, a lector or a deacon or a priest. In the beginning, the reader read directly from the appointed book of the Bible, as in the synagogal liturgy, and especially from a book containing the four Gospels. It was easy to use the Bible or an evangeliary as long as a "continuous reading" or "sequential reading" (*lectio continua*) of the biblical text was practiced, or even a "semi-continuous reading" (i.e., with some omissions). (We may recall how, until the recent liturgical reform, this ancient practice was reflected in the formula with which the reading of the Gospel at Mass always began, namely, "*Sequentia sancti evangelii secundum* . . . ["Continuation of the holy Gospel according to . . ."].) For the previous reading from the New Testament, there was another book that contained chiefly the Letters of St. Paul and therefore bore the name *Apostle (Apostolus)*.

At times it was difficult and bothersome to locate the correct readings, or pericopes as they were called, especially since the readings were becoming increasingly shorter and less and less continuous. Consequently, instead of complete books of the Gospels and Letters, books that were unnecessarily heavy and also expensive to have copied, more practical books of readings came into use. In these the readings followed the order proper to a specific Church or region (the *capitulare lectionum*); for the non-Gospel readings there was an epistolary (or lectionary); for the Gospel readings, an evangeliary (in the narrow liturgical sense of the term) or evangelistary.

Once Missals came into use, the various books of readings, as well as the books for the chant parts of the Mass, all became part of the one inclusive book, although the separate books continued to be used in Offices celebrated by deacons and in solemn pontifical Masses. Comparable to the latter were the books of readings in the vernacular for use at the Latin Mass in recent decades. The lectionaries of the new reformed liturgy have happily become much larger because of the increased number and length of readings from the Bible. They have once again become separate entities from the celebrant's book, so that we have now returned to the ancient liturgical tradition according to which altar and lectern each have their own special books.

In antiquity and the Middle Ages, veneration for the Lord's word led not only to the very careful copying of the lectionaries but also to their embellishment with colored initials and miniature paintings; the bindings as well were often carefully made and costly. During the liturgy of the word, the evangeliary was given the respect due to the Lord himself, being accompanied with candles and incense during the procession, and kissed after the passage was read. Evidently a close parallel in dignity was seen between word and sacrament, evangeliary and altar.

To the extent that the acclamations sung by the people became more artistic, it became necessary in the course of time to introduce a specially trained group of singers (the *schola*) with a precentor (*cantor*) at its head. In the process, of course, the direct participation of the people in the celebration was notably lessened. The schola had its own book of melodies, which was known by various names: cantatory (*cantatorium*), antiphonary (*antiphonarium*), gradual (*graduale*), etc. The variety of such songbooks is extraordinary, the various types often reflecting quite local traditions and customs. They contain solo pieces for a single cantor, as well as the necessary Mass chants (processional songs such as the introit, offertory, and communion; gradual, tract, alleluia, and sequences; recurring texts such as the Kyrie, Gloria, Credo, and Sanctus). Many of the manuscripts contain the earliest examples of musical notation and are extremely important for the history of music.

The master of ceremonies acquired his own special book of regulations, the Order (*Ordo*), as it was called; in it the structure and course of a liturgical action was described. Especially significant were the *Ordines Romani* of the seventh to the fourteenth centuries, which contained the rites, the ceremonies, and the opening words (*initia* or *incipit*) of the liturgical texts for the Mass and the other sacraments, for the dedication of a church, for special occasions such as Holy Week, and so on. The oldest Roman liturgical books, the sacramentaries, had contained only texts and gave very few if any indications as to how a given ceremony was to be conducted. However, once the originally simple ceremonies became richer and more complex, and especially when the Anglo-Saxons in the seventh century and the Franks in the Carolingian period introduced a liturgy "according to the Roman manner," it became necessary to codify rituals that had hitherto been passed on by word of mouth. Such codification became all the more necessary since the Roman liturgy was being carried into a new and quite different socio-cultural context.

Because of their purpose, these books of ceremonies usually contained no texts but only descriptions of ritual that were later incorporated into the Missal; in the latter, they were printed in red ink (and therefore were known as "rubrics": Latin *rubricus* = red) between the texts that had been brought together from sacramentary, antiphonary, lectionary, and evangeliary. In a similar manner they were incorporated into the "breviary," or book containing all the texts needed for the Liturgy of the Hours. Unfortunately, the *Ordines*, which in the beginning were a great help, did much later on to rigidify the ritual and produce the canonical rubricism of unhappy memory. Meanwhile, especially in the tenth century and especially at Mainz, the *Ordines* were expanded by the inclusion of the texts themselves and not just their *initia*; they thus became the basis for the Romano-Germanic pontifical (book for episcopal liturgy) that was brought to Rome under the Ottonian emperors. The *Ordines* thus expanded also developed, in another direction, into the episcopal book of rites (*Rituale*) and book of ceremonies (*Caeremoniale*).

The appearance of such *Ordines*, or sets of regulations, was characteristic of a development with important consequences for the Roman liturgy. The relatively simple celebration of the early centuries, for example in the time of Justin Martyr, had gradually become a precisely regulated ceremonial that imposed officially prescribed movements and actions on the numerous participants in the sanctuary. Meanwhile, the congregation in the body of the church was reduced to a group of mute spectators. The living interaction of presiding minister and community had in the course of time been reduced to an overly objective cultic act taking place on an elevated platform before the eyes of the faithful.

The causes of this shift did not reside in the celebration of the Mass itself, but lay outside of it; the root was the new, constitutional position occupied by the pope. During the peace that ensued after the age of persecution, the bishops, and especially the Roman bishop, became an integral part of the civil administrative and judiciary system. As a result, the relation between clergy and people gradually changed, and this change was reflected in the liturgy. In the Constantinian period, the bishops acquired civil privileges: they belonged now to the highest level of the senatorial bureaucracy, had their own jurisdiction, were granted corresponding insignia and outward honors, the title of "Your Excellency," etc. After the empire was divided in the fourth century, the authority of the pope became even greater, since the imperial office in the West Roman Empire soon became extinct.

We must be careful here not to falsify history. The development we have been describing did not initially result from a quest of power by the Church, but from the duty the popes assumed of protecting the people of Rome who suffered terribly through wars and barbarian invasions, sackings and famines. Concern and protection easily elicit gratitude and respect; respect brings power with it, and power, which is not an evil in itself, quickly finds a corresponding outward expression. From this point of view, the later (counterfeit) "Donation of Constantine," according to which Constantine, when he moved his residence to Constantinople in the East, ceded Rome and the West to the pope, is simply a subsequent juridical approval and consolidation of a situation that already existed.

In any event, it is not surprising that elements of court ceremonial should find a place in the solemn Mass celebrated by the bishop of Rome, and that numerous details of the celebration should be modeled on the ritual of the imperial court at Constantinople. Thus there were special clothing, including shoes and episcopal cap (the *phrygium*, or Phrygian pointed cap, out of which both the miter and the tiara developed), insignia on the garments to indicate rank in the hierarchy, a code of colors, retinue with candles and incense, right to an elevated throne and a baldachin, ceremonial supporting of the bishop's person by acolytes, greeting of him by entrance hymns, kissing of objects to be handed to the bishop and acceptance of them back with covered hands, bowings and genuflections, array of titles, and so on. This development can be seen full-blown by 700 in the so-called *Ordo Romanus I*; it has, however, already been very much spiritualized and adapted to the circumstances of public worship, so that the various things we have mentioned could strike the faithful as quite appropriate for the patriarch of the West.

In the ninth/tenth century, a redactor at the Ottonian court or at a synod added to *Ordo Romanus II* the notation: "Bishops in their dioceses are to act like the pope in all matters."[8] The prescription had, however, long been followed in practice, for, ever since the Carolingian period (around 800), the Roman liturgy had been the sole liturgy, marking the unity of the empire, and the bishop's Mass had been fully assimilated to the papal Mass, with its special elements of courtly ceremony. This assimilation was justified by the juridical situation in the Frankish empire — but justified by that alone! — since in the Carolingian period the clerics of the chapel at the imperial court were favored when it came to filling episcopal sees, while from the Ottonian period on, bishops became princes of the realm and, from the High Middle Ages into the Baroque period, actually exercised civil authority.

It is a waste of time approving or condemning this whole development, whether in its general manifestations of ecclesiastical "triumphalism" or in its particular manifestations in the pontifical liturgy as we knew it until very recently. The development was a historical fact that cannot be changed. Reflection on the kind of outward manifestations proper to the episcopal office began long ago; in areas in which the Church is being persecuted, there is and can be no question of how the bishop's office should find expression! It can certainly be said that the present-day practice of the bishop concelebrating with his priests, with the solemnity of the ceremony corresponding to its locale (domestic chapel or cathedral), is far more appropriate to the episcopal office than many of the forms created in the past. Meanwhile, in June 1968, Pope Paul VI greatly simplified the various pontifical insignia, without going to the other extreme of a drab puritanism.[9] The Church does not yet seem to have found a style suited to our time in the matter of outward manifestation and festal solemnity. But then, the same can be said of democracy in the civil sphere!

Unfortunately, not a single presbyteral *ordo* has been preserved from the distant past — for example, an *ordo* followed in a Roman parish church or titular church in the time of Gregory the Great. If one had come down to us, the liturgy it reflected would be much closer to that of Justin or Hippolytus than to a papal Mass. It would surely be solemn and dignified, but not rendered pompous and alien to us by courtly ceremonial such as we find in the papal Mass of late antiquity.

---

[8] *Ordo Romanus II*, no. 10; text in Michel Andrieu, *Les Ordines Romani du Haut Moyen Age* 2 (Spicilegium Sacrum Lovaniense 23; Louvain, 1948), p. 116.

[9] Paul VI, apostolic letter motu proprio *Pontificialia insignia* (June 21, 1968), in *AAS* 60 (1968) 374–77.

C. The Mass Among the Franks
(Eighth to Tenth Centuries)

1. THE FRANKS ADOPT THE ROMAN LITURGY

Around 500, the Franks who had entered Gaul under Clovis accepted Christianity and, unlike other Germanic tribes, most of which became Arian, accepted it in its Catholic form. The decision of the Franks was of great historical importance, for it meant that invaders and the conquered now professed the same faith, and that national differences would not be aggravated by religious ones. It was precisely this latter barrier that prevented the Ostrogoths, Lombards, and Vandals from putting down roots in their new country, and ultimately led to their downfall. In the case of the Franks, on the contrary, conditions from the very beginning favored their settling down and remaining in Gaul.

There is a point worth noting that is often overlooked: The Franks accepted Christianity about a century before the influential liturgical activity of Pope Gregory the Great (590–604). At the time, the Old Gaulish Liturgy (often wrongly called the ''Gallican''), which was relatively independent of the Roman, was flourishing. The language of worship, like the language of everyday life, was a decadent Latin, but the liturgy itself was not Latin-Roman. It was a distinct West Roman–Eastern form that included, among other things, many details taken from the Eastern Churches, for the old links of Lyons and Marseilles with the East by sea — at that time the easiest route — were still strong, being as yet unhindered by Islam as they would be from the seventh century on.

As a matter of fact, in the sixth and seventh centuries Rome itself, once the West Roman Empire had collapsed, looked more or less to Byzantium (Constantinople) for protection against the Arian Visigoths and against the Lombards who, initially at least, were extremely intransigent. As early as about 500, the Sicilian-born Pope Gelasius, who did so much for the Roman liturgy and gave his name to a whole group of sacramentaries, was as much a Byzantine as a Roman in outlook.

The evangelization of the Franks was gradually accomplished by the centralized Gaulish clergy, once Bishop Remigius of Rheims (ca. 436–533) had baptized the Frankish king Clovis and his grandees at Christmas 498/499. The Bishop's well-known words, ''Humbly bow your head, Sigamber; worship what you burned, burn what you worshiped,''[10] were certainly a handy slogan, but short indeed even as a ''Short Formula of the Faith''! In fact, the ensuing two and a half centuries were certainly not a brilliant period in the life of the Gaulish-Frankish Church. Hardly one of

[10] Gregory of Tours, *Historia Francorum* II, 31.

the Frankish overlords died a natural death; disorder was widespread. The Church itself in good measure reflected the general decadence of morals and brutalization of human relationships; the formation of an indigenous Frankish Church was a slow and wearisome process. Outstanding figures such as Venantius Fortunatus and St. Radegund were few and far between in the life of the Church.

Itinerant monks from Celtic Ireland and Scotland aided in missionary and pastoral work. Naturally, they brought with them the customs, often monastic in character, of their homeland, and these were soon adopted in Gaul. Especially important for the future was their penitential discipline, which was quite different from that of the early Church. Absolution was not deferred until after public penance had been done, but was given immediately upon the confession of sins, provided the penitent promised to make "satisfaction" later on.

In the beginning, it was exceptional to find the Gaulish liturgy showing any significant connection with the long established Roman liturgy, but this situation changed as more and more pilgrims visited Rome. Because the Princes of the Apostles had suffered martyrdom and were buried at Rome, the City fascinated and thereby came to influence the Franks. As time went on, Rome increasingly came to be seen as the source of a possible consolidation of the Frankish Church, especially since the island kingdom of the Anglo-Saxons had already adopted the Roman liturgy as sole model (*ca*. 600) and had, since the middle of the seventh century, been sending more and more missionaries to the Continent, thus gradually and, finally, almost completely replacing the Irish and Scotch apostles who had been spreading the customs and liturgy of their homelands.

Utrecht was the continental base for the Anglo-Saxons in their work of evangelization and reform. It was no accident that before beginning their apostolic work, many Anglo-Saxon missionaries went to Rome, where they were consecrated bishops for the mission lands and where they adopted Roman names. Thus Wynfrith became Boniface, Willibrord became Clement, and so on. Also typical of their approach was their close collaboration with the Frankish kings or majordomos, especially with Pepin III, son of Charles Martel and father of Emperor Charlemagne. Pepin aided Pope Stephen II against the Lombards; the Pope then anointed him king at St. Denis in 754 and named him *Patricius* and Protector of Rome. The result of these political developments was that the Franks looked more toward Rome, not only in civil matters, but in ecclesiastical and liturgical matters as well.

From this point on, Roman liturgical material flowed into Gaul. The result was the hybrid liturgy reflected in the "Later Gelasian Sacramentaries," which we mentioned earlier. In this liturgy, old and new stood side by side; the distance between the Old Gaulish and the Roman liturgies could not yet be overcome, because there were not enough scriptoria in operation to carry out quickly the unification after the Roman model which the central royal authority wanted. A man who exercised an important influence during this period was Bishop Chrodegang of Metz (742–766), who went to Rome in 753 to study the liturgy and to bring authentic Roman customs back to the Franks.

Charlemagne pursued the work his father had begun. In 785 he received from Pope Hadrian I (772–795) a Gregorian sacramentary (the "Hadrianic Sacramentary"), which he decreed should be for the future the sole authentic and binding model (the "Aachen Original"). This codex was a precious gift indeed in terms of its material make-up, but unfortunately its contents were incomplete, since it contained the liturgy only for those days on which the pope himself celebrated it. It required an appendix, therefore, and Alcuin, an Anglo-Saxon chaplain at the court, supplied it. In compiling the appendix, Alcuin drew chiefly on the Later Gelasian Sacramentaries, and added the feasts and rites hitherto customary in Gaul. This appendix, originally kept separate, was soon incorporated into the authentic Roman model for ease in use; the result was a new hybrid, although one whose content was essentially Roman and "Gregorian." It was this hybrid, imposed for the sake of a unified liturgy by both the political authorities and the bishops, that became the basis for almost all liturgical practice in the West.

Liturgical pluralism, with all its undeniable disadvantages, was thus brought to an end. The result was unity, but a unity that soon repressed all creative innovation and development. Any developments that did occur were relegated to the rank of paraliturgy, which elicited widespread popular enthusiasm but also missed being shaped by the spirit of the early liturgy, as we shall see.

2. ENRICHMENT OF THE ROMAN LITURGY IN GAUL

The Franks not only adopted the Roman liturgy; they also fostered it and devoted loving study to it. We have proof of this in the writings of Amalarius of Metz, Walafrid Strabo, Alcuin, and many others. Nor did these scholars forget that the liturgy must take root among the people; lyric, dramatic, and hymnic elements were all added to the more sober Roman base and were enthusiastically adopted by the people.

In our own day we may bemoan the fact that the Church in Gaul did not throw down the language barrier and enable the Franks, and later the other German tribes, to achieve a much greater degree of identification with their liturgical worship. But this very idea was impossible at that time. The dialects spoken by the various tribes were not yet thought of as

apt for literary use; that is why the ancient tribal legislations were translated into Latin, and no one thought of translating the Latin liturgy into a
vernacular that might have been generally understood. By the time a
German literary language did develop, the Latin liturgy had come to be
thought of as untranslatable. By this I mean that it had come to be regarded as a structure of objectively holy rites that could not be tampered
with, since only in its inherited form did it guarantee and mediate salvation. Liturgy had come to be simply a mystery over which men had no
control; people thought of it as having been willed by the Church and even
by God himself in its present form.

In the early Carolingian period, the people by and large frequently
experienced the liturgical celebration as a moment of intense emotional
devotion. This was because the clergy initiated them into it and gave them
solid instruction. The liturgical seasons of Holy Week and Eastertide
were especially popular because they gave such scope for the imagination
as the people celebrated the Palm Sunday procession with its singing; the
washing of the feet on Holy Thursday; the veneration of the cross on Holy
Friday, with the unveiling of the cross, the acclamations, and the Re-
proaches; the Paschal Vigil, with the impressive lighting of the new fire,
the carrying of the "Light of Christ" into the dark church, the *Exsultet*
with its intense emotion, and the blessing of the Easter candle and the
baptismal water; and Easter day, with its dramatic elements, out of which
would later develop the Easter plays with the apostles and holy women
coming to the tomb, and so forth. Recent research has shown that these
elements were not taken over from the pre-Gregorian Roman liturgy but
were added in the Carolingian period, although not without the influence
of the Jerusalem liturgy.

Another characteristic of the period is the preference for solemn
hymns. The more sober and coolly rational Rome of late antiquity moved
in quite a different atmosphere, for at Rome there had always been great
reserve toward ecstatic verve and charismatic enthusiasm. The use of
hymns in worship met with general opposition, unless they could pass as
"Ambrosian" or were used only by restricted groups, for example the
Benedictine monks. Initially, the Gloria was reserved for the pope's
Mass; only in the Franco-German sphere did it become part of the liturgy
for Sundays and feastdays. We may think of the Carolingian liturgy as
being in general quite festive and enamored of singing.

The Old Testament became important as an anticipatory reflection of
the fulfillment to be found in the New Testament. Not only did many
churches take over the seven-branched candelabrum, but it was also at
this period that numerous anointings — of priests, kings, churches —
were introduced. There is no mistaking the fact that the archaic character
of the Old Testament rites appealed to these young people. Evidently, the

symbol as powerful sign met their needs more than did the more recent kind of liturgy that was rationally shaped and emphasized the verbal.

An important step was taken during this period as regards the development of separate books intended for different kinds of liturgical use. The old sacramentaries contained not only the texts for the Mass but also the prayers for the administration of most of the other sacraments. Now, in tenth-century Mainz, for example, practical books were compiled for the celebration of the sacraments and for the sacramentals, dedications, and blessings. The formularies were taken from the old collections, augmented, and accompanied by suitable directions; separate books were compiled for the bishop and for the parish priest. These productions became the bases for the later Ritual and Pontifical; in fact, even these names were used at that period. The books originated at this period; later, they were brought to Rome and became liturgical books for the Church at large.

3. THE FRANCO-GERMAN CONTRIBUTION IS BROUGHT TO ROME

The development we have been sketching took place mainly in the area between the Meuse and the Rhine, especially in Mainz, which was the metropolitan see of the greatest of the early medieval ecclesiastical provinces. But many other cities — Metz, for example — were also very important.

At Rome, the ninth and especially the tenth century — the "dark ages" — were not a propitious time for liturgical development, to say the least. The Roman urban patricians held all power, and the papacy reached its lowest point in history. No wonder, then, that the clergy celebrated the liturgy in a negligent manner, and that the people took little part in it. Liturgical books were not even copied as needed. In comparison with the northern countries, then, a void was being created that needed to be filled. It was then that the Ottonian emperors from Saxony undertook a reform of the liturgy as well as of Church politics; in the liturgical sphere, they promoted the transfer of northern customs to Rome. One story sums up the situation: When St. Henry II was being crowned emperor at Rome in 1014 by Pope Benedict VIII, he interrupted the Mass and demanded that the Creed, by now customary in the North, be recited at the end of the liturgy of the word; he went further and got it introduced into the Roman Mass.

The monks of Cluny in Burgundy played an especially significant role in refurbishing and revitalizing the Roman liturgy according to the Franco-German pattern. Burgundy, in the southern part of the Meuse-Rhine area, achieved great cultural and ecclesiastical importance in the Middle Ages;

it became, in Huizinga's phrase, "the crucible of Western culture." The Benedictine Cluniac monks restaffed many monasteries of central Italy (Farfa, for example) and of Rome (St. Paul's Outside the Walls, for example), and brought with them the liturgy of the lands north of the Alps. The Italians and the Romans received it willingly and even enthusiastically.

The Cluniac reform reached the zenith of its influence under Pope Gregory VII (1073–85), who had become a monk of Cluny in 1047 and had come to Rome in 1049 with Leo IX; in 1059 he became archdeacon of the Roman Church, and 1073 he was elected pope. In the spirit of the Cluniac reform, Gregory took strong measures to purify the Church of all that was unworthy and to win her freedom from the tutelage of the State. The Pope's basic tendency to create a strongly centralized government for the Church showed with special clarity in the liturgy, and since his day the improved liturgy of the older Roman Church has been, without qualification, the liturgy of the Latin Church in its entirety. At the same time, however, his influence could not stop the liturgical decadence of the medieval period. The spirit of a new age was making itself inexorably felt; the structural laws proper to the Roman liturgy went unrecognized, and medieval subjectivism won the day.

On the whole, we can accept Theodor Klauser's judgment on the ninth and tenth century, as far as the liturgy is concerned: "It would be no exaggeration to say in conclusion that during a critical period, the Franco-German Church succeeded in saving the Roman liturgy not only for Rome itself but for the entire Christian world of the Middle Ages."[11]

D. The Shift to the Subjective

1. THE BREAKDOWN OF EXPERIENTIAL LITURGICAL COMMUNITY

Theodor Klauser characterizes the early and high medieval period — the five hundred years between Gregory VII and the Council of Trent in the sixteenth century — as a time of "dissolution, elaboration, reinterpretation and misinterpretation."[12] This negative development was ultimately due to the fact that conscious communal participation in the liturgical celebration had increasingly weakened. In the course of time, not only because of the language barrier but very much by means of it, the Mass had become simply the priest's Mass. The people were silent spectators; they were pious, but their piety was not liturgical; they did not pray the Mass, but prayed during it.

[11] Theodor Klauser, *A Short History of the Western Liturgy: An Account and Some Reflections*, translated by J. Halliburton (New York, 1969), p. 77.
[12] *Op. cit.*, p. 94.

From the theological viewpoint, the event taking place at the altar was still a means of salvation, and the people still regarded it with deep devotion, but as worship it had become excessively objectified. Its language and ceremonies were hardly, if at all, intelligible any more, and therefore were no longer a concern of the people as a whole. The vital interaction of president and congregation had been broken off, at least as far as the outward sign of the sacramental unity of all the actions was concerned. Now priest and people were simply together in the same place, and only an occasional bell — at the consecration, for example — called the attention of all present to certain set actions of the celebrant.

There were many reasons why priest and congregation thus simply coexisted at Mass. The chief reason, however, was that the actions proper to the congregation had been severely limited or suppressed. For example, the Offertory procession at the preparation of the gifts had formerly been important both spiritually and as a caritative self-expression of the community; this procession had now disappeared. In addition, since the Carolingian period, the daily bread of the worker's day was no longer the material for the sacrifice of the Mass; it had been replaced by an unleavened bread that was alien to his experience and quite different in character.

The spiritual countermovement of the Communion procession had likewise almost disappeared, because people rarely received the Lord's body at Mass. That is why the Lateran Council of 1215 had to impose the strict obligation of receiving Communion at least during the Easter season. Communion from the chalice had still been practiced, at least occasionally, as late as the eleventh/twelfth century, but now it had fallen completely into disuse; from the late Middle Ages on it was strictly forbidden, a move that drew strong resistance from the Hussites, Wycliffites, and others.

The acclamations, short actions that could easily be performed even by a liturgically untrained community, had been taken over by the servers of the Mass.

All in all, then, the community awareness proper to the territorial church had dissipated, and had been replaced by many other structures that were feudal (such as the system of the privately owned church, or *Eigenkirche*) or based on class (for example, the guilds and corporations) or concerned with devotion or caritative social action (such as the numerous confraternities). In the cathedrals, collegiate churches, and monasteries which had their own clerical liturgy, clerical liturgy and liturgy for the people were increasingly separated. The stone screen in front of the choir was a visible symbol of the new situation: clergy and people did not want to disturb one another. True enough, in front of the screen there was usually an altar for the people ("altar of the cross" was the name often given to it), but it was only one altar among the many located in side chapels or attached to the column of the now far too large churches and meant for the use of the confraternities or for Mass endowments.

The activity of the more recently founded religious Orders, especially the Mendicants, certainly represented a pastoral improvement, but it also further undermined the traditional parochial system; the latter also suffered greatly from the cancerous effect of the benefice system. The pastors, appointed from above, took the revenues of their office — and indeed the revenues of many parishes simultaneously — but often fulfilled their corresponding obligations through substitute curates who usually had little theological training and often celebrated the liturgy in a negligent manner.

To balance the picture, we must admit that during this period there were many deeply religious men among the clergy, men who worked hard in their pastoral ministry and were genuine "priests of the people." But even they thought of the liturgy and its authentic, meaningful execution simply as a "means of grace" that remained unintegrated with the rest of their piety. But all this darker side of the Middle Ages is well known, and we need not go into it further here.

A chief cause of the trouble was that hardly anyone had a theological grasp of the liturgy in its true nature. In keeping with the predominantly juridical outlook of the time, the liturgy was reinterpreted as the collection of officially regulated rites by which men were to give God the "honor due him" and which communicated "God's grace," conceived, frequently, in a very material and quantitative way. The rites and vocabulary of the liturgy itself were, however, in the last analysis unintelligible; they no longer spoke directly to men, but existed only as an objective reality set apart from everyday life.

In order to give the faithful some kind of access to the liturgy, those working at the pastoral level fell back on "symbolism," that is, an allegorical explanation of each and every detail of the service. Unfortunately, the explanation rested, not on a biblical and historical foundation, but on liturgically unjustified and arbitrary constructions and misinterpretations. Secondary details often became the focus of attention. Thus if the choir of a cruciform church happened, perhaps because of the nature of the ground on which it was built, to be not completely perpendicular to the transept axis, the slight bend was interpreted as a representation of Christ's head drooping to the side as he hung dead on the cross. Since the altar represented Christ, the lector or subdeacon had to face the altar rather than the people as he read (in Latin) the Old Testament passages, these being regarded as all pointing to Christ. The Mass in its entirety was often interpreted as a play-like representation of the history of salvation from paradise to final judgment. Calderón's well-known dramatization *The Mysteries of the Holy Mass* is a baroque echo of this tradition.

This symbolico-allegorical literature began as early as about 1000, but achieved its most luxuriant growth in the twelfth century with Honorius of Autun's *Gemma animae* (Jewel of the Soul) and *Speculum ecclesiae* (Mirror of the Church), Rupert of Deutz's *De divinis officiis* (Divine Services), and John Beleth's *Rationale de divinis officiis* (Explanation of Divine Services), and in the thirteenth with Sicard of Cremona's *Mitrale* (The Miter) and especially with the *Rationale divinorum officiorum* (Explanation of Divine Services) of William Durandus the Elder, canonist and bishop of Mende. The last-named work is an able compilation based on the previous literature and can be regarded as a summa of this kind of liturgical commentary. Countless copies of it were to be found in all medieval libraries, and it thereby exercised a very extensive influence on the way the liturgy was celebrated. The work is of great historical importance and conveys to us as no other can a sense of the true state of the medieval liturgy, as a liturgy which was greatly venerated but whose signs were not understood and were therefore misinterpreted.

The medieval liturgy had in good measure lost its power to shape popular private devotion. It had hardened into a set of prescribed formularies for prayer; in the popular mind it was immensely important, but it was experienced only in the distorting mirror of an allegorization that was more misleading than truly explanatory. The human subject of the liturgy, namely the community in the New Testament sense of the word, was overlaid by other social substructures. Popular piety was left to its own resources and therefore inevitably turned to what was accessible: the events of the history of salvation, and especially the earthly life of Jesus (his birth, miraculous cures, passion, cross, resurrection, and ascension). This was a source at which the imagination could slake its thirst; here pious and even mystical absorption in God became possible.

The *Imitation of Christ* of Thomas á Kempis (1399–1471), one of the finest witnesses to late medieval piety, shows both the admirable impulses of meditative empathy that were at work in this piety, and its sacramental weakness. In this book the reader is drawn to Christ in a moralizing way, and especially through emotion and subjective feeling; he is aroused to follow Christ as his model, yet at the same time he may well neglect the sacramental access to Christ. In this respect, the *Imitation* was the forerunner of the pietism that stood apart from both Church and liturgy.

It is easy to understand how for people in this frame of mind, love for Mary and veneration of the saints could become extremely important; also how such piety could easily lead to an excessive preoccupation with relics and to an ideal of holiness as based on a multiplication of external works, for example pilgrimages and processions. The late medieval altar tells us a good deal about the times: the bread and wine are still to be found there, of course, although they are adored rather than eaten; but above them on the beautiful devotional retables is depicted an imagined world of holiness that appeals to, and expresses the inner longings of, the believer who is not really participating in the worship proper.

2. THE PRIVATE MASS

In the early Church, Mass was celebrated for limited circles as well as for large communities. Masses of the former kind were distinguished from the Sunday celebrations chiefly by the fact that they could be celebrated on any workday, especially for small groups and even for personal intentions, and therefore in simpler form, without a large body of clerical officiants, and in quite diverse places (dwellings, votive spots, etc.). "Votive" Masses (*votum* = promise, intention, wish) originated in these Masses for small groups. They are fully legitimate liturgical forms, since at no period in the history of the liturgy has the private been absorbed by the general; if it were, the "general" would be mistakenly identified with the "collectivist". Vital community springs naturally from vital groups and individuals.

Such Masses in a small circle of people must, however, be distinguished from the private Mass that we find in use at the end of the first millennium. The private Mass has a quite different theological basis and quite different motivations. It is a Mass celebrated by a cleric without a congregation and with only a server present. The justification for this private Mass cannot be challenged even today, although we must assign it a different value than men did during the almost one thousand years that it flourished.

The private Mass probably originated in the monasteries. In the beginning, of course, monasteries were communities of lay people living according to an idealistic democratic rule and under an abbot whom they chose as their spiritual father. St. Benedict, for example, permitted approved monks to be ordained for his monasteries by the competent bishop only if there was a real spiritual need; these ordained monks took no precedence over the other monks except in the liturgy (cf. *Rule*, ch. 64).

However, once the monasteries became the favorite source of missionaries for pagan lands (as early as Gregory the Great and the mission to the Anglo-Saxons), the situation changed. The number of priest-monks necessarily increased very rapidly, since only priests could exercise a full missionary and pastoral apostolate in the foreign country. The Scottish monastery of Melrose, for example, had only four priests around the year 650; yet around 784, during the extensive missionary activity of the

Carolingian period, the monastery of St. Peter at Salzburg had twenty-two priests out of ninety-seven monks, or almost a quarter of the community.

In the tenth century there were monasteries with over a hundred priests. Some of these priests exercised a pastoral ministry in the surrounding countryside, but on the whole the number of priests was far greater than required by the needs of the monastery. Even if each priest had taken a turn presiding over the monastic liturgy, he would have been called on to celebrate only two or three times a year. Subjective devotion, however, and especially the newly developed theological doctrine of the "fruits of the Mass" logically led to the wish to celebrate more often, and even daily if possible, and daily celebration did in fact quickly become the rule.

The secular clergy soon imitated the monks, especially since such a practice fitted in nicely with the wish of the faithful to have the fruits of the Mass applied to the individual salvation of the living and the dead. It is here, too, that we find the beginnings of the "Mass stipend," that is, of gifts of money or kind to the clergy for the celebration of Mass, as well as of endowments for Masses and altars, that lasted beyond the death of the giver. The person giving the stipend asked that the special fruits of a particular Mass be applied to himself and his relatives or friends. Attention was focused not so much, if at all, on the Church as a whole, in communion with which the individual lived and within which he was incorporated for his salvation, as on the subjective personal salvation of an individual or group or limited community. The medieval shift to the subjective is as clear here as is the loss of the New Testament consciousness of a community that is grounded in Jesus Christ and celebrates the Eucharist before the face of God.

Given the large number of priests desirous of celebrating their individual Masses in the monasteries and in the urban communities with their confraternities, various other groups, and Mass endowments, profound changes came about in the traditional ceremonies of the Mass. The ideal, of course, was to surrender as little as possible of the sacred rite, since its form was regarded as sacrosanct and unchangeable. Inevitably, however, the form was curtailed. Little space was available for each priest because of the numerous side altars (in the beginning the traditional principle that an altar should be used only once on any given day — the principle of "fasting," as it were, as applied to an altar — was observed). This limitation of space, together with the need to be considerate of others celebrating simultaneously in the same church, forced some reductions that were important for the future.

The singing of the choir at each Mass had to be dropped, and their chants were now simply read in a low voice by the priest himself. There was neither the room nor the manpower for numerous assistants with diversified functions. The movements possible in a spacious sanctuary had to be curtailed, and all the ceremonies previously performed at the pulpit now had to be performed at the altar, where only the distinction of "Gospel side" and "Epistle side" could still be maintained. There was no longer need of a presidential chair, since the priest stood at the altar throughout the Mass.

The sermon had long since disappeared. The Offertory procession was now dropped, because it was replaced by the private stipend, although the washing of the hands remained obligatory despite the fact that it had lost its purpose, inasmuch as the priest no longer touched any of the gifts produced by nature.

The acclamations, hitherto spoken aloud but now found distracting, were spoken quietly by the server. By and large, the extreme quietness of the celebration was the most striking thing about the new form of the Mass, and the latter was therefore justifiably described as the "silent" or "read" Mass. The priest read his part in a low voice; the people stood in silence near the altar, separated from it only by the "Communion rail," although the latter fulfilled its function only infrequently. Communication between the quietly praying priest and the silent bystanders had been broken; "active participation" had become an illusion. The faithful might pray privately "during Mass," but they did not share vitally in the celebration of the rite (even assuming that they did not find the multiplicity of Masses on workdays too demanding and simply stay away). It could even happen that, lacking a server, the celebrant had to address his "The Lord be with you" to the empty air and supply the answer "And with your spirit"!

The new customs adopted in the private Mass soon influenced the Sunday worship of the community; in fact, from the thirteenth century on, the private Mass became the normative form of celebration. The private Mass of the simple priest even set the pattern for the bishop's private Mass and the pope's in the *Sancta sanctorum* chapel of the Lateran. Only the solemn pontifical Mass on special occasions and the occasional High Mass in the parish (with the assistance of a deacon as a faint reminder of the splendor of bygone days) were maintained for special circumstances. Even on these occasions, however, the ceremonial of the private Mass exerted its influence, since the celebrant now had to say quietly all the parts that others had taken in earlier times; thus he had to say the words being sung by the choir and the readings which the deacon or subdeacon chanted.

Mass as celebrated by a single unassisted priest had won the day, and concelebration, except at Masses of ordination, had disappeared. Thus, if a priest took the part of a deacon or subdeacon at a Mass with assistants, he did not receive Communion at that Mass, but celebrated privately in advance. Monks and canons were obliged to celebrate their private Masses before attending the conventual Mass in monasteries or the pontifical Mass in cathedrals.

It is not known with certainty just when the ritual of the private Mass was first codified. Customary law probably developed during the tenth century, perhaps initially at Mainz or in the monastery of St. Gall. In 1243, at a Chapter of the Franciscan Order at Bologna, we hear of a fixed Ordo, or description of ritual, that begins with the words *Indutus planeta* ("Having donned the chasuble") and was proposed by Haymo of Faversham, General of the Order.[13] John Burckard of Strassburg, who became papal master of ceremonies in 1483, wrote an Ordo that was published in 1502 and quickly adopted everywhere. It was taken over into the post-Tridentine Missal and was normative until recently.

3. THE PRIEST'S MISSAL

The formation of the Mass book, or Missal, at least in its basic shape, was closely connected with the phenomenon of the private Mass. Previously, a variety of officiants had participated in the celebration of the Mass, and each had his own special book. In the private Mass, however, the single celebrant had to fill all the roles; consequently we find all the texts which previously had been distributed among several books gathered into one book — the Missal. Thus the Missal contained the presidential prayers from the old Hadrianic Gregorian Sacramentary, which had been meant for the use of the presiding celebrant; the readings from the lectionaries used by deacon and subdeacon; the chants from the old antiphonaries or graduals used by schola or choir; and finally (written or printed in red and therefore called "rubrics") the old Ordo, or book of regulations, for the master of ceremonies, who saw to it that the individual officiants did what they were supposed to do at the proper moment and that the whole ceremony proceeded according to rule. Such a comprehensive Mass book was ideal for the needs of the private Mass.

From around 700 we have the Bobbio Missal, and from around 800 the Stowe Missal, both intended as small-format Missals for traveling monks. These Missals, however, had been compiled only to meet special, limited needs. After many variations and intermediate stages, the development of complete Missals reached a provisional terminus at the end of the tenth century. These complete Missals were originally meant for use only in monasteries, but from the twelfth century on they everywhere replaced

[13] Text in S. J. P. van Dijk (ed.), *Sources of the Modern Roman Liturgy: The Ordinals of Haymo of Faversham and Related Documents (1243–1307)* (Leiden, 1963), 2:3–14.

the old specialized liturgical books. Beginning in the thirteenth century, they became obligatory, since even in a sung Mass the celebrant had to read all the texts which others were also reading or singing.

Initially, various ecclesiastical centers (Milan, Mainz, Cologne, Lyons, Braga, Toledo, etc.) and religious Orders (the Cluniacs since 1080, the Cistercians since 1134, the Carthusians, and the Dominicans) all had their special Missals. Then, in an act pregnant with consequences, Francis of Assisi in 1223 adopted the Missal of the Roman Curia for use in his Order and prescribed it as obligatory. This "Missal According to the Custom of the Roman Curia," a title later abbreviated to "Roman Missal," quickly spread throughout the West. In 1277, Pope Nicholas III ordered its use in all the parish churches of Rome, and it was then adopted in many places, Because it was so widely used (the *editio princeps* was printed at Milan in 1474), it later became the basis for the post-Tridentine Missal of 1570.

4. PRIVATE PRAYER IN THE MASS

Since the Missal was from the very beginning a book intended only for the priest's use, subjective private prayers made their way into it from an early date. The outward manner of reciting these was distinguished by the fact that the priest did not, as in reciting the official prayers, extend his hands but instead clasped them. He spoke the prayers, not in the name of the community (which did not answer them with an "Amen"), but in his own name and for his own intentions. They served his personal need of recollection or a proper frame of mind, as for example before the readings and before his Communion. They also helped allay his sense of personal unworthiness, as for example at the beginning of Mass and from time to time throughout the rite. At times, especially in the eleventh century, such confessions of sins, or "apologies" as they were called, were introduced in large numbers throughout the Mass, as were prayers of thanksgiving.

It was typical of the new conception of, and attitude toward, the liturgy that within the great prayer of thanksgiving which the Eucharist is, short private prayers of thanksgiving should seem necessary. The reason for this was that Christians of that age thought of the Mass as a pregiven rite into which they laboriously and even scrupulously endeavored to enter; they no longer saw it as an appropriate self-expression of the celebrant.

Frequently the private prayers were variations (in the first person singular) of older prayers, many of them from the Gelasian Sacramentary and even from other Liturgies; frequently, too, however, they were new compositions. To them were added other private prayers that interpreted the liturgical action, often following the lead of medieval symbolism. They might interpret actions which were originally performed without verbal accompaniment, as for example the preparation of the bread and wine during the Offertory, the mingling of the wine and water, the washing of the hands, etc. The theological inadequacy of the prayers thus introduced showed clearly in formal expressions of oblation that could easily be misunderstood (*Suscipe; Offerimus*), and even in an epiclesis, or invocation of the Spirit (*Veni, sanctificator*; this was the only such epiclesis in the Missal of the time), that equivalently introduced a ''Little Canon'' into the preparation for the sacrifice.

Such explanatory private prayers, meant as a help to the celebrant, were felt to be necessary to the extent that the ceremony and its gestures were no longer directly intelligible. The desire to introduce meaning showed with special clarity in the various prayers that accompanied the incensing of the altar and the gifts. And yet the more these prayers became part of the rite and were stereotyped through daily use, the more they failed in their purpose, since they were said by rote and ceased to be a real help and stimulus to thought.

The importance given to private petitions during the Canon warrants mention in this context. Personal needs experienced each day had led to the multiplication of private Masses and the creation of the stipend system. There is no question, of course, but that petition has its place in the Eucharist. Petition is not opposed to thanksgiving; on the contrary, in making petitions I acknowledge the power of him who can grant them, for no one prays to someone who is powerless. But the new importance given to the petitions clearly manifests a new outlook. Originally the individual unquestioningly thought of himself as included in and caught up by the saving prayer of the Church as expressed in the great intercessions that closed the liturgy of the word, and especially in the pauses for reflection that were an invitation to personal prayer. Now, however, a special place was required for personal petitions, which soon overloaded the Canon.

The Canon was chosen as the place for these prayers, because thus one came as close as possible to the consecration, which was felt to be the climactic moment in the mystery. This is why the consecration was surrounded by numerous memento prayers. For this reason, too, until quite recently the people often prayed aloud in the vernacular all during the Eucharistic prayer. When I was a chaplain, immediately after World War II, I found out that the ''Prayer for a Good Harvest'' had to be said daily from Easter into the autumn, and in the winter months the ''Prayer for Those Making Their First Communion'' (on the next Pentecost), this latter usually being read by a student in one of the upper forms. At the monthly Communion Days of my students in the Kolping Society, I tried unsuccessfully to shift the ''Prayer for the Beatification of Father Adolf Kolping'' from its fixed place immediately after the elevation of the chalice to a more suitable location. At the time, I bowed to the express wish of the community, because otherwise they would simply have been hurt; without a long, slow liturgical education, their devotion would have suffered rather than profited by the change.

There is a pastoral lesson to be learned from the set of questions we have been touching on, and it is this: If private concerns and needs cannot be voiced at the celebration of the Mass, they will find a less satisfactory outlet elsewhere. Once the general intercessions had been eliminated at a fairly early stage and replaced by the Kyrie litany, and once the latter had been reduced to the simple Kyrie, private intentions invaded the Canon and finally almost overwhelmed it, or else they sought expression completely outside the Mass. It was then that the pilgrimage, for example, became a more popular and more intensely experienced form of petition and thanksgiving than the Mass itself. The Mass was celebrated, of course, at the place of pilgrimage, but in terms of devotion it was entirely secondary to the intentions of the pilgrims.

Private prayer should never be eliminated from the liturgy; on the contrary, it must be taken up into the liturgy in a suitably ecclesial form and made to contribute its own vitality to the liturgy.

5. THE GAZE THAT SAVES

The Middle Ages spent a lot of time discussing the question, "At what precise point in the Canon does the transformation of the bread and wine into the body and blood of Christ take place?" Interest in the question was, however, more practical than speculative. It arose out of another question: "What is to be done if, for some reason (for example, the sudden death of the celebrant), the Canon is broken off? Up to what point may the bread simply be removed? From what point on is it consecrated?"

As the reader probably knows, the Eastern and Western Churches still disagree on the answer to the above question as formulated in different words: "Does the consecration take place through the epiclesis, or does it take place through the 'words of consecration,' which are spoken as a declaration rather than as a simple narration of a past event?" The Eastern Church maintains the first of these two views, while Latin theologians maintain the second, although the Church has never issued a dogmatic declaration on the point. This second view became common in the West around 1200, when it was accepted that the change in the bread was accomplished once the relevant "words of institution" had been pronounced, and therefore before the words over the chalice were uttered.

As a result of this view, it soon became customary for the celebrant to genuflect in adoration immediately after the consecration of the bread, and to do the same after the consecration of the wine. Since, however, the priest's body hid the holy signs from the people during the Canon, he elevated the consecrated species, so that the people might kneel and gaze and offer their own adoration. It would have been natural, of course, for the priest to turn to the people while elevating the host and the chalice. Such a turn was thought to be impossible because of the law of orientation that applied to the Canon, and a rather curious alternative solution was found: the priest raised the species so high that the people could see them above his head, even though his back was to the congregation.

The elevation of the Eucharistic species of bread and wine soon became very popular, for it fitted in nicely with the general delight in gazing at things. Intellectual piety and authentic participation in the celebration of the mysteries had become very restricted in the course of time, and now eye and feeling demanded their satisfaction. The desire to look upon the Lord's body led to a theory of "communion through the eyes," that is, a saving contact with Christ that consisted simply in gazing on him. The priest was asked to keep the host elevated as long as possible; people willingly gave him a larger stipend for doing so, or supplied him with assistants who would hold up his arms if he grew weary.

In the large urban churches and cathedrals, where as many as forty altars belonging to corporations and confraternities were to be found, a favorite arrangement was to have the showing of the sacred species take place at one Mass after another in close succession; processions of people would move from elevation to elevation in order to attain (according to current popular belief) a cumulative and richer enjoyment of the fruits of this holy gazing. The theologians did not teach such a quantitative concept of grace, but it played an important part in the consciousness of the faithful and motivated them accordingly.

This same delight in gazing had already found an earlier outlet in connection with the relics of the saints. These were no longer kept locked up in boxes or wallets which one could only touch in one's attempt to come as close as possible to the relics. Instead, they were made visible in glass cyclinders. The existence of such ostensoria was an invitation to treat the sacred host in the same way as relics, and as a matter of fact, the earliest Eucharistic monstrances are indistinguishable from the ostensoria used for relics. By means of monstrances, the elevation at the consecration could be perpetuated as the sacred body of Christ was "exposed" for long periods of adoration.

The visions of St. Juliana of Liège (1192–1258) led to a special feast of the Body of Christ, which was established in 1256 by Bishop Robert for the Liège diocese. As early as 1264, Pope Urban IV (1261–1264), who had previously been Archdeacon of Liège (1242–1247), ordered the feast to be observed throughout the Church. Because this Pope died so soon after, the feast was not everywhere accepted. Especially north of the Alps, however, it was everywhere welcomed; the first Corpus Christi procession at Cologne took place in 1277, the first at Benediktbeuern in 1286.

In such processions, the Blessed Sacrament was carried through the city in a monstrance, often under a canopy or on a litter. It was followed by priests garbed in Mass vestments and carrying candles or relics or chalices, along with singers, musicians, choirboys, and the entire community. There had been similar processions through fields and city on such occasions as Palm Sunday, the transfer of relics, the solemn administration of the last rites, etc. The general festive joy and the decoration of the streets are still echoed in such German names for Corpus Christi as "Sparkling Day" (*Prangtag*) and "Garland Day" (*Kränzeltag*).

At an early date, tableaux depicting the sufferings of Christ were introduced and carried on floats; it was out of these and the dialogue used to explain them that the Corpus Christi plays evolved. The guilds vied in providing floats for the occasion; sometimes there were forty or fifty of these, with the floats of the miller and the baker — the men who provided the hosts — sharing the place of honor.

The feast is a vivid example of medieval piety. Its point of departure was the liturgy, but the liturgy did not, in the last analysis, serve as its norm and shaping force. One consequence of this piety was a belief in the apotropaic, or demon-defeating, effects of the procession: "The devils shall see it and tremble." It was because of this belief that the clergy would carry the Blessed Sacrament through fields threatened by bad weather and thus dispense a blessing for good weather. According to legend, St. Clare of Assisi (1194–1253) defended her sisters and her convent from the attacking Saracens (1240/41) simply by holding up the monstrance toward them; that is why the ostensorium is her usual attribute in Christian iconography.

By the late Middle Ages it was necessary to eliminate occasional abuses connected with the feast, but in 1551 the Council of Trent defended the feast itself against the Reformers as being a suitable external way of venerating "the triumphant victory of his [Christ's] death": "It was right that the victorious truth should celebrate a triumph over lies and heresy, so that its adversaries, confronted with such splendor and with the Church's great universal joy, might either be rendered powerless and sink to the ground as broken men or be filled with shame and confusion and recover their senses."[14]

This example of medieval piety illustrates, to our way of thinking, the unfortunate combination of a religious basis or motive, such as we expect to find in an inclusive Church, with the kind of spectacle the people love.

[14] Council of Trent, Session 13: Decree on the Most Holy Eucharist, ch. 5 (*DS* 1644).

In modern society, popular custom and folklore, bands and exhibits, have come to be associated with a different kind of occasion. In the Middle Ages, however, the Church was still the leaven of society. The chief civic festivals were the Church's feasts; the dedication of a church or a church fair not only had a religious side but were also popular festivals. We would, however, be entirely lacking in historical sense were we simply to hail the past before the tribunal of an "enlightened" modernity!

It is easy today, in the present "more ecumenical climate of opinion," to give a new interpretation to the Tridentine statement (which in any case was not a dogmatic statement!). After all, the dynamics of processions and parades can even in our day provide a needed corrective to the worshiping community's long periods of silent sitting in church; the community — and not just the young — often feels restless and needs to move about. Certainly one of our tasks today is to find forms of worship that are not conceived solely with the intelligentsia in mind. Reform does not mean simply cleaning house and throwing things out without replacing them; it means turning in new directions while observing basic and tested norms.

E. Uniformity Replaces Unity-in-Multiplicity: The Roman Missal of 1570

The sad state of the liturgy at the end of the Middle Ages and on the eve of the Council of Trent (1545–1563) was due essentially to a failure to grasp the real nature of the liturgy. Numerous excrescences upon the liturgy itself, as well as abuses and one-sidedness in popular piety, largely hid the foundations of the liturgy from view; or, to change the image, a luxuriant ivy covered walls that in any case were not very solid. In addition, there was the decadent condition of the Church as a whole: the great schism, the antipopes, the lack of education of many clerics, the trade in offices, and the general low state of morals that was due in many instances to wars, selfish political interests, and social upheavals. The call for "reform in head and members" was being issued on every side, and no one could claim not to hear it. No pope or bishop alone, however pious and ecclesial-minded, could have prevented the evil situation.

The primary focus of attention was on the damage that had been done to the Church as a whole. For this reason, the Council of Trent dealt only incidentally with liturgical reform; its concerns in this area were, negatively, the elimination of open abuses, and, positively, the improvement of the Missal and especially of Church music and Church hymns.

Other factors to be considered were a kind of theological uncertainty and, above all, the attacks of the Reformers on the ecclesiasticoscholastic doctrinal structure, attacks often inspired by the way the liturgy was being celebrated and the sacraments were being administered. This is not the place to inquire how justified Luther was in thinking that the importance for salvation of Christ's one redemptive sacrifice on the cross was being relativized and obscured by the many sacrifices of the Mass that the Church offered; that God's word in Scripture was not being preached but was "in chains"; that popular "work piety" had eliminated faith; that ritual was hindering rather than helping the spiritual life; and that the claim of clergy and ecclesiastical officials to be a separate and special class was repressing the community's legitimate awareness of itself as God's priestly people. To discuss such questions would take us too far afield.

Calvin's and Zwingli's denial of the real presence of Christ in the Eucharist and their judgment on offices and sacraments were in the last analysis direct attacks on the whole traditional manner of celebrating the liturgy. The Council of Trent, which had been convened only after much effort and which even then was frequently interrupted, regarded it as its first and principal task to shed theological light on the doctrinal controversies of the Reformation, although even in so doing the Council always had its eye on the practical needs of Church life.

Early on in the Council (1546), Bishop Thomas Campeggio[15] suggested that as the entire Church used a single translation of the Scriptures (the Vulgate), so it should use a single Missal. Initially, the suggestion was rejected, chiefly because many of the Council Fathers worried about infringing on the rights of the bishops. It also became increasingly clear, however, as time went on, that the Council in any case was not, or would not have been, in a position to introduce and carry through an authentic and radical reform of the liturgy. Councils, too, after all, are children of their time. For the moment, then, the Fathers were reduced to eliminating what was negative and harmful. To this end, in their final session (1563), the Fathers, now impatient with the eighteen-year-long synod, expressed to Pope Pius IV (1559–1565) a wish that was pregnant with consequences for the future, namely, that he would establish commissions for the redaction of the liturgical books. The Pope quickly did so, and his action was confirmed by his successor, St. Pius V (1566–1572).

A chief participant and soon the head of the reform commission was the scholarly Cardinal Guglielmo Sirleto (1514–1585), a friend of the reforming St. Charles Borromeo of Milan, himself a nephew of Pius IV. The reform commission did its work thoroughly and speedily: the reformed Roman Breviary was published in 1568, and the new Roman Missal in

---

[15] According to Hubert Jedin, Campeggio represented conservative curial thinking. See Jedin's *History of the Council of Trent*, translated by E. Graf, Vols. 1–2 (St. Louis, 1957, 1961), *passim*.

1570. In 1588, under Sixtus V (1585–1590), the commission was entrusted with all liturgical matters and established as the Congregation of Rites, the highest Roman authority in this sphere. The Roman Pontifical, which deals with all the sacramental actions performed by a bishop, was published in 1596, and finally the Roman Ritual, intended for the use of priests in the pastoral ministry, appeared in 1614. At this point, the Tridentine reform was essentially complete.

It is significant that all these books carry the adjective "Roman." The rites had been purified as much as was possible at the time, but the price paid was that the liturgy was also made uniform in accordance with a central model, and its wording was strictly determined. Admittedly, any diocesan liturgical customs that were more than two hundred years old could be continued, but only a few sees (Milan, Toledo) and religious Orders in fact preserved their ancient customs over the long run. At this point in history, everyone was apparently satisfied with the reform that had been achieved, and glad to be finally rescued from the sad liturgical situation of the past.

The new Roman Missal of Pope Pius V (1570) was first and foremost a purified Missal. Gross abuses were eliminated; there was a greater simplicity and stylistic discipline in the liturgical texts; the unity of the Latin Rite was restored; the rubrics (from the old manuals of the masters of ceremonies) were clear and unambiguous, even if overly juridical, insufficiently adaptive, and, from the viewpoint of the history of the liturgy, occasionally quite problematic. In all probability, however, everything had been done that was possible at the time.

We would be ill-advised to pass a one-sided judgment today on the centralization imposed at the time, even though it was inconsistent with the relative independence which the bishops of the early Church had enjoyed over against the Successor of Peter, and with the pluralism in liturgical practice that likewise marked the early Church. The centralization was probably a historical necessity. At a time when the national States were emerging, each with its ambitions for a State Church and with its bishops pursuing their special interests while showing little concern for the general good of the Church, a papacy purified of the evils of the Renaissance period and endowed with a new vitality was certainly the lesser evil in terms of Church polity. Gallicanism in France is all the evidence we need on this point! A weak papacy, moreover, could not and cannot be a source of help to hard-pressed local Churches. It is not for us here to raise the question of the criteria according to which this central power should and must be exercised if it is to be faithful to the nature of the Church.

The positive line taken by the reform commission was a return to antiquity and "the primitive rule for prayer" (*ad pristinam orandi regulam*), that is, to the period before the medieval excesses. In the view of the commission, this meant, concretely, a return only to the time of Pope Gregory VII, in the latter part of the eleventh century. The customs followed in the city of Rome "in the good old days" were evidently taken as the ideal. The attention of the theologians of the day was directed to controversy with the Reformers, and the latter were attacking a "tradition" that, at least in part, was quite recent. These theologians were unable to think in terms of going back even further than the eleventh century; their mental outlook did not allow them to see that neither the history of the Mass nor any fixed point in its development, but only Christ's own institution, should be the criterion for reform. Like a council, a theologian is a child of his time; only when men achieve a certain distance from hotly debated issues can they attain to a more complete vision of truth and justice.

A chief characteristic of the Tridentine reform, then, was that it simply eliminated the most scandalous and frequently chaotic excesses. First and foremost, the reformers did away with a large number of inappropriate votive Masses, some unduly subjective sequences and other hymnic elements, and many prefaces that had departed in style from the ancient models. Another important step was to abridge drastically the calendar of the saints, which had become coextensive with the Church year and had assigned a feast to every day. Klauser points out that in the period between 1200 and the Council of Trent alone, about two hundred new feasts of saints entered the Missal. In the reformed calendar, at least half of the year was free of saints' feasts, especially the period of the forty days' fast in March and April. In determining which saints were to be celebrated, the primary allegiance was given to those who had been venerated at Rome during the first millennium. The local Roman atmosphere came through in an especially clear way in the revived practice of indicating the stational church in Rome for each feast or liturgy. The information meant little to the Church at large, but occasionally it did supply the reason for the choice of texts or shed some light on the interpretation being given to them.

From our contemporary viewpoint, the Roman Missal of 1570 failed to accomplish the long overdue restructuring of the entire Mass so as to meet the requirements of God's people assembled for worship. The private Mass continued to be the ideal, as is clear from the document that introduced the Missal, "The Ritual To Be Followed in the Celebration of Mass" (*Ritus Servandus in Celebratione Missae*). In this document, attention was focused entirely on the celebrating priest and his action at the altar, where the whole celebration, including the liturgy of the word, took place. There was little that was communal about the celebration: the Offertory procession was not restored, except in the minimal form of the contribution for "the basket"; a server or, in more favorable circumstances, a choir spoke the acclamations, while the choir saw to it that the solemn Mass was much more of an esthetic musical experience than an action of the congregation.

The participation of the people continued, then, to be devotional rather than liturgical, as is clear from the singing (which obscured the Mass proper), the devotions during Mass, or the praying of the Rosary while the Mass proceeded. The old intercessions at the end of the liturgy of the word were not restored, although to a degree the frequently used "Universal Prayer" of St. Peter Canisius replaced them. Variable petitions could have relieved the Canon of its burden of petitionary prayer and could have helped give private petitions a more liturgical character or bring them into proper perspective. It was probably the lack of general intercessions that accounted for the multiplication of presidential prayers — as many as seven collects, secrets, and postcommunions!

The structural components of the Mass, each possessing its own character, were likewise obscured. For example, the entrance rites ran into the liturgy of the word without any break, since after the prayer of the day the priest stayed in the same place and immediately began the reading. The beginning of Mass was made up of heterogeneous remnants of older and more comprehensive liturgical actions that were simply lumped together: private preparatory prayers, entrance song, fragment of a litany, and Gloria, with the greeting — "The Lord be with you" — coming only after the Gloria!

The reading of the lessons in a foreign language prevented any authentic proclamation of them. We must bear in mind, of course, that, at least in that period, Latin did seem to be a bond uniting the Church. Nonetheless, since the Scriptures were read in Latin, the reading became simply part of a rite, not a real proclamation. It was occasionally followed by a sermon, but the latter frequently had nothing to do with the Scripture reading.

Eucharistic piety continued to be characterized by static adoration rather than by participation in the celebration. This trend was strengthened by the fact that Communions were infrequent, and even then were often separated from the Mass proper, so that people received for the most part either before or after Mass or entirely apart from Mass. In these circumstances, the significance of Communion as an integral part of the Mass was lost sight of. Frequently it was something juxtaposed to the Mass; worst of all, it was thought of, at times, in wholly objective terms as something one "received" and could "offer up" for the living and the dead.

The baroque Mass, at least the High Mass, was also characterized by stress on a solemnity and ostentation that were intended to counteract the Reformers' lack of appreciation for the Mass. The Roman edifices built by the Jesuits in the sixteenth century (the Gesù and San Ignazio at Rome) provided a program for the future. Grandiose altars, with the tabernacle in the middle, filled the rear wall of splendid interiors that were conceived as imposing royal basilicas. The screens that had divided medieval churches were almost everywhere removed so that the eye could travel unhindered to the main altar and the tabernacle. In the sanctuary, which, deliberately or indeliberately, was modeled after the stage of the theaters of antiquity, a sacred drama could unfold, with the clergy, in their rich but excessively ornamental and hardly functional brocades, as the actors. Numerous candles and a great deal of incense and gleaming gold gave even further solemnity to the celebration. The ceremonies were carried out in a strictly rubrical manner and could vie in splendor with the pageantry of any secular court or absolute monarchy. All the forms of art — architecture, sculpture, painting, the handicrafts, and music — vied in glorifying this liturgy and augmenting its magnificence.

Amid all this splendor, there is no mistaking the fact that an excessive objectivization of the event at the altar still hindered the congregation from taking any active part. The usually fixed seating arrangement in the body of the church (seats arranged as in a theater!) directed everyone's attention to the altar but did not draw the person attending Mass into a properly liturgical involvement. As a matter of fact, it limited the person — especially in the more normal circumstances of the parish church, where the solemnity was much diminished and the possibilities more limited — to his own subjective adoration and devotion. These almost inevitably sought in processions and pilgrimages a more active expression than was possible at Mass.

It would be unjust, of course, to dismiss all these outward forms simply as "triumphalism." No, there was an honest effort to find subjective satisfaction through forms of devotion, especially devotion to the Hearts of Jesus and Mary. The trouble was that all these devotions lacked a real, conscious relation to that which is the source and origin, the center and summit, of Christian life, namely, the vital celebration of the Eucharist. Such a connection was not present in the theological consciousness of the baroque period; the people of the time calmly did what was in their power and what was felt in their day to be liturgically appropriate.

One achievement of the Missal of Pius V was soon offset, as a new growth in the number of saints' feasts occurred. In this phenomenon we must certainly see an index to Catholic self-awareness: in increasing the number of feasts, the Church was showing herself to be the Church of proven saints. Between 1570, the year of Pius V's calendar reform, and 1914, one hundred eleven new feasts were introduced, usually as higher-ranking feasts ("doubles") that were superimposed on the liturgical seasons and did much to obscure the true character of the liturgical year. The increase in the number of feasts for Doctors of the Church — those representatives of doctrine in its pure state — was especially notable: there were only four such feasts in the middle of the sixteenth century, but thirty by 1959.

Another factor that was important in the post-Tridentine period was the excessive development of liturgical law. From the seventeenth to the twentieth centuries, juridical formalism and liturgical casuistry increasingly took priority over the liturgical life itself, especially because of the private and the officially published decrees and responses of the Congregation of Rites and because of the commentaries on rubrics that proliferated. Not without justification does Klauser call the three centuries between the establishment of the Congregation of Rites and the pontificate of Pius X a "period of stagnation and rubricism."[16] The result was the theologically startling fact that in the authoritative liturgical manuals of the early twentieth century (J. J. Navatel, Ph. Oppenheim, etc.), only that was regarded as "liturgical" which was prescribed in the official books. The fact of being prescribed made an action liturgical! Every new decision made was cemented into place; any further development could take place only within the channels of the juridically prescribed and pregiven. Necessary reforms were lacking or were swallowed up by the system.

F. The Modern Liturgical Renewal

At the end of this age of rubricism, the liturgy was once again very much in need of reform, especially since the twentieth century was gradually restoring a more profound theological grasp of the nature of liturgy and of the Mass in particular. Christians were realizing that the liturgy is the communal, salvific celebration of God's hierarchically organized people of the new covenant, who gather in Jesus' name and as a body, though with each member playing a distinct and irreplaceable role, actively, consciously, and devoutly celebrate the mysteries.

The long desired breakthrough was finally achieved in our time at the Second Vatican Council, which thus carried a step further the reform to which the Council of Trent had been challenged but for which the time was not yet ripe. We must be aware of the continuity implied in this last statement, for the liturgy of our time is not an absolute novelty, but deliberately stands within the tradition which the Church has preserved from the beginning. That is the point which Pope Paul VI makes, in response to the objections of some extreme traditionalists, in his Intro-

---

[16] Klauser, *op. cit.*, p. 129.

duction to the General Instruction on the Roman Missal: The new Missal is "a witness to the unchanging faith" and represents, not a break with tradition, but an adaptation to new conditions.[17]

Simplifying somewhat, we may say that the reform initiated by the Council of Trent proceeded from above, while that of Vatican II proceeded from below. After Trent, a new set of revised liturgical texts and books was issued, and its use was juridically regulated and indeed made obligatory; the means, however, namely good order, gradually became the end, and finally did away with all spontaneity. The reform of Vatican II, on the other hand, was more concerned with life; its chief, though not exclusive, motivation was pastoral. The conciliar reform had to overcome a great deal of opposition and suspicion; this, however, had the advantage of forcing the reformers to an ongoing self-criticism and constant reflection on their positions. Finally, the reform, set within the framework of a critically elaborated doctrine on the Church, was officially adopted.

The earlier reform was almost inevitably subject to the dangers of juridicism. The recent reform, on the contrary, has almost inevitably been exposed to the dangers of scandalous indiscipline and occasional capriciousness. Though we do not approve of such a swing of the pendulum, it is easy to see the historical and psychological reasons for its occurrence. The impulses to reform had long been contained, as it were, by a dam that was threatening to burst; once the waters were released, it was inevitable that they would not be easily channeled. The cure for the ills attendant on the reform is surely not a new juridicism or rubricism, but a deliberate balancing of freedom and restriction, spontaneity and order, and a concern for the underlying and necessary structures of the liturgy. Only in such an approach will it be possible to respect the tradition inherited from the Fathers of the Church, while also taking into real account the needs of our time.

The reform is by no means a finished business; in fact, it can never be a finished business. For it is only by preserving the permanently valid basic structures of liturgy, while revising their socio-cultural expressions from age to age, that the liturgy will remain vital and be a suitable sign of salvation to every generation.

1. The Liturgical Movement

The recent liturgical reform was not due to a sudden legislative act, but had matured slowly over a long period. From one point of view, we may

---

[17] The Latin text is in *Missale Romanum*, editio typica (Vatican City, 1970). The Introduction or Preface (*Cenam paschalem*) has fifteen sections; the words quoted here are the title of sections 2–5.

think of it as the progressively elaborated expression of unease and a desire for reform in the face of the immobilism that characterized the post-Tridentine forms of worship. A number of the changes seem indeed to be startling in their extent, but we must bear in mind that over a long period there had been an unsatisfied desire for many smaller reforms.

It was only in the twentieth century that the desires for reform began to be voiced in the Church at large. The reasons behind these desires are many — some historical, some pastoral, and, above all, some theological.

Historical studies and the editions of ancient texts made people aware of liturgical riches no longer known in modern times. This applied both to the range and variety of prayers and to the vitality possible in the celebration of the liturgy. Such historical studies began in the seventeenth century; some of the more important names are the French Benedictines Jean Mabillon (1632–1707) and his disciple Edmond Martène (1654–1739), and the German Benedictine Martin Gerbert of St. Blasien (1720–1793). The historical bent of nineteenth-century romanticism did much to spread the knowledge of liturgical history, and the stream of editions and studies has only increased ever since.

The history of the liturgy could have provided a good corrective to the rubricist attitude of mind much earlier, but unfortunately the consciousness of history was obscured, especially in the second half of the nineteenth century, by another orientation of the same romantic movement, namely, a concern with legitimacy and restoration. This did not, however, prevent scholarly work from continuing its task of bringing to light and making known the rich treasures of the great Latin liturgical tradition. It is difficult to overestimate the importance of the work done by historians of the liturgy, for to the ensuing liturgical movement, which at times was tempted to a somewhat visionary enthusiasm, the historians gave solid foundations and careful criteria for healthy development. Without exaggeration we can say that none of the promoters of Vatican II's Constitution on the Sacred Liturgy could have done his work without the knowledge, for example, of the monumental *Missarum Solemnia* of Josef A. Jungmann (1889–1975).[18]

Of special importance for the celebration no less than for the study of the liturgy was the renewed enthusiasm for Gregorian chant in the Mass and Office that was fostered by the Abbey of Solesmes (Department of Sarthe, in northwestern France). The chief inspiration here came from Prosper Guéranger (Abbot of Solesmes, 1837–1875) who promoted both liturgical music and a liturgical spirituality. The celebration of the liturgy and the Church year was the dominant mark of the monasteries of men that Guéranger founded throughout western Europe.

[18] *The Mass of the Roman Rite: Its Origins and Development (Missarum Solemnia)*, translated by F. A. Brunner (2 vols.; New York, 1951–55).

In Germany, Beuron (re-established in 1863) became especially important under the Wolter brothers, Maurus and Placidus, who drew their
inspiration from Solesmes. Beuron was soon seconded by Maria Laach in
the Eifel hills, and by its later abbot, Ildefons Herwegen (1874–1946;
abbot from 1913). The monasteries of the Beuron Congregation became
gathering places for those concerned with the liturgy, especially educated
people. They also exerted a strong influence at the parish level through
their liturgical books and especially their popular missals (for example,
the Latin-German missals of Anselm Schott of Maria Laach, first published in 1883; 67th edition in 1964). The choral singing promoted by
Solesmes received its seal of approval from Piux X in 1903, since the
Vatican edition of the liturgical chant books was based on the work done
at Solesmes. Singing — done, for the time being, by a monastic community or a schola — became the forerunner of greater active participation
by the community of the faithful.

Desires for liturgical reform at the *pastoral* level go back to the time of
the Enlightenment, before and around 1800. Recent scholarship is now
ready to do greater justice than previously to that period of Church history, especially since we have now gained sufficient distance from the
evident weaknesses and limitations of that age. Thus, a proper evaluation
of the episcopal office at the present time is proving to be a needed and
effective safeguard against the particularist and episcopalist tendencies of
the Enlightenment period. It must be said, however, that the didactic
penchant of the Enlightenment did lead to better and more frequent sermons, even if the themes of preaching were often limited to morality and
good behavior; it also led to methodical catechetics in Church and school.
Demands for the use of the vernacular, especially in the liturgy of the
word, were already being made at that time, in the interests of enabling
the faithful to take a knowledgeable, "rational" part in the celebration.

The Enlightenment reacted — rightly so, in large measure — against
all that was excessive, one-sided, and "unintelligible" in worship, against
the purely quantitative increase in the number of Masses, and against an
excessive attention to processions, pilgrimages, relics, and indulgences.
On the positive side, it sought to promote liturgy at the parish level
("German High Mass," Vespers in German); it reformed the ritual for the
administration of the sacraments; and it endeavored to promote the continuing education of the clergy through study, pastoral conferences, and
pediodicals. In this area we need mention only the names of Johann
Michael Sailer (1751–1832) and Ignaz Heinrich von Wessenberg (1774–
1860).

Even these fruitful efforts, however, were ignored by the nineteenth-
century restoration, though for reasons that had to do with ecclesiastical
politics rather than pastoral practice. A more rigid centralization seemed

at the time to be the only effective weapon against revolution, democratization, and nationalism, all of which were attacking the temporal power of the papacy. The priority given to considerations of ecclesiastical politics had a negative effect on the pastoral life of the Church at large. Here again, however, the passage of more than a century has enabled us to reach a more objective judgment on that period.

The breakthrough for a pastoral liturgy came with the Communion decrees of Pope Pius X (1903–1914), which promoted the more frequent reception of the Eucharist and lowered the age required for first Communion. Though the liturgical implications of these decrees were not realized at first, they were in fact the point of departure for recovering the concept of the Mass as being a meal as well as a sacrifice.

In Pius X's motu proprio on Church music, *Tra le sollecitudini* (1903), the liberating words "active participation [of the faithful]" occurred for the first time. The idea inspired the gifted Benedictine monk Lambert Beauduin (1873–1960) when he issued his challenge at the Catholic Congress of Mechlin in 1909: "The people must share in the liturgy" (*Il faut démocratiser la liturgie*). The speech had such an influence that nowadays we rightly think of 1909 as the real beginning of the liturgical movement. Many monasteries of Beauduin's own Order gladly got behind his program. But the chief role in the reform was played by charismatic individuals and pastoral workers whose contribution is still often unappreciated and frequently contemned.

The liturgical movement reached the peak of its effectiveness in German-speaking lands after the First World War, as more and more small streams ran together to form a mighty river. In Austria, the chief figure was Pius Parsch (1884–1954), a Canon Regular of Klosterneuburg, who, while a military chaplain at Kiev, experienced the transforming power of the liturgy for the first time, especially at the Easter celebrations of the Orthodox Church. On returning home, he established his little "liturgical community" at St. Gertrud. He devoted himself especially to a "people's liturgy," in which the whole community participated ("people's liturgy" is really a tautologous phrase, since the word "liturgy" already contains the word "people" [Greek *laos* = people]).

Parsch saw the Bible and the liturgy as together providing the basis for the Christian life (*Bibel und Liturgie* became the title of a journal he published, 1926–). He brought the historically evolving liturgical signs to life by a mystagogical catechesis, and freed them from a narrowly ritualistic interpretation by showing how they spring from everyday life, when the latter is seen through religious eyes. He was an effective organizer, and his own publishing firm, Liturgische Apostolat (Liturgical Apostolate), issued millions of pamphlets and books to spread his message throughout the German-speaking world.

Other vital centers of the liturgical movement were everywhere to be found in the German-speaking lands, especially in the cells of the Catholic Youth Movement, out of which the younger clergy emerged, men who in some cases founded oratories (e.g., at Leipzig) and in every case propagated the message among the people. (Among the Catholic Youth Movement groups we may mention *Neudeutschland*; *Quickborn*, which had its center at Burg Rothenfels on the Main River and did its pioneering work under the leadership of Romano Guardini; and *Katholische Jugend* under Ludwig Wolker.) The crisis through which the Church passed in the Nazi period and World War II brought communities together around the altar with greater awareness and gave living proof of the rightness and pastoral necessity of liturgical reform. As a result, the bishops took up the cause with great determination and overcame the obstinate polarizations of opinion.

We may mention, as one example of the many important stages in the liturgical movement outside of German, the establishment of the Centre de Pastorale Liturgique at Paris in 1943; this organization quickly developed a fruitful liturgical apostolate.

In the *dogmatic* area, the newly rediscovered doctrine of the Church as the Mystical Body of Christ proved helpful and clarifying to the liturgical movement. The Church is more than a socially constituted community, more than simply a "perfect society." The latter is only the outward sign of the Church as "primal sacrament." The Church, which is "Christ spread abroad" (Bossuet), makes visible both God's saving action in the world *and* the sacrifice of praise offered to God by believing mankind. The Church is the incarnate Christ continuing to live and work among men. As Pope Leo I put it, "What formerly had been visible in our Redeemer now took the form of sacred rites."[19]

The theologians and the entire Church were made more aware of this doctrine by Pius XII's encyclical *Mystici Corporis* (June 29, 1943). As a result, there was a new appreciation of the place of the liturgy in the life of the Church. The encyclical *Mediator Dei* (November 20, 1947) harked back to the liturgical reform of Pius X and made it clear that the liturgy was essentially a participation by the Church in the priestly activity of Christ. The encyclical rejected the one-sided view of the liturgy as "prescribed ceremony":

> It is an error consequently and a mistake to think of the sacred Liturgy as merely the outward or visible part of divine worship or as an ornamental ceremonial. No less erroneous is the notion that it consists solely in a list of laws and prescriptions according to which the ecclesiastical Hierarchy orders the sacred rites to be performed.[20]

---

[19] *Sermo* 74. 2 (*SC* 74:140).

[20] *Mediator Dei*, no. 25; Vatican Press translation (Washington, D.C., n.d.), p. 13.

The Pope expressly approves the "commendable private initiative" to which the liturgical movement owed its rise, and especially "the zealous and persistent labor of several monasteries within the distinguished Order of Saint Benedict" "toward the end of the last century and . . . through the early years of this one."[21]

The liturgical movement now began to have the weight of the Church's authority behind it, with the encyclical *Mediator Dei* as the Magna Carta of reform. A series of practical steps quickly followed: rituals with texts in the vernacular were approved; a new translation of the Psalms from the original language was published; the liturgies of Holy Week and Easter were revised; evening Mass was permitted; the law of Eucharistic fast was modified so that it ceased to be an obstacle to more frequent Communion; instructions on sacred music paved the way for, and encouraged, the more active participation of the community in public worship.

In his address to the International Congress on Pastoral Liturgy at Assisi in 1956, Pope Pius XII described the liturgical movement as a clear and palpable "movement of the Holy Spirit in His Church."[22] In a provisional, interim move, Pope John XIII simplified the rubrics, but he left it to the coming Council to undertake a sweeping reform of the liturgy on a biblical and patristic basis, with greater pastoral effectiveness as the goal. From the Council he expected an updating (*aggiornamento*) of the Church; even now, however, this updating is a goal not yet fully attained.

2. VATICAN COUNCIL II
AND THE NEW MISSAL OF POPE PAUL VI (1969)

The definitive reform of the liturgy resulted from the work of the Second Vatican Council. The first great document produced by the Council was the Constitution on the Sacred Liturgy (*Sacrosanctum Concilium*), which was promulgated on December 4, 1963. Pope John XIII had evidently thought that deliberations on questions of liturgy were best calculated to clarify and provide a solid basis for the dogmatic and practical goals of the Council. Events proved him right, since all the later discussions and debates were to a great extent given their theological and pastoral cast by this first Constitution.

On the other hand, it must be recognized that this first Constitution could not explicitly state all that was later to be discussed, formulated, and set down in further Constitutions, Decrees, and Declarations. Everyone who deals with the liturgy will therefore be well advised to keep in

[21] *Mediator Dei*, no. 4; translation in *op. cit.*, p. 4.
[22] *Vous Nous avez:* Address to the International Congress on Pastoral Liturgy at Assisi (September 22, 1956); translated in *TPS* 3 (1956) 273.

mind the total conciliar context of the Constitution on the Sacred Liturgy; this holds especially for the Dogmatic Constitution on the Church and the Pastoral Constitution on the Church in the Modern World.

It is only when we read the Constitution on the Church that the importance of the liturgy in the Church's life becomes fully clear. In this Constitution we are told that the liturgy is only *one* of the three self-expressions on the Church, the other two being preaching (kerygma) and service to the world (*diakonia* or *caritas*). This is true even though "the liturgy is the summit toward which the activity of the Church is directed" and "also the fount from which all her power flows" (*CL*, no. 10; Flannery, p. 6; cf. no. 9). The three ways in which the Church is at work in the world are therefore always to be seen as closely related; only then will we see the whole picture and not limit our vision to particular aspects.

There is need, then, of locating the liturgy squarely within the mystery of the Church and seeing in it the action that both constitutes and express-es the Church as sacramental, that is, as effective agent of salvation. The whole first chapter of the Constitution on the Liturgy emphasizes that very point, as it tells us that God manifested his universal salvific will (1 Tim. 2:4) to the patriarchs (Heb. 1:1) but has now fully revealed himself in Christ, the mediator between God and men (1 Tim. 2:5), "for his [Christ's] humanity united to the Person of the Word was the instrument of our salvation" (*SC*, no. 5; Flannery, p. 3).

In accordance with God's will, Christ's mission is continued in the preaching of the Church (*SC*, no. 6) and in the liturgy, which "is rightly seen as an exercise of the priestly office of Jesus Christ . . . under the guise of signs perceptible to the senses" (*SC*, no. 7; Flannery, p. 5). "From this it follows that every liturgical celebration, because it is an action of Christ the Priest *and* of his Body, which is the Church, is a sacred action surpassing all others. No other action of the Church can equal its efficacy by the same title and to the same degree" (*ibid*.; italics added).

This description of the liturgy as the Father's saving action through Christ (add: in the Holy Spirit) *and* the expression of the faith of God's people through Christ (in the same Holy Spirit) liberates it from the one-sided and erroneous approaches of the past and connects it (not merely on ritual points) with the neotestamental and apostolic sources and founda-tions. Consequently, in pastoral practice the liturgy cannot be simply something some people like and prefer; it is rather an essential action of the Church in the interrelation and interaction of God and man within the communion of the Church. God and the people of God who were united to form the Church are partners in a dialogue and a "new covenant in

Christ's blood." The "ecclesial character" or "ecclesial dimension" of the sacraments, that is, their close connection with the mystery of the Church, has become the subject of new theological awareness, as has the relation of the faithful to the Church as the primal sacrament.

Given this context, *pastoral practice* likewise takes on a new character, corresponding to the fact that the basic desire of the Council was to give a new vision of "the Church existing for the sake of mankind." Thereby a second or "anthropological" dimension of the liturgy has acquired a new and radical importance. The saving action which the Church performs in the name of Christ and which is experienced both in transparent signs and in the word that proclaims and makes actual is for the sake of man: men are to be enabled, in faith, to express themselves in the liturgical action and to recognize the liturgy as their own. The revised liturgy is meant to give new vitality to both the signs and their anthropological dimension, to sacrament and faith alike.

Here our reflections in the first section of this book are at an end. We are back to what we presented in our Introduction, in the form of a commentary on the opening articles of the General Instruction of the Roman Missal, as the sound teaching of the Church. In his own preface to the General Instruction, in which he is replying to some hyperconservative opponents of the reform, Pope Paul VI says that these principles reflect the institution Jesus left us, as well as the tradition of the magisterium and the Fathers, and are a suitable response to the pastoral needs of the present time. They are principles that must always be the point of departure for the theology, the form, and the celebration of the Mass. The hierarchically ordered people of God are to take an active, conscious, full, fruitful, and devout part in a liturgy that is a dialogue in which the Father effects men's salvation through the Son in the Holy Spirit, and in which the Church, for her part, inspired by faith, hope, and love, offers to the Father, in, with, and through Christ and in the Holy Spirit, a sacrifice of praise and self-giving.

The second part of this book is intended to make that kind of participation more feasible; to this end it makes use of the directives given in the new Missal. Our aim in the following reflections is to preserve a balance between order and freedom; the *order* that is signified by the vertical-temporal dimension of tradition and the horizontal dimension provided by the communion of the Church throughout the world (in other words, the basic identity of yesterday–today–tomorrow and here–elsewhere), and the *freedom* of action proper to a concrete community in the here-and-now, with its particularized range of ideas and expressions, so that its liturgy may find a form that does justice to its situation. The task of the presiding celebrant is to adapt the liturgy to the community's power to grasp and shape. Only then will both the community and the Church be experienced in the liturgy; only then, too, will the individual know and feel that the liturgy is addressed to him and that he is an active agent in it.

The signs used in the liturgy are almost all "signs that have evolved" (*gewordene Zeichen*). This is to say that the meaning of the signs and the manner of their use are more easily understood in the light of tradition. For this reason, we shall draw a good deal on history as a means of understanding. We will thus be telling the faithful who join in the celebration, not only that they should act thus and so, but also why earlier generations did things this way.

Part Two

The Community Mass

INTRODUCTION

By the mid-second century at the latest (see the account given by Justin Martyr), but probably as early as the late apostolic age, the community Mass had two parts: the liturgy of the word and the Eucharist. The framework provided by various introductory rites and a somewhat briefer conclusion is partially of more recent origin, yet is also, both functionally and psychologically, a necessary part of the celebration.

"In a sense the Mass comprises two parts: the liturgy of the word and the liturgy of the Eucharist. These however are closely connected with one another and form but a single act of worship. For in the Mass the table both of God's word and of Christ's body is spread so that the faithful may be instructed and nourished. There are also rites to begin and end the celebration" (*GI*, no. 8).

As a result, the outline of the celebration is today, and has been for centuries, the following:

      I. Opening
     II. Liturgy of the word
    III. Celebration of the Eucharist
    IV. Conclusion.

Of these, the second and third are the principal parts, while the first and fourth provide a framework.

The recent reform of the liturgy has made the structure of the Mass more clearly recognizable by introducing noticeable breaks and transitions. Thus, for example, the liturgy of the word and the liturgy of the

Eucharist each has its own proper place where its functions are performed: the lectern and the altar. The obligatory use of the lectern is especially important. Previously, the liturgy of the word could be carried out at the altar or from the pulpit; now, since the place for proclamation is fixed, the independent significance of the liturgy of the word emerges more clearly.

In the older community Mass, the transition from introductory rites to liturgy of the word was hardly noticeable, since after the prayer of the day (which was the last of the introductory rites) the celebrant began the reading (the first act in the liturgy of the word) while standing at the same place, using the same book, and maintaining the same position (his back to the people). Now the change of situation is clearer, because the president and the people sit down in their proper places (presidential chair and benches of the congregation), and the reader then goes to the lectern for the first reading, while president and congregation are assembled together under the word of God. The transition from liturgy of the word to liturgy of the Eucharist is likewise made evident by the shift of attention and action from lectern to altar. This clearer structuring of the celebration makes its meaningful execution much easier.

On the other hand, the close connection of lectern and altar in the one sanctuary makes it equally clear that the liturgy of the word and the liturgy of the Eucharist belong together — certainly clearer than did the traditional distance between pulpit and altar. The differentiation and connection of the two parts of the Mass are now made impressively manifest. The singleness of the service that embraces all these individual parts is further brought home to the participants by the architectural shape of a functional church.

In order to give an overview of the course of the celebration and to bring out the meaning and function of each part, we shall here set down the pertinent articles from the General Instruction, which offers authoritative explanations.

> I. *The actions preceding the liturgy of the word*, namely, the entrance, the greeting, the act of repentance, the Kyrie, the Gloria, and the collect, together constitute a prelude, an introduction, and a preparation.
> The purpose of these rites is to permit the assembled faithful to establish a communion among themselves and to dispose themselves for listening to the word of God in the proper frame of mind and for celebrating the Eucharist in a worthy manner (*GI*, no. 24).
> II. The main components of *the liturgy of the word* are the readings from Sacred Scripture and the chants between the readings. The homily, the profession of faith, and the general intercessions, or prayer of the faithful, develop the readings and chants and bring them to a conclusion. In the readings, which the homily explains, God speaks to his people, reveals the mystery of redemption and salvation, and provides food for the

spirit; moreover, Christ himself is present in the midst of the faithful by means of his word. The people make this divine word their own by means of the chants, and express their adherence to it in the profession of faith. After being nourished by it, they pray, in the general intercessions, for the needs of the entire Church and for the salvation of the entire world (*GI*, no. 33).

III. At the Last Supper, Christ instituted *the paschal sacrifice and meal*, by which the sacrifice of the cross is made constantly present in the Church, since the priest, who represents Christ the Lord, performs the same action which Christ did and which Christ bade his disciples do in his memory.

Christ took the bread and the cup, gave thanks, broke the bread, and gave it and the cup to his disciples with the words: "Take, eat, drink; this is my body; this is the cup of my blood. Do this in memory of me." The Church has so ordered the entire celebration of the Eucharistic liturgy that its parts correspond to these words and actions of Christ. This is to say that:

1) At the preparation of the gifts bread, wine, and water are brought to the altar, these being the material elements Christ took into his hands;

2) In the Eucharistic prayer, God is thanked for the whole work of salvation, and the gifts are made into the body and blood of Christ;

3) The breaking of the one bread points to the unity of the faithful; in communion the faithful receive the body and blood of the Lord just as the apostles received them from the hands of Christ himself (*GI*, no. 48).

IV. *The concluding rite* comprises:

a) the greeting and blessing of the priest, these being enriched and given fuller expression on certain days and occasions by a prayer over the people or some other more solemn formula;

b) the dismissal, by which the people are sent away so that each member may go back to his good works, praising and blessing God (*GI*, no. 57).

It is evident that the new General Introduction intends to do more than did the rubrics of the earlier Missals. It represents an explanation of the Mass that is based on solid theology and history, and is in the service of pastoral practice. It has the disadvantage of being repetitive, inasmuch as Chapter 2 ("The Structure, Components, and Parts of the Mass") provides a general overview of the parts of the Mass (articles 22–57), while Chapter 4 ("Various Ways on Celebrating the Mass") gives a description that overlaps with the first, of the basic form of "Mass with the people," that is, Mass with a congregation (articles 82–126). In addition, the "Order of Mass with a congregation" is accompanied by brief ritual instructions, printed in red ("rubrics") that are in fact short extracts from the two descriptions already mentioned. In the following pages, I shall make these rubrics the basis of my exposition, while at every point bearing in mind and giving references to the two chapters of the General Instruction.

1 THE BEGINNING OF THE MASS

The introductory rites are among the more recently added parts of the Mass. In their present form they are, for the most part, relics and short-ened versions of what were originally more extensive rituals, that is, of processions, litanies, penitential acts, hymns, and, especially, set forms of greeting. In the Tridentine Missal, the fragmentary and accumulative character of the rites was even more evident and was especially to be seen in the fact that the greeting — "The Lord be with you" — came only after the Gloria. The recent reform did not entirely eliminate the impression of accumulation, but the structure has on the whole been rendered more logical and easier to put into practice, especially when use is made of the various options offered.

If we were to judge by Justin Martyr's account[1] or the liturgy of Good Friday (before 1955), we might conclude that originally the Roman Mass began with the readings. And yet penitential rites, at least on certain days,[2] as well as greetings or other ways of establishing the right mood, must always have suggested themselves and been found functionally necessary. From the standpoint of the psychology of prayer, it seems obvious that some preparation is needed, since the dispositions of body and soul with which the celebration is begun will pretty much characterize the whole of it. The early Church liked to have an atrium (an open, usually colonnaded court) at the front of its basilicas, since a forecourt was needed if people were to be fully prepared for entering the church. Passing through the atrium, they left behind the hectic pace and noise of everyday

---

[1] *Apologia I*, 67.   2 Cf. *Didache*, 14, 1.

life, and recollected themselves for their encounter with God. The orderly
and harmonious architecture helped to this end.

The introductory rites play a similar role. It is worth noting that the
General Instruction describes these rites as an "introduction" (*exordium*;
GI, no. 24) and does not use the old designation "entrance" (*introitus*),
since the "entrance" was and is, in fact, only one part of this section of
the Mass. Attention is now focused not on the entrance but on the formation of a worshiping community that is capable of properly hearing and
celebrating (*GI*, no. 24b).

1. Entrance and Opening Song

The "assembling" or coming together of the community is usually accomplished today in an informal manner; in an age when everyone has a
watch, it takes only a short time for people to assemble so as to begin at a
set time. Not so in earlier ages, when a lengthy period might elapse before
everyone had assembled. The praying of the psalms, the recitation of
Terce before the medieval pontifical liturgy in the cathedrals, the recital of
the Rosary before the Sunday High Mass, and other practices were often
exercises intended to pass the time of waiting and to put the participants
into the proper mood. To avoid disturbances, each person went quietly to
his place. This silent entrance into the church is the normal thing today.
Yet it would not be a bad thing if members of the community greeted one
another in a suitable manner. The community might also arrange to help
the handicapped, for example, and lead them to their places. There are
numerous other possible interactions that would eliminate or lessen any
anonymity.

The priest emerges from the sacristy with those who are to perform
various services during the Mass: reader, cantor, servers. The servers
may carry a cross, candles, and censer; the reader (or deacon) may carry
the book of the Gospels (cf. Rubrics).

The way from the sacristy to the sanctuary may be the shortest possible. However, according to the layout of the church and the degree of
festivity of the day, a longer route may be chosen, so that the procession
comes up the middle aisle of the church. In the early centuries the sacristy
and similar service-rooms were usually located near the entrance of the
church, but in the Middle Ages they were transferred to a point near the
apse of the sanctuary. This was initially done in cathedrals and monastic
churches so that those obliged to sing the Office in choir might more easily
don their choir robes and then have only a short distance to go to the
"choir," the name often used for the sanctuary since that time. Soon
parish churches imitated the practice. As a result, the procession, which

had been the rule, especially at episcopal and papal services in antiquity, fell into disuse. There is no doubt, however, that this manner of entering can be valuable as a way of setting the tone; for this reason, it is rightly being restored in many places.

The cross and the utensils carried in the procession are set down in the sanctuary: the candlesticks on or near the altar or even on a table at the side, the book of Gospels on the altar, and the processional cross most appropriately in a floor socket or similar holder behind the altar, so that the community can see it throughout the Mass (unless, of course, the presidential chair is behind the altar, in which case the cross is best placed to one side). If there is already an immovable cross set in the sanctuary or hanging there or depicted in painting or mosaic on the back wall, the processional cross should not be introduced as a double. There is no regulation that the cross must have a corpus (the use of crucifix dates only from the Middle Ages). In fact, a cross adorned with precious stones or enamel work is far more traditional and better symbolizes the link between cross and resurrection.

"The priest approaches the altar as an *entrance song* is sung" (Rubric; cf. *GI*, nos. 25 and 82). This song has several purposes. First of all, it calls attention to the fact that the celebration is beginning (cf. *GI*, no. 25). The experience of pedagogues suggests that it is a very good thing to open a function or ceremony with communal singing. This action makes it clear that something special is beginning. The deeper breathing required for singing helps the participants to be better disposed in body and mind; it is less easy to be distracted; and the concentration on text and melody prepares the congregation for what is coming. The General Instruction observes: "Singing is a sign of a joyous heart (cf. Acts 2:46). That is why St. Augustine rightly says: 'Singing is the sign of a lover,' while antiquity already had the proverb: 'He who sings well prays twice'" (no. 19).

We should bear in mind that all processional songs, including those at the preparation of the gifts and at Communion, have a very practical value as shown by long experience: they prevent people from getting restless, and they also tend to give bodily movement a dimension of inwardness. Processions by their nature can easily disturb the devotional spirit and cause restlessness (this does not apply only to children). Singing has power to order and harmonize and is better able than praying — which can easily be drowned out — to lessen and alleviate unwanted distractions. On the other hand, it helps to move about from time to time at divine service so that there is no feeling of being constricted (again, it is not children alone who may feel this).

According to ancient liturgical tradition, a procession regularly ends with a prayer. For this reason, the entrance procession is already related, across the intervening introductory rites, to the prayer of the day.

Singing also fosters consciousness of community; indeed, in the context of worship, it is already a communal action. Coming together and being together acquire a new emotional dimension through singing together.

The content and form of the song should suit the mystery of the liturgical season and the degree of festivity. Its theme, too, should be somehow related to the celebration. When the General Instruction lists as the final function of the song "to accompany the procession of priest and servers" (no. 25), it alludes to a historical fact. In the Constantinian period, the primary purpose of the song was to honor the bishop as he came in; the same custom was observed for officials of high or consular rank. The entrance song was thus part of the "royal ceremonial" and a homage to the bishop. This aspect of the entrance song, however, was soon played down in the Church in favor of more pastoral considerations. Nonetheless, even today the hymn *Ecce sacerdos magnus* ("Behold, a great priest") is sung to honor the bishop when he comes for his visitation and on other occasions. The shouts of *Evviva il papa!* ("Long live the Pope!") that accompany a pope's entrance are similarly meant as an honorific greeting.

There are many ways of handling the introductory song, but the main one to consider is the responsorial singing of schola (and/or cantor) and congregation. This form is to be preferred because it best brings out the fact that everyone present shares in the celebratory action. For centuries the traditional entrance song frequently took the form of the choir singing each verse of a psalm, and the congregation singing the responsorial antiphon after every verse or every other verse. A shortened version of this ancient practice is what we see in the older Missal at the Introit, where we find antiphon, verse, Gloria Patri, and repetition of the antiphon. The reduction of the psalm to a single verse was due to the disappearance of the procession, which had lasted long enough for the singing of many verses or even the whole psalm.

The antiphon for the day that accompanies the entrance is always a short, pregnant, easily retainable, and musically simple verse which the congregation can be expected to sing without a great deal of practice. The verse is often taken from the psalm that is sung, or suggests in turn that the psalm from which it is drawn is a suitable one to choose for singing. The verse could, however, and still can be taken from elsewhere in the Scriptures; now and then it is a new composition but reflects the dominant idea of the feast. In earlier times, we find (in the dating of documents, for example) that the opening word of the antiphon for a given day also supplied a name for that day: for example, in Lent, Invocabo Sunday, Reminiscere Sunday, Oculi Sunday, Laetare Sunday. The antiphons in the new Missal have been very carefully chosen, and, especially when they are not sung and might therefore easily be passed over inattentively, they provide good starting points or themes for the short introduction to the Mass of the day that follows upon the opening greeting.

Instead of the antiphonal or responsorial singing of schola and congregation, songs with regular stanzas are preferred in many places. They are preferred because everyone knows them, and they require no lengthy practice. Care must be taken, however, lest they be too general and not well adapted to the feast being celebrated. In many cases, only one stanza of a song is really suitable.

A song by the choir alone — a motet, for example — should be the exception, since the congregation is more or less excluded, and little is done to build up the desired community and sense of communal participation. We must not, of course, underestimate the power of music; it remains a fact, nonetheless, that we are rendered active more by acting than by simply receiving what is given to us. The same remarks hold for organ playing — for example, a variation on a song that is suited to the theme of the celebration. One possibility, however, is to have the organ play a prelude, and the congregation then sing a stanza of the song.

An old tradition in German-speaking countries is the Kyrieleis songs. If one of these was used, the Kyrie could be dropped, making the introductory rites seem more compact.

The rubrics in the new German Missal allow the priest to approach the altar in silence. This practice will be suited chiefly to Masses for small groups on weekdays. A silence that is truly filled by active devotion depends on conditions that are not always present in large congregations, especially at the beginning of the service.

2. HOMAGE TO THE ALTAR

When the priest and his attendants reach the altar, they pay homage to it. It represents Christ, and the president of the community thereby greets the head of the house, as it were, before the celebration begins.

The General Instruction lists the acts of homage: profound bow (or genuflection if the Eucharist is reserved in the tabernacle there), kissing of the altar, and, in some cases, incensation of the altar (no. 84).

The profound bow, as distinct from the simple bow of the head (cf. *GI*, no. 234), is older, in the history of worship, than the genuflection, and, in the East, has since ancient times been preferred to the genuflection. It is noteworthy that in the description of the papal Mass of around the year 700, the pope, on entering the sanctuary, makes a profound bow to the *sancta* (the "holy things," i.e., the remnant of the Eucharistic bread from a previous Mass that will be put into the chalice before Communion),[3]

---

[3] *Ordo Romanus I*, no. 48; Andrieu, *op. cit.*, 2:82–83.

whereas genuflections (derived from court ceremonial) are made to the pope himself. Originally, then, the profound bow was no less a sign of reverence than the genuflection, although today we usually regard it as the lesser sign. The genuflection is now made only to the Eucharistic species and on this account is regarded as the higher expression of veneration. If the tabernacle is located on the altar (an exception, according to *GI*, no. 276) or close to it, the celebrant and attendants are to genuflect to it; this rule holds also if the procession passes in front of the reserved sacrament (*GI*, no. 233).

After the bow, the priest (and concelebrants, if there be any) approaches the altar and kisses it (*GI*, no. 85); he extends his arms a bit, places his hands on the altar, bends, and touches the altar table with his lips. Like the bow or genuflection, the kiss is given to the altar and to Christ himself as represented by the altar. The kiss is an expressive bodily gesture that symbolizes a union desired or achieved, and is almost always accompanied by an embrace. This brotherly kiss has a very ancient tradition behind it. It is still customary in the East when greeting a friend and especially a guest, while in the Latin countries it persists in the form of the accolade or ceremonial embrace; especially in socialist countries it is used as a sign of friendship between politicians and bureaucrats.

The embrace or kiss is frequently accompanied by friendly words and wishes: *salaam*, *shalom*, *pax tibi*. In pagan rites the kiss was given not only to persons but to holy objects: idols, the thresholds of temples, door-hangings. Popular devotion in many religions has been and still is familiar with it, although custom varies widely according to time and place. The kissing of things probably came into the Christian liturgy by way of court ceremonial, according to which any object handed to the ruler must first be kissed, just as gifts received from the ruler's hand must be taken in a hand covered with a cloth.

In the old Missal, the devotional kissing of objects was much more frequent than it is now. The celebrant kissed the paten at the preparation of the gifts; the deacon kissed the base of the chalice and the cruets of wine and water; each vestment was kissed before it was donned in the sacristy. In order to bring out the real meaning of these acts of veneration, a small cross was attached to the chalice and paten and sewn or appliquéed onto the vestments (amice, stole, maniple, etc.). The altar was also kissed more frequently: before every *Dominus vobiscum*, during the Canon, and so on. Reducing the number of kisses makes the kiss at the beginning of the celebration (and at its end, though only by the principal celebrant at this point; cf. *GI*, no. 208) more expressive, meaningful, and solemn.

As we have already remarked, the kiss is intended for the altar both as an altar and as a symbol of Christ. In earlier times it was also directed to the relics of confessors and martyrs that were enclosed in the altar. This intention was suggested by the prayer which the priest said after finishing the prayers at the foot of the altar and while ascending to the altar platform: "We pray you, Lord, through the merits of your saints whose relics are here [he kisses the altar], and all the saints, to forgive me all my sins. Amen." This prayer is omitted from the new Missal, and relics are no longer required, except in a solemnly consecrated main altar (*GI*, no. 266), whereas in the past relics had to be present even on unconsecrated altars, in the altar stone that was inserted at the center under the altar cloth. The new liturgy pays no attention to the presence of relics in the altar. It is thus made clear that the kiss is an act of homage to altar alone.

The incensation of the altar is optional: "As occasion suggests, the priest incenses the altar" (*GI*, no. 27); "Then, as occasion suggests, he circles the altar and incenses it" (*GI*, no. 85). Incense may be used in *every* form of Eucharistic celebration (*GI*, no. 235), and thus even in a Mass for a small group; on the other hand, it is not prescribed even for solemn functions. The priest puts the incense in the censer and blesses it with a sign of the cross, without any accompanying words (*GI*, no. 236). It is more appropriate to do this in the sacristy before entering the church and the sanctuary. After kissing the altar, the priest circles it with the censer. According to the General Instruction, an altar attached to the wall so that it cannot be circled will be an exception; if this happens to be the case, first the right side, then the left, is to be incensed.

"If there is a cross on the altar or beside it, it is to be incensed first, if it is behind the altar, the priest incenses it when he passes in front of it" (*GI*, no. 236). This emphasis on incensing the cross (which is a more readily grasped symbol of Christ than the altar is) calls attention once again to the Christological significance of incensing the altar.

The incensation or non-incensation of the altar is a matter of judgment, but a judgment that depends not only on the celebrant's wishes but on local custom and on the community or its liturgy committee. For a while it looked as if incense were going to disappear completely from worship; at present, however, it seems to be coming back into favor. I would urge that it not be simply eliminated, for ecumenical reasons if nothing else, since it is very much favored in the Eastern Church and has been since earliest times. Whether St. Ephraem the Syrian actually mentions it in a hymn as an existing practice or simply uses it as a symbol is disputed.[4] The same can be said of St. Ambrose in his explanation of the Third Gospel.[5]

In the Roman West, incense was not used for a long time; its absence may reflect the Church's memory of the fact that in the Decian persecution (*ca*. 250), the incensing of the symbols of the State and the pagan gods had signified a rejection of the faith, so that apostates from the faith were

---

[4] Cf. his *Carmina Nisibena*, no. 17 (written *ca*. 363).

[5] *Expositio Evangelii secundum Lucam*, I, 28 (*SC* 45:61).

simply called *thurificati*, i.e., "those who offered incense [*thus*]". Such a
memory, at least at the literary level, was quite possible. Incense, like the
kissing of the altar, seems to have been introduced into the Western
liturgy by way of court ceremonial. In the ancient world, for quite practical reasons, people of rank would be conducted through the unlighted
streets by a servant with a torch; in case the torch was extinguished by
wind or rain, another servant was there with a brazier of hot coals to
relight it. This custom was then modified for courtly use indoors, for
example, in throne rooms or consular halls, where a candle replaced the
torch, and a thurible the brazier. Thus candlesticks and censers became a
mark of honor for those in high social position.

It is easy to understand that the incense carried in the procession and
the attendance of seven candlestick bearers should be marks of honor
given to the pope as he entered the church,[6] and that these marks of honor
should then be given also to the altar and the book of the Gospels, both of
which represent Christ. Incense became customary in the Western liturgy
only in the post-Carolingian and early medieval periods; its use was possibly fostered by closer contact with the East in the period of the
Crusades. In the old Missal, incensing was prescribed for a solemn Mass,
but also permitted only on that occasion.

In the history of religions, incense was used by the pagans as an apotropaic, that is, as a means of warding off evil spirits, as, for example, at
burials and exorcisms. It has also been used to purify and expiate, as in
the incensation of the chalice in the Ethiopian Liturgy. It is a sensible sign
of sacrifice, especially in the Old Testament. Thus the passage from the
prophet Malachi which is often quoted as a prediction of the New Testament sacrifice mentions not only "a pure offering" but also "incense . . .
offered to my name" (1:11; cf. also Exod. 30:34; Lev. 2:1, where the
frankincense accompanies a cereal offering). Incense evidently has the
same symbolic value as the cloud; the glory of the Lord is manifested by
the cloud (Exod. 16:1, and frequently), and the cloud is the dwelling or
shekinah of God (1 Kings 8:10, and frequently). In the art of the Ottonian
period, the cloud or the hand reaching from the cloud is a symbol of God.

After paying homage to the altar, the priest and his attendants go to their
seats (Rubrics; cf. *GI*, no. 86). The priest's or president's chair is a new
and not always fully understood piece of sanctuary furniture. The word
"new" is not used absolutely here, of course, since in fact we have only
gone back to a very ancient practice of the Church. The presidential chair
has no connection with the *sedilia* (seats) that used to be customary, that
is, the small seats on which the celebrant and his assistants used to sit
during parts of the Mass that involved lengthy singing by the choir (e.g.,
Gloria and Creed) at a solemn Mass. Those seats were simply concessions

[6] According to *Ordo Romanus I*, no. 46; Andrieu, *op. cit.*, 2:82.

to the fatigue of the celebrant; they were a work of mercy. The presidential chair, which is set up opposite and in the sight of the congregation, is, on the contrary, an expression of the hierarchic structure of God's people. In the person of his minister, Christ himself presides over the service (cf. *CL*, no. 7); the celebrant represents him.

The original presidential chair continued to be used only at pontifical Mass and in cathedrals (the word "cathedral" derives from the Latin *cathedra*, i.e., "[bishop's] chair"). Once the private Mass had become the rule, the presidential chair of a priest was eliminated, because the priest now stood at the altar throughout the Mass. Because of the law of orientation at prayer, the bishop's chair changed its position in the course of time; it used to be in the apse or against the back wall, but later was moved to the side of the sanctuary. Even in antiquity and in the synagogue, sitting on a chair or professorial seat was the prerogative of teachers. Thus the president of the synagogal liturgy sat on "Moses' seat" (Matthew 23:2), facing the congregation; this chair distinguished him and showed him to be an ordained rabbi in Israel. That is why rabbinical literature has the stereotyped formula: "Rabbi so-and-so sat down, opened his mouth, and taught" (cf. the description of Jesus' action at the beginning of the Sermon on the Mount, Matthew 5:1).

The presidential chair is the normal place for the celebrant, just as the nave of the church is for the congregation. The celebrant sits there when he himself is not performing any function, as for example when the reader is carrying out his function at the lectern during the liturgy of the word. The president can, however, also carry out some of his own functions from this place, as during the introductory and concluding rites. At the community Mass, the priest's chair thus plays the same role as the bishop's chair at a pontifical Mass: It is not simply a utilitarian piece of furniture but has a theological significance in relation to the community. Therefore, while being practical, suitable, and unostentatious, it should not, in false modesty, be put where it will not be noticed; the office it represents is part of the community's life.

3. THE SIGN OF THE CROSS

"The priest and the faithful, still standing, make the sign of the cross on themselves, while the priest, facing the people, says: 'In the name of the Father and of the Son and of the Holy Spirit' " (Rubric; cf. *GI*, no. 28; in *GI*, no. 86, the "Amen" is explained as an acclamation and response of the people).

In the old Missal, the sign of the cross was made at the start of the prayers at the foot of the altar (which were regarded as the beginning of the Mass), and it might be considered to be, at the present time, a relict of those now omitted introductory prayers. Such a supposition is unnecessary, since the sign of the cross as an introduction to prayer has a long tradition behind it, which regards the making of the sign on oneself as an act of self-blessing before prayer. When the cross is properly and devoutly traced from forehead (seat of understanding) to breast (seat of heart and feelings) and then from shoulder to shoulder (the points from which spring the arms and hands with which we work and bear fruit), it is certainly an eloquent and expressive gesture of prayer, faith, and devotion.

In the liturgy, the sign of the cross occurs elsewhere as an action consecratory of persons and objects, especially in the administration of the sacraments and sacramentals. The formula of blessing that accompanies the sign at the beginning of Mass comes from the baptismal mandate in the Gospel of Matthew (28:19b). Unfortunately, the connection between the sign of the cross and baptism has been lost in the popular mind, but it can and should be revived. "Signing" and "sealing" were for a long time names for "baptizing" in the early Church. In addition, the sign of the cross is based on a mysticism of the cross that has been known from the time of the Fathers and has good theological grounds, namely, that all salvation comes to us through the cross of Christ[7] and that the sacraments spring from the wound that pierced the side of the dead Christ on the cross (John 19:34).

4. Greeting of the Congregation

From his place the president greets the congregation with gesture and word: the gesture of outstretched arms and a wish for blessings. Both elements — gesture and word — occur in the greetings we use in everyday life, where we may make some kind of expressive sign and speak words that further interpret the sign. The extension of the arms can have two meanings (we are not speaking here of the quite different gesture of prayer used during the presidential prayers). It can be a gesture of invitation, in which case the opened hands are inclined upward a bit; or it can be a stylized form of embrace offered to the entire congregation, in which case the palms of the hands are held perpendicular and facing each other. The inherent meaning of both forms is readily understood even today, especially if the gestures are not excessively restrained and ritualistic, but are authentic expressions of an inner attitude and are marked by ease and affability.

[7] Cf. St. John Chrysostom, *Homiliae in Matthaeum*, 54, 5 (*PG* 58:537), and Tertullian, *Adversus Marcionem*, III, 22, 5–7 (*CCL* 1:539–40).

The pervasive sacramental structure of all ecclesial action (sign and word, "matter and form") is to be found in this greeting, where the gesture is specified and given an unambiguous meaning by the accompanying wish for blessings. As in everyday life, so in worship a greeting can become a formality. It will not become that if the heart is in it and if the usual formula is changed or expanded occasionally. The Missal helps prevent formalism by bringing out the theological meaning of the greeting through the accompanying words and by providing a number of formulas.

The liturgical greeting is not simply an expression of personal good will and friendliness. "The mystery of the assembled Church is manifested by the greeting and the congregation's answer" (*GI*, no. 28b); "The purpose of these [introductory] rites is to permit the assembled faithful to establish communion among themselves" (*GI*, no. 24b). The English Missal provides three formulas of greeting. The German Missal provides eight, most of them taken from the conclusions (2 Cor. 13:13) or openings (Rom. 1:7; cf. the constant pairing of "grace and peace" in 1 Cor. 1:3; 2 Cor. 1:2; Gal. 1:3; Eph. 1:2; etc.; cf. Apoc. 1:4) of St. Paul's letters. The special character of the feast may also be brought out in the greeting.

The Latin Missal likewise offers three formulas, the last being the ancient and long customary "The Lord be with you," or "Peace be with you" if the celebrant is a bishop. The greeting is based on Scripture, where it is the greeting the risen Lord gives his disciples on Easter (Luke 24:36; John 20:19, 21; etc.). We must recall that "peace" means more than the absence of war and conflict; it is the summation of eschatological salvation, the expression of God's rule (Rom. 14:17), and a fruit of the Spirit (Gal. 5:22). Moreover, this peace is identical with Christ: "For he is our peace" (Eph. 2:14). In intention, then, the greetings of both bishop and priest are the same; it is only ancient custom that words them differently.

The congregation's answer is literally "And with your spirit." From a purely philological standpoint, the phrase is simply a Semitic expansion of "And also with you." "And also with you" is the translation that has been adopted in the official English Missal. When the German Missal was being redacted, it was frequently suggested that this simpler everyday form be used, but it was finally decided not to use it on the grounds that it would impoverish the meaning of the greeting. Just as the president's greeting is not simply an expression of his personal good will and readiness to communicate with the congregation, but is a proclamation of salvation in the name of Christ, so too the congregation is not responding to an individual person with a human function but to the minister who is a "servant of Christ and steward of the mysteries of God" (1 Cor. 4:1). The greeting and response help form a human community, but this community itself is oriented toward "the presence of the Lord to his assembled community" (*GI*, no. 28). On ecumenical grounds, too, the expanded response, which marks a certain separation from everyday life, was preserved as in the past.

The exchange of greetings, together with the kissing of the altar, used to be regarded as an introduction to the priest's official prayers (the opening and concluding prayers) and comparable to the lengthy summons to prayer just before the prayer over the gifts. It is not possible to take this view today, even though the Canon still begins with the same greeting, "The Lord be with you," in the dialogue before the preface. It is more important and profitable to compare the structure of the greeting in the introductory and concluding rites of the Mass. In both places, the exchange of greeting is accompanied by a somewhat lengthy wish for blessings (provided the celebrant makes use of the longer blessing formulas at the end and the longer greeting formulas at the beginning), as well as by a gesture of communication and the naming of the Trinity. The fact that Paul begins and ends his letters with similar formulas provides the real basis for the liturgical tradition.

5. INTRODUCTION TO THE CELEBRATION

"The priest, deacon, or other capable minister can say a few words introducing the faithful to the Mass of the day" (Rubric; cf. *GI*, nos. 29a and 86b). This introduction to some extent continues the work of the greeting inasmuch as it fosters the sense of community in the celebrating congregation and makes it easier to experience the mystery. But the introduction should not duplicate the greeting by using similar words, for that would only devalue and cheapen the solemn liturgical contact which the greeting represents. It is always possible, however, to go beyond the official greeting to a more personal one, or to welcome some particular individual, provided his or her presence is significant for the entire community and the greeting is not meant simply to honor him or her as an individual. This kind of introduction is appropriate when one or other sacrament — baptism or marriage, for example — is to be administered in connection with the Mass.

The speaker of the introduction is usually the celebrant of the Mass, since this is one of his constitutive tasks. It will be an exception, therefore, to have someone replace him — an eventuality for which the rubric provides. Yet the nature of the introduction as a mystagogy (initiation into the mysteries of salvation) may make the substitution desirable on occasion. We may think also of the parish priest speaking the introduction when the bishop presides over the liturgy (at confirmation, the dedication of a church, etc.).

The introduction is not a part of the liturgy of the word, and it would therefore be out of place to allude to the coming readings from Scripture, unless the order of readings suggests a theme for the whole service. In general, it is more appropriate to refer especially to the entrance antiphon, either because it has been sung and there is spiritual profit to be derived from dwelling on it for a moment, or because some other song has replaced it and the antiphon may therefore be easily overlooked. The entrance antiphons, as we observed earlier, have been carefully chosen for the new Missal, and the experience of many shows that they are almost always worth a meaningful comment.

The introduction is to consist of "a few words" (Rubric). In general, people today are afraid of the liturgy being excessively rationalized and verbalized; this they find reprehensible. This introduction should therefore not be allowed to turn into a first sermon. The better prepared it is, the shorter and more pregnant the introduction can be!

6. GENERAL CONFESSION OF SINS AND PENITENTIAL ACT

An act of repentance before Mass is appropriate because man is sinful. The synagogue long ago occasionally celebrated a penitential liturgy before the regular service; the *Didache* speaks of breaking bread "after you have confessed your sins."[8]

In the old Missal, a pentential rite involving the Confiteor was a fixed part of the opening of every Mass, although it was only at a relatively late date that the rite was transferred from the sacristy to the foot of the altar. Other penitential rites were also used on occasion, as, for example, the prostration on Good Friday, when the priest and his deacons lay face down on the floor before the altar. This particular penitential act has been retained on Good Friday in the new Missal, and it is certainly an impressive ceremony. We should note, however, that in its origins (in Persian court ceremonial), the prostration was more an act of devotion and submission than a confession of guilt. Similarly, the Greek term for "prostration," *proskynesis* (from the word *kyōn*, "dog"), suggests an act of self-humiliation rather than an admission of moral guilt. It must be admitted, however, that admission of sin and submission to God are really not so far apart.

According to the new Missal, too, the penitential act is an integral part of the introductory rites, at least as a rule; in this, the Missal reflects an inner necessity. The new Order of Mass, however, shows a welcome adaptability that was lacking in the old. For penitential seasons, the first penitential act provided in the Missal seems the most appropriate; it al-

[8] *Didache*, 14, 1; text in Hänggi-Pahl, *op. cit.*, p. 68.

lows a pause for an examination of conscience, and then contains an explicit confession of sins in the form of a revised Confiteor. (The Confiteor had largely lost its impact in the old Missal because it had been used in every Mass, even on great feasts such as Easter.) A second form of the penitential act, containing verses from the psalms, is perhaps best suited to Sundays and feastdays. The third variation, with its several versions of a revised Kyrie litany, fuses penitential act and litany (two parts that in themselves are independent each of the other) and thus lessens the feeling we may have that too many small rites are being packed into the introductory part of the Mass. The German Missal expressly allows for replacing either of the first two types of penitential act with a song expressing repentance.

The greeting and the confession of sins are omitted when another liturgical action immediately precedes the Mass, for example, a procession on Corpus Christi; likewise, when candidates for baptism are brought in, or at weddings which have their own forms of introduction to the service. Otherwise the penitential act would be repeated at a baptism within a Mass, since the baptismal rite has its own proper renunciation of sin and profession of faith in God.

The old Asperges procession has happily been given an honorable place once again and can replace the penitential act. The Asperges is a renewal of the Christian's memory of his baptism, and for a long time it was a very popular part of the introduction to the Sunday Mass. It can, of course, quite rightly replace the penitential act, because baptism is the basic repentance or "change of heart" (*metanoia*). The celebrant's task is to make full use of the rich options given him and thereby to give ever new vitality to the spirit of repentance and the confession of sins.

The rite of the confession of sins has, as we indicated, three forms or variants, each with its four-part structure: invitation; short silence for reflection and examination of conscience; confession of sinfulness; request for pardon. The structure is a logical one, and is suggested by the nature of things.

In all three forms, the priest's invitation to repentance aptly expresses the liturgical point of the rite, which is to prepare for celebrating the mysteries and to draw down God's mercy. In their content, the three formulas of invitation are almost identical; as need arises, they may be modified somewhat. All three simply give nuances of the same basic idea and intention.

In order that the penitential act may be not simply a ritual formality but a conscious, authentic interior action, the second moment in the four-part structure — the short silence — is psychologically indispensable. It must be long enough but not too long. An old liturgical custom suggested "the length of an Our Father." This led, however, to the actual praying of the

Our Father at this point (and, for a long time, at the corresponding point in Compline in the divine Office). The *preces* or intercessions in the old Breviary originated in the same way; in fact, a parallel phenomenon occurred wherever there were pauses for reflection. This misunderstanding meant, of course, that the beneficial pause for reflection was really not being used, but instead was filled in with the Our Father, which served as a jack-of-all-trades prayer. All this has now fortunately been changed and improved. And yet the suggested length of the pause reflects long experience; it has a spiritual tradition behind it and can properly be used in the future as in the past.

The actual confession of guilt has three possible forms, based on the traditional Confiteor, on some penitental psalm verses, and on a Kyrie litany.

The old Confiteor, which was brought from the East, probably in the sixth/seventh century, was in general use in the Frankish liturgy ever since the early Middle Ages. Originally, however, the priest said it privately in the sacristy as part of his preparation for Mass. In the course of the Middle Ages, it was transferred to the beginning of Mass, and was used for centuries in the Missal of Pius V in the form of a twofold confession by priest and servers, the latter representing the congregation.

The prayer in its older form had a strictly symmetrical structure: confession before God and the saints and the brethren (or priest) who are present; admission of guilt while striking the breast three times as a sign of repentance; prayer to the saints and the brethren (or priest) that they would intercede with God. The prayer gave clear expression, more so than did the sacramental rite of private confession, to the theological and ecclesial dimension of repentance. The list of the saints in the confession and in the plea for intercession could vary somewhat; thus until quite recently the members of the old religious Orders included the names of their saintly founders.

The new form of the Confiteor has eliminated the separate confessions of priest and people, since all without exception or difference are sinners. At the same time, the use of the first person singular allows each person to express his personal guilt, not only (as in the old Confiteor) because of sinful acts — thought, word, and deed — but also because of the often more serious omission of the good he should have done. In addition, the old strictly symmetrical structure has been changed. Now the confession is made before God and the brothers and sisters of the ecclesial community, while the prayer for intercession names the Blessed Virgin, the angels and saints, and the brothers and sisters of the community. There is no problem about the priest not being named as an intercessor, but we may ask why Christ, *the* intercessor and mediator, is not named. The explicit confession of sin at the center of the prayer, with the threefold striking of the breast, has been taken over unchanged. This first form of the penitential act with its circumstantial self-accusation is felt by people generally to be especially impressive; it is therefore especially suited for use in the penitential seasons and on days of penance.

The second form of confession comprises a double pair of psalm verses: "Have mercy on us, Lord, / for we have sinned against you. / Show us your mercy, Lord, / and grant us your salvation." The structure of this short prayer is not unlike that of the Confiteor inasmuch as it contains both a confession of guilt and a plea for mercy. And yet experience shows that this form is not very popular, though it should be, since it is short and rich, and helps keep the introductory section of the Mass from seeming too much an accumulation of at times somewhat disparate rites. This form is therefore well suited for use at Sunday Masses, except during the penitential seasons.

The third form of confession is a Kyrie litany that has been given a new function. We shall be speaking shortly of the Kyrie itself and of the litany as a liturgical form. This new version of the Kyrie differs from the old by the fact that the petitions are not directed to the Father, as the Kyrie litany originally was in the Eastern and Western Churches, but to Christ. The classical order of liturgical prayer has, of course, at all times been: to the Father, through Christ the mediator, in the Holy Spirit. In other words, in the dialogue of salvation, liturgical prayer is the human response to God's redemptive and revelatory action which comes from the Father, through the Son, in the Holy Spirit. At the same time, however, it is a fact that prayers to Christ have been numerous in the Mass, especially in the form of acclamations.

The litany form has also been changed: instead of the usual statement of the content of each petition, followed by the community's imploring cry, there is now a statement praising Christ, after the manner of the old "tropes," followed by a cry of repentance. The Kyrie was originally not a penitential cry (it did not say "Lord, have mercy *on us*"), but rather a cry of homage and petition ("have mercy," that is, "be gracious," "hear our prayers"). It would be unreasonable, however, to fault the new form of Kyrie litany simply because of the changes it represents; the historical forms produced by a given age are not sacrosanct but must be adapted to new needs.

All three forms of the confession of sins include a plea for forgiveness, which is modeled on that of the old Missal (*Misereatur, Indulgentiam, Aufer a nobis*). All three petitions are deliberately put as wishes, that is, they are not formulas of absolution but petitions for pardon, even though it is a priest that speaks them. They are certainly not words of sacramental absolution for sins that require confession, but there can hardly be any doubt of their theological and sacramental significance for repentant sinners.

As we noted earlier, at Sunday Mass the penitential act may be replaced by the blessing of, and sprinkling with, holy water. The old custom of the Asperges procession (named after the first word of the opening antiphon, from Psalm 51:9) was very widespread and popular from the Middle Ages on. It was both a recall of baptism and a penitential rite, but was used only at the principal Mass on Sunday (though it must be remembered that in earlier times this Mass was likely to be also the only Mass). The extension of the rite to all Sunday Masses, including the anticipated Mass on Saturday evening, is an adaptation to new circumstances.

Immediately after the liturgical (and perhaps a personal) greeting to the community, the priest faces the people and, with the container of water in front of him, urges the congregation to join him in prayer, reminding them that the sprinkling with the blessed water will be a renewal of their baptism. After the pause for silent reflection, he blesses the water, using one of the three prayers provided (the third of them, for use in the Easter season, refers more expressly to the paschal mystery). According to the custom of the place, he may mix some salt with the water. He then sprinkles himself, the servers, the clergy, and the congregation with the holy water; he may do this from his place or during a procession through the church.

During the sprinkling, the congregation sings one of the three songs provided for Sunday within or outside of the Easter season. These songs are taken from Scripture. The antiphons are based on Psalm 51:9 (the old, somewhat modified *Asperges* verse that is put on the lips of David after he has sinned with Bathsheba), on Ezekiel 36:25-26 (the outpouring of clean water as a prophecy of baptism), and on 1 Peter 1:3-5 (who praises the mystery of Easter as celebrated on each Sunday). During the Easter season, the texts are the *Vidi aquam* (based on Ezekiel 47:1-2, 9) that was used in the past, or the praise of God's choice of the priestly people of God (based on 1 Peter 2:9), or the water flowing from Christ's side (cf. John 19:34) as a symbol of paschal and sacramental salvation. Like the other penitential acts, the *Asperges* rite ends with a petition for the forgiveness of sins.

7. The Kyrie

After the penitential act the *Kyrie eleison* is begun, unless it has already been used in the penitential act. It is a song in which the faithful acclaim the Lord and ask for his mercy; therefore it is usually to be sung by all, that is, by the congregation as well as the schola or cantor.

Each acclamation is normally repeated once, but, depending on the native genius of the various languages, on the musical form, and on circumstances, it may be repeated more often, or a short trope may be added. If the Kyrie is not sung, it is to be recited (*GI*, no. 30).

The Kyrie eleison as we have it is but a remnant of a litany. A litany is so constructed that after each petition is announced (usually by a deacon), the congregation gives a stereotyped answer. The form is very simple and practical, for it makes few demands on the congregation. These litanic forms — "ectenies," as they are called in the Eastern Church — are numerous in the Byzantine liturgy. Those who have participated in a Greek or Slavic liturgy will probably never forget the polyphonic *Kyrie eleison* (Slavic: *Gospodi pomilui*).

The litanies originated in the secular liturgy of late antiquity, in which acclamations to the emperor were used. A cantor would utter some praise of the emperor, and the people would come in with a cry of homage or petition, their cry being frequently supported by the polyphony of a water-organ. From the late Constantinian period on, it was thought appropriate to make use of these political or courtly forms in the worship of the Lord Christ and of God, especially since the form was simple and yet had a certain grandeur about it. The disadvantage of such litanies is that between the invitation to pray and the response no pause for personal prayer and personal appropriation of the petition is allowed. It must be noted, however, that in the Byzantine liturgy a strong atmosphere of prayer is felt throughout the ectenies; this is probably due above all to the singing.

The Kyrie litany originated in the East. Pope Gelasius I (492–496), a Greek from Sicily, introduced it into the Roman liturgy to replace the older intercessory prayers at the end of the liturgy of the word (see Good Friday, for example). A litany of its nature can contain as many intentions as desired — five, ten, twenty — although as soon as the litany became a fixed part of the Mass, set schemata of intentions and petitions were inevitably established. The Gelasian Kyrie litany later fell victim to Gregory the Great's well-known desire to shorten the liturgy; he eliminated the naming of the intentions, and reduced the sole remaining part of the litany, namely the acclamations, to three times three, while establishing the alternation *Kyrie eleison, Christe eleison, Kyrie eleison*. By so doing, he provided the basis for the Trinitarian interpretation of the acclamations: three each to Father, Son, and Holy Spirit.

It is difficult in fact to decide which divine person was originally and primarily being referred to as *Kyrios*. It would doubtless be more likely that in all the acclamations the Father or simply God was intended. In the Septuagint, the Greek translation of the Old Testament made by the Jews of Alexandria, *Kyrios* is always a translation of "Yahweh" (God). The old liturgical law that all prayers were to be directed to the Father through Christ would also make such an interpretation more likely (it is the interpretation retained in the Byzantine liturgy down to the present time).

In the New Testament, however, especially in Paul, Christ is regularly called "*Kyrios* Jesus," the title *Kyrios* being used to indicate his divinity. In addition, during the conflicts with the Arians (Arius held that Jesus is like God but not fully and properly divine), the Western anti-Arians in particular chose, for obvious reasons, to emphasize prayer to Jesus. It is notable that the acclamations of the people during Mass are directed to Christ. This is true even in the Eucharistic prayer, despite the fact that the latter is in its overall structure directed to the Father through Christ. Thus when the priest, immediately after the consecration, bids the people proclaim the mystery of God, they answer with acclamations addressed to Christ, although, at least externally, such a practice is a marked stylistic break in the continuity of the Canon.

As acclamations, the Kyries would by their nature be spoken only by the people; the priest would have no part in them. This natural reservation of acclamations to the congregation was, however, obscured at an early date, when the priest and the servers (congregation) began to alternate in uttering them. Here difficulties often arose because the acclamations were in threes, while there were only two parties praying. I recall that in the days when we served Mass, we were much more concerned to use the right acclamation at every point than to pray devoutly for God's mercy!

Today's generally followed practice of having priest and people each say the *Kyrie, Christe*, and *Kyrie* once is much more sensible; even better is to have cantor and people say them. But it is also possible to have cantor (priest), schola, and people each say each of the three acclamations. In any case, the number of the acclamations is not fixed, any more than it was in the old litany tradition. In keeping with that same tradition, tropes or short verses can be inserted; the new form of Kyrie litany as used in the general confession of sins is an example of this use of tropes.

The acclamations may use either the untranslated *Kyrie/Christe eleison* or a translation of it. The Greek words, which were kept untranslated in the old Latin Mass, are also printed in the new Missal. There are good reasons for this, in terms of the universal Church and of the ecumenical spirit. It can be taken for granted that the Greek words are everywhere understood.

The important thing is that the congregation be involved in the acclamations. To bring the schola in as well, as a third party, makes sense, but to have a choir alone take the part of the congregation (as in "polyphonic Masses") is hardly defensible, even though the activity of the choir might appear to be delegated to them, as it were, by the congregation. Short acclamations like the Kyrie or the Amen or the response to the greeting of the celebrant should not be spoken by substitutes but by those to whom they belong.

There can be no doubt that the sung acclamations are in every case to be preferred to the spoken.

To avoid duplication, the Kyrie is always omitted when the penitential act has taken the form of a Kyrie litany (third form) or when a *Kyrieleis* song (a song with *Kyrieleis* as the refrain) has been sung at the beginning of Mass. The addition of *Kyrieleis* to early German hymns (which were therefore called *Leisen*) was very popular and continues even today.

8. THE GLORIA

> The Gloria is a very old and venerable hymn by which the Church, gathered in the Holy Spirit, glorifies and petitions God the Father and the Lamb. It is sung by the congregation or by the congregation alternately with the schola. If it is not sung, it is to be recited by all in unison or alternately.
>
> It is sung or said on Sundays outside the Advent and Lenten seasons, as well as on solemnities and feasts and at special more solemn celebrations (*GI*, no. 31).

The Kyrie and the Gloria are closely connected both theologically and historically; they are similar in structure, and both are acclamations. At the same time, the Gloria contrasts somewhat with the Kyrie, because the former is a hymn of praise, whereas in the course of time the Kyrie was abbreviated and came to be regarded less as an acclamation of homage (which it originally was) than as a cry of repentance and a plea for mercy (this especially in more recent centuries). In view of this change in the character of the Kyrie, there was evidently a need of finding an outlet for joy, especially on feastdays.

It is not clear just when the Gloria was introduced into the Roman liturgy. A prototype of the hymn already appears in the *Apostolic Constitutions*,[9] but for internal reasons and on the basis of the history of forms, we must say that the Gloria as we know it was introduced only after Gregory the Great, and after the Kyrie had been given the Trinitarian interpretation which goes back to him. The Gloria is to be seen as a prolongation of the Kyrie as thus interpreted.

In the Gregorian sacramentaries, the bishop intones the Gloria on Sundays and feasts; a priest does so only at Easter. (We should note that although the hymn opens with the angels' song [Luke 2:14], it was not originally a Christmas hymn, as people often suppose.) Since the early Middle Ages, however, the priest too has prayed the Gloria on Sundays and more important feasts outside the Advent and Lenten seasons. The

[9] VII, 47–49; the work originated around 400 in the region of Antioch.

hymn is one of the few to be found in the Latin Missal, and from the Carolingian period on was very popular, even outside of Mass; thus when Charlemagne brought Pope Leo III in state to the Imperial Diet at Paderborn (799), the people sang the Gloria.

In the *Apostolic Constitutions*, the Gloria, with its numerous biblical citations, has a clear tripartite structure (three stanzas). In its traditional Latin form, however, it seems to lack a logical progression and to be unclear or, possibly, not fully developed. The Trinitarian scheme is very clear in the Greek prototype: "To you, O God, is honor due: to the Father, through the Son, in the Holy Spirit. Amen." [10] There would have been many advantages in rewriting the Latin hymn, but evidently the reform commission was unwilling to tamper with this "very old and venerable hymn" (*GI*, no. 31), perhaps because of all the musical settings made for it from the period of Gregorian chant through the Palestrinian and classical periods down to the present time.

The first part of the Gloria is a cry of praise to God. It begins with the angels' song (Luke 2:14), which was regarded, along with the "Holy, holy, holy" (Is. 6:3) as being "an authentic heavenly song of praise"; its use at the beginning of this hymn is therefore very appropriate. The angels' song, in the Latin text, follows the Vulgate version, which divides it into two parts: "Glory to God in the highest — and peace on earth to men whom he favors." The Greek text, however, is divided into three parts: "Glory to God in the highest — and peace on earth — grace to men." [11]

The English text implicitly keeps the optative form of the verb "to be": "Glory [be] to God. . . ." This is not the sole possible interpretation of the original text; the indicative could just as well be used in translation ("Glory is to God . . ."), since all forms of praise of God from the Jewish period emphasize the fact that God is being glorified; they are not just wishes that God may be glorified in heaven and on earth.

To the revealed acclamation, five further acclamations have been added (in the Latin text) by the Church and Christians at prayer: "We praise you, we bless you, we worship you, we glorify you, we give you thanks for your great glory." Such exclamations of praise are an ancient and long-standing practice in the liturgy. They had been used in the public cultus rendered to the emperors, and they occur in an ecclesiastical context in, for example, the Passion of St. Polycarp of Smyrna (*ca.* 150). They are also found in the Eucharistic prayer of the early Eastern Liturgies.

These acclamations are in fact addressed to each of the three divine Persons. The object of them is, of course, in the first place, God the Father, who is described (according to a literal translation of the Latin

[10] *Apostolic Constitutions*, VII, 48, 3.   [11] *Apostolic Constitutions*, VII, 47, 1.

text) as "Lord God, heavenly king, almighty God the Father." The second Person of the Trinity is then named: "Lord — only-begotten Son, Jesus Christ, Lord God, Lamb of God, Son of the Father."

At this point we would expect the Holy Spirit to be named, as he is in the version of the Gloria that we find in the Bangor Antiphonary and in a recension from Milan. Instead, the allusion to redemption that is contained in "Lamb of God" (cf. John 1:19, 36) leads the author of the hymn to speak of Christ's redemptive activity in a further, three-membered acclamation added in the form of relative clauses: "who take away the sins of the world, have mercy on us; who take away the sins of the world, receive our petition; who sit at the right hand of the Father, have mercy on us." These new acclamations in turn lead effortlessly to a three-membered doxology addressed to Christ: "For you alone are holy, you alone are Lord, you alone are Most High, Jesus Christ," to which is immediately added the obligatory Trinitarian ending: "with the Holy Spirit, in the glory of God the Father." Only in this final praise is the Holy Spirit named. There is thus a certain similarity in structure and sequence of thought with the Apostles' Creed, for in this latter, too, the section on the Father is relatively concise and that on the Son is quite detailed, while the Holy Spirit is simply named at the end.

The doxology in praise of Christ has its parallel in the Eucharistic prayer or anaphora of the Liturgy of St. John Chrysostom. In this the priest calls out at the elevation of the species: "The Holy to the holy!" and the choir answers: "One is holy, one is Lord: Jesus Christ, in the glory of God the Father." These acclamations all have their origin in Scripture, the first coming from the Book of Leviticus (11:44), the others from the First Letter to the Corinthians (8:6) and the Letter to the Philippians (2:11).

Similar praise already occurs at the same point in the Mass of the "Clementine Liturgy."[12] There too it is closely linked to the "Glory to God in the highest." From all this we can see that the description "very old and venerable" (GI, no. 31) is not just a rhetorical flourish. In the Gloria we are indeed praying in accordance with very ancient liturgical tradition.

It is less easy to decide how this hymn should be handled in the community's liturgy. The rubric in the Latin Missal says simply: "When prescribed, the hymn is sung or recited." The rubric in the German Missal says: "The Gloria is sung by all or in antiphonal fashion by community and choir or by the choir alone." The General Instruction likewise suggests various ways of starting the Gloria: "The Gloria can be intoned

[12] *Apostolic Constitutions*, VIII, 13, 13; text in Johannes Quasten, *Monumenta eucharistica et liturgica vetustissima* (Florilegium patristicum 7; Bonn, 1935–37), pp. 229–30.

by the priest or the cantors or it can be begun by all together'' (*GI*, no. 87). The important thing is the principle that the Gloria belongs to the people. If the priest intones it, he does so legitimately as leader of the congregation. He will do better, however, to leave the intoning to the cantor as representative of the congregation, in accordance with the axiom that each person is to do that, and only that, which belongs to him. If there is no cantor, the intoning can readily be left to the priest.

One further point: If the cantor or priest sings or recites only the first few words, as used to be customary in the choral office or at a Mass with a choir singing polyphony, he breaks up the biblical song of the angels in an unattractive way. It would be better for whoever intones the Gloria to sing or recite the whole beginning of the hymn, and for the congregation to join in then with the further acclamations.

In addition, the alternation of congregation and choir (or cantor) that is suggested by the General Instruction should not take the form of a mechanical alternation from verse to verse as in the psalms. This is what people are mostly used to, but the uneven distribution of acclamations, which are in groups of three or five, forbids such a mechanical process, at least if we do not want to destroy the esthetic and theological structure of the hymn. This is to say that in this part of the liturgy we must pay greater attention to formal structure than we have usually done in the past. For this reason, if the hymn makes excessive demands on the capabilities of the congregation, the best solution for the time being may be to leave the singing of it entirely or chiefly to the choir. Perhaps this would soon lead to musical compositions in which the people could have short acclamations as their contribution.

The rubric also allows the congregation to recite the Gloria, but such a practice is really not esthetically satisfying; in addition, it is hardly acceptable from a spiritual point of view, at least as a long-range solution and in view of the tendency of the congregation to reel off the Gloria in a monotone. The third part of the rubric found in the German Missal (and only there) reads like a resigned acceptance of the second-best: "The Gloria may be replaced by a Gloria song." This immediately confronts us with a problem, since in the new German Hymnal (the *Gotteslob* or "Praise of God") it would be difficult to find a suitable "Gloria song." The ones offered are usually much poorer in content than their great model, and offer at most one or other thought from the rich treasure of praise contained in the Gloria.

We suggest that it would be rewarding task for composers to write musical pieces that can be easily sung while nonetheless keeping the proper content and structure, and that will involve cantor, choir, and congregation is a way that makes sense and is not merely mechanical.

Only then will the Gloria, with its rich content for meditation, become fully the possession of the people that it should be as the sole hymn in the Order of Mass.

9. THE PRAYER OF THE DAY

The prayer of the day concludes the introductory part of the Mass. It is a universal law of liturgical structure that each liturgical celebration, and each relatively independent part of a celebration, should end with a prayer. We find this law followed in each part of the Mass (prayer of the day, intercessions, prayer over the gifts, prayer after Communion), in the Liturgy of the Hours, in independent liturgies of the word, and so forth. All spiritual experience suggests that imagination must be filled and faith awakened (chiefly through the word of God) before man turns to God in prayer.

Today we can regard the prayer of the day simply as the conclusion of all the introductory rites, without delving into the history of the liturgy and asking which specific part of the introduction the prayer is to be regarded as concluding: a procession, a litany, a penitential act, or a hymn. Yet originally the prayer of the day certainly did have that kind of specific role. If we were wrongly and mechanically to string together the old traditional ways of beginning the Mass (and the ways provided in the new Missal), we would not do justice to the introductory rites as we have them today. The General Instruction in fact bids us set a very definite tone in the introduction, depending on the character of the day (degree of festivity, season of the liturgical year, connection with the administration of a sacrament, or some other liturgical action).

I would therefore advise every celebrant to come to grips with this necessary variation of the introductory rites by starting with the pre-scribed or chosen prayer of the day and, then, with an eye on that, deliberately shaping the entire introduction. In this way, this prayer, which is also rightly called a "collect" or "summarizing prayer," will in fact sum up and conclude the main theme of the introduction and the basic mood of the day. The sections of the introductory rite will then not be mere parts added together, but will form an organic whole that can create a specific attitude and spirit in the congregation, after the manner of a musical overture.

It is a general fact of experience, including religious experience, that the beginning determines what a thing will be. The repeated complaint that the many introductory rites are too disparate and are simply strung to-gether is justified only when no effort has been made to shape them into an organic whole. The large number of options provide the celebrant with a great opportunity, since he now has far more extensive means of achieving variety, proper accent, and nuances, even if he does no more than observe the rubrics in a meaningful way, since the rubrics are no longer simply negative boundary markers but are intended as positive helps.

The prayer of the day, along with the prayer over the gifts and the prayer after communion, is one of a group of "orations" that are always "presidential prayers," that is, official prayers of the presiding celebrant. The latter must speak or sing these himself, and cannot delegate them to anyone else, for example a reader or a concelebrant. The Latin word *oratio* (English "oration," as a general synonym for prayer of the day or collect, prayer over the gifts, and prayer after Communion) is derived from the verb *orare*, which can mean not only "to pray" but also "to speak, teach, proclaim." *Oratio* might, therefore, be better translated as "prayer-speech." In the early Church, the chief charism of the priestly office, and a criterion applied in determining whether or not a man was called to the priestly office, was the ability to be both a preacher and a pray-er in the liturgy of the word. As we have already seen, however, prayer formulas were soon collected and put together in *libelli* ("booklets"), which served as models for prayer. Individuals either learned such prayers by heart or used them as patterns. Only in the course of a rather long period of time was the text of the presidential prayers fixed and made obligatory.

The orations are the Roman formulas of the Missal. From their first appearance (in writing from the seventh/eighth century, but in oral form at a much earlier date — the fourth/fifth century), they show an astonishing wealth of content and a classical form: not a superfluous word; an artistic perfection and elevated speech that show the sure Roman sense of style. These prayers are the end-result of a long rhetorical tradition. Their formal perfection has won them high regard from the historians of literature. They have always been enthusiastically praised, and rightly so, for they are linguistic jewels — striking, clear, full of meaning, polished in wording, lapidary in form. Their language is quite different from everyday speech and has been purified of all that is flat and crude. It supposes in many cases a congregation that has a biblical and theological formation, and frequently too a congregation of ascetics and monks.

It is just as unmistakably the case, however, that these great advantages are offset by many drawbacks: an excessive emotional reserve, a relatively difficult conceptual content, a poverty of scriptural and imaged expression, and, as a result, a number of intellectual difficulties for simple believers and the ordinary Christians of the community. Yet the fact that the petitions are couched in very general terms and lack concrete detail is hardly a fault, and has made it possible for the prayers to have a long life. A prayer aimed very specifically at a particular situation often fits only that occasion and, even then, may not be expressive to all who hear or use it. A certain generality of formulation, on the other hand, allows a prayer to be acceptable and usable on many occasions.

There is no doubt that the precision and characteristic Latin form make these prayers difficult to translate. An effort has therefore been made in the official translations to enrich the prayers without making them too wordy, since that would go directly against their spirit and tradition.

The orations have a set structure: invitation to prayer; moment of silence; prayer with Trinitarian conclusion; Amen of the community.

The invitation to prayer is as short as possible: "Let us pray." By reason of its conciseness, this invitation fits every occasion, since it indicates no specific intention for the prayer. The hearer knows that the intention will follow, since the prayer of the day is also called a "collect" or "summarizing prayer." Suggestions have been made to expand the invitation, as for example in the general intercessions on Good Friday. In the first of these, the invitation runs: "Dear brothers and sisters, let us pray for the holy Church of God that our Lord and God would bestow peace upon the entire world, unite and protect that world, and grant us peace and security to the glory of his name." Such an invitation would provide a specific content for the silent prayer that follows. The disadvantage, of course, is a certain repetitiousness in the invitation and the prayer proper.

The function of the moment of silence is indicated in the General Instruction: "Together with the priest all observe a brief silence, so that they may become aware they are standing in God's presence, and may formulate their petitions in their hearts" (no. 32).

Silence and stillness are a part and structural element of the liturgy. The Constitution on the Sacred Liturgy (no. 30) emphasizes this point, as does the General Instruction (no. 23). The latter also indicates the various functions of the moments of silence: reflection at the confession of guilt and after the invitation to prayer; short meditation after readings and homily; interior prayer of praise after Communion. The prayer of the congregation is truly worship in Spirit and truth (John 4:23) only when it is supported and permeated by private prayer. The Instruction on Sacred Music of 1967 says:

> Through it [a reverent silence at times] the faithful are not only not considered as extraneous or mute spectators at the liturgical service, but are associated more intimately in the mystery that is being celebrated, thanks to that interior disposition which derives from the word of God that they have heard, from the songs and prayers that have been uttered,

and from the spiritual union with the priest in the parts that he says or sings himself.[13]

We should note that according to the Missal, the pause for silent prayer is now obligatory and no longer merely optional. It must therefore never be omitted, and should be of suitable length.

The celebrant speaks or sings the prayer of the day, in which he sums up the prayers of the congregation. In addition, "in it he gives expression to the special character of the celebration" (GI, no. 32), that is, of the Sunday, the season of the liturgical year, a memorial of a saint, a remembrance of the dead, and so on. It was formerly a custom, and for a time even a prescription, that in, for example, Masses connected with a sacrament — a wedding Mass, let us say — there be commemorations of the season and any saint's feast, as well as various other obligatory prayers, which might number, in all, as many as seven. All these other prayers have now been dropped. It is permissible, when there is a good reason, to introduce a "commemoration" into the greeting at the beginning of Mass or to introduce into the general intercessions petitions that would once have been the subject of additional prayers.

The prayer proper of the classical Latin oration follows a more or less fixed plan: address, frequently extended by an adjective (or even two; praise of God, in an appositional addition or a relative clause; petition, usually beginning with one or other word for "grant" (*praesta*; *concede*; etc.); conclusion, in which the form depends on whether the addressee of the prayer is the Father or the Son; the "Amen" acclamation of the community.

Here is an example (collect for Palm Sunday):

> Omnipotens sempiterne Deus,
> qui humano generi, ad imitandum humilitatis exemplum, Salvatorem nostrum carnem sumere et crucem subire fecisti,
> concede propitius,
> ut et patientiae ipsius habere documenta et resurrectionis consortia mereamur.
> Per Dominum nostrum Iesus Christum Filium tuum, qui tecum vivit et regnat in unitate Spiritus Sancti, Deus, per omnia saecula saeculorum.
> Amen.

And here is an English translation that is intended to mirror the structure of the Latin original:

> Almighty everlasting God,
> Who, in order to give mankind an example of humility it might imitate, caused our Savior to take our flesh to himself and to endure the cross,
> in your mercy grant

---

[13] Sacred Congregation of Rites, instruction *Musicam sacram* (March 5, 1967), in   *TPS* 12 (1967) 177.

that we may be found worthy to have the proofs of his patience ever
before us and to share in his resurrection.
Through Jesus Christ, your Son, our Lord, who lives and reigns with you
in the unity of the Holy Spirit, God, for ever and ever.
Amen.

In the early Church, prayers were always addressed to the Father. As
we mentioned earlier, prayers addressed to Jesus were introduced only at
a later date, often under the influence of an anti-Arian theology. The new
Missal attempts to restore the older practice as far as possible. Therefore
the General Instruction says: "The prayer spoken by the priest is addressed, in the Holy Spirit and through Christ, to God the Father" (no.
32). Prayers addressed to the Holy Spirit, though quite possible from a
theological viewpoint, were extremely infrequent even in past centuries
(they occurred, for example, in some formularies in the consecration of
virgins) and have been completely eliminated in the new Missal.

The spiritual content of the orations is very rich. After the address to
God and the mention of an attribute that is determinative or at least
especially relevant to the feast (omnipotence, eternity, love of men,
fatherhood), a sentence or appositional clause names the great deeds of
God in the creation and conservation of the world, as well as in revelation
and redemption. In this respect, the orations resemble the psalms and
their piety, for a favorite theme of the psalms is praise of God for his
dealing with his people. The reason for now approaching God is his fidelity and the fact that what he has done in the past he will continue to do in
the future. Men may petition him with confidence that he will keep his
promises (cf. Matthew 7:7-8; Luke 11:9-10), especially when men ask in
the name of the mediator, Jesus Christ (John 14:13-14; 15:16; 16:23, 26).
This is why all the orations end with "*through* Jesus Christ, our Lord."

"The people unite themselves to the priest's prayer; they give their
assent to it and make it their own with their acclamation, 'Amen' " (*GI*,
no. 32).

We shall end this section with some remarks on bodily posture in
prayer. The celebrant offers the prayer of the day and all the presidential
prayers while using the gesture of the orant, that is, with his arms extended and his hands held open, palms upward. The Missal no longer
gives any detailed instruction on just how this gesture is to be made. The
customs of various cultures can exercise a legitimate influence here.

In the history of religions — depending, of course, on the world-picture
of a given culture and period — the raising of the hands has been an
eloquent expression of prayer to the "gods above." On the other hand,
reverence for the chthonic divinities (those whose abode is in the earth)
would naturally be shown by bowing and opening the hands downward
toward the earth. The history of religions shows that alongside elevated

altars dedicated to "the heavenly gods" there might be underground chambers where sacrifice was offered to the gods of the earth.

Investigation into universal human gestures has also shown that among all peoples the extension and showing of the open hands, which cannot hold a weapon or anything harmful, is a sign of peace; signs made with the open hand, even in the Fascist and Nazi greetings, draw their power in the last analysis from this basic human gesture. Prisoners of war knelt in an attitude of submission and raised both weaponless hands; at the same time their unprotected breast was an appeal to the victor to be magnanimous and not use his sword. Hands raised and open are thus a universal human gesture of peace, trust, and petition, whereas the clenched fist is a threat and a declaration of war. In the Old Testament it was customary to raise the hands to God (Exod. 9:29, 33; Pss. 28:2; 63:5; 88:10; etc.), but also to direct them toward the sanctuary of the Temple (1 Kings 8:38; etc.).

This Jewish gesture of prayer was evidently taken over by Christians for use in private as well as public prayer. Tertullian refers to it. The Jews, he says, are conscious of their guilt and therefore do not dare raise their hands to the Lord; but "for our part, we not only raise our hands, we also open them, and by thus imitating the Lord's passion, we confess Christ even by our manner of praying."[14]

The oldest representation of the crucifixion that we have is to be found on the wooden doors of the church of St. Sabina on the Aventine in Rome (sixth century). The details here are still very restrained, because to the Roman mind crucifixion was such a scandalous kind of death. The crucified Jesus is shown with arms slightly bent and nailed hands extended; the cross itself, however, is not explicitly depicted, and it is almost as though Jesus were standing before the wall of a house. His attitude is exactly that of the orant as Tertullian describes it. When the Christian prays in this manner, the Father sees in him, as it were, his own Son dying on the cross. This explanation of the orant's gesture is of course secondary and allegorical, but it is also typical and rich in implications.

It is possible that in the early Church the whole community prayed in this manner, for example at the Our Father, and that this may have led to difficult situations and disturbances, so that finally only the celebrant used the gesture. Such reductive developments, in which a gesture or action becomes restricted to the celebrant, have not been rare in the history of the liturgy. It is possible that the crossing of the arms on the chest likewise originates in Tertullian's mysticism or in ancient views generally. The gesture was strictly obligatory among the Byzantines from the ninth century on (Pope Nicholas I explicitly approves of it in his letter to the

---

[14] *De oratione*, 14 (*CCL* 1:265).

Bulgarians in 866[15]); it is to be found today in Latin countries and occasionally in Germany among the young.

The pressing together of the open palms in the private prayers of the
priest at Mass, and on other occasions too, as for example when people
come to Communion, probably originated in feudal custom and was
meant as a gesture of dedication and fidelity. It occurs with this meaning
in priestly ordination, in the rite wherein the candidate makes his promise
to the bishop. The clasping of the hands or interlocking of the fingers,
which is very common today, is likewise quite old. St. Gregory the Great
describes St. Scholastica, as using it; as she prayed, "she placed her
hands, with fingers interlocked, on the table."[16] All such gestures in the
liturgy have profound expressive power and are well worth reflecting on
(cf. *GI*, nos. 20–21). The person praying can use them as an expression of
devotion, but, when deliberately used, they can also increase the person's
devotion.

The prayer of the day and the Amen of the congregation bring the
introductory rites to a close. They are a sign that the whole of the preparatory activity has been carried on under the influence of the Spirit and that
their purpose has been achieved: "to permit the assembled faithful to
establish a communion among themselves and to dispose themselves for
listening to the word of God in a proper frame of mind and for celebrating
the Eucharist in a worthy manner" (*GI*, no. 24).

At this point, everyone sits down at his place, and the reader approaches the lectern. The whole community is united under the word of
God; God is now coming to his people through his word.

[15] Nicholas I, *Epist.* 97: *Responsa ad consulta Bulgarorum* (*PL* 119:1000).

[16] Gregory the Great, *Dialogorum libri*, II, 33 (*PL* 66:194).

2 THE LITURGY OF THE WORD

1. THE SPIRITUAL STRUCTURE OF THE LITURGY OF THE WORD

The opening rites are an introduction and preparation for the entire Mass, which is made up of the liturgy of the word and the Eucharist, and for the twofold coming of God in word and sacrament. These rites are, however, directly and immediately a preparation for the liturgy of the word, and a help to that readiness to listen properly which the liturgy of the word presupposes.

> When the Sacred Scriptures are read in the Church, God himself speaks to the people, and Christ, who is present in his word, proclaims the Gospel.
> For this reason, the readings from the word of God, which are a very important component of the liturgy, are to be heard by all with reverence. The word of God as contained in the readings from Sacred Scripture is directed indeed to the men of every age and is intelligible to them, but its effectiveness is increased by a living explanation (the homily), which is also part of the liturgical action (*GI*, no. 9).

The General Instruction is here building upon the teaching of the Second Vatican Council: "He [Christ] is present in his word, since it is he himself who speaks when the holy scriptures are read in the Church" (*CL*, no. 7; Flannery, p. 5); "In the liturgy God speaks to his people, and Christ is still proclaiming his Gospel" (*CL*, no. 33; Flannery, pp. 11–12). These conciliar statements are not examples of fanciful allegorizing, but express the reality which faith apprehends.

The structure of the liturgy of the word corresponds to the process of faith, that is, to the fact that God alone can initiate man's salvation, and that without him we can do nothing (John 15:5). "Faith comes from what is heard, and what is heard comes by the preaching of Christ" (Rom. 10:17). The content of the message is the reconciliation of man with God as effected once and for all in Christ.

> All this is from God, who through Christ reconciled us to himself and gave us the ministry of reconciliation; that is, God was in Christ reconciling the world to himself, not counting their trespasses against them, and entrusting to us the message of reconciliation. So we are ambassadors for Christ, God making his appeal through us. We beseech you on behalf of Christ, be reconciled to God (2 Cor. 5:18-20).

Anyone who hears the message and accepts it in faith is saved: "If you confess with your lips that Jesus is Lord and believe in your heart that God raised him from the dead, you will be saved. For man believes with his heart and so is justified, and he confesses with his lips and so is saved" (Rom. 10:9-10). But "no one can say 'Jesus is Lord' except by the Holy Spirit" (1 Cor. 12:3).

The liturgy of the word follows this "logic of faith."

> In the readings, which the homily explains, God speaks to his people, revealing the mystery of redemption and salvation and providing spiritual nourishment. Christ moreover is present through his word in the midst of the faithful. The people make this divine word their own by means of songs, and gives their adhesion to it in the profession of faith. After being nourished by it, the people pray in the general intercessions for the needs of the entire Church and the salvation of the entire world (*GI*, no. 33).

We may illustrate the point once again with the beautiful image from Isaiah that we cited earlier (Is. 55:10-11). The word of God comes down like rain on the earth in the proclamation of the readings; like rain it sinks in and penetrates the heart of a man as he reflects on what he has heard and as he listens to the explanation and actualization of the message in the homily. The rain of the word makes the earth of the soul "bring forth and sprout, giving seed to the sower and bread to the eater." The believer then responds with a profession of his faith and with intercessions which he offers in the name of the entire world. Later on, he receives the bread God provides for the eater.

The liturgy of the word thus has its own irreplaceable dignity and importance. But it also stands in very close relation to the Eucharist, though it is not on that account to be regarded simply as a "Fore-Mass."

> In the Christian community . . . the preaching of the Word is required for the sacramental ministry itself, since the sacraments are sacraments of faith, drawing their origin and nourishment from the Word [cf. *CL*, no. 35.2]. This is of paramount importance in the case of the liturgy of the

> Word within the celebration of Mass where there is an inseparable union of the proclamation of the Lord's death and resurrection, the response of its hearers and the offering itself by which Christ confirmed the new covenant in his blood. In this offering the faithful share both by their sacrificial sentiments and by the reception of the sacrament (*PO*, no. 4; Flannery, pp. 869–70).

In many documents of the Second Vatican Council and in the General Introduction, this association of word and sacrament is expressed by the allegory of the two tables: "table of the divine law and of the sacred altar" (*PC*, no. 6; Flannery, p. 615); "the double table" (*PO*, no. 18; Flannery, p. 896); etc. The term "table of the word" may at first hearing seem strange, but it has for its basis and presupposition the biblical contrast between bodily nourishment and nourishment from the word of God. Thus, "man shall not live by bread alone, but by every word that proceeds from the mouth of God" (Matthew 4:4; cf. Luke 4:4), verses that are a citation from the Book of Deuteronomy (8:3). The prophet Amos speaks of a famine that is "not a famine of bread, nor a thirst for water, but of hearing the words of the Lord" (8:11). Man lives by and from God's word, which is a food for him and a source of strength. The image of the two tables is frequently found in ecclesiastical literature from the patristic period (beginning with St. Hilary of Poitiers) down to Thomas à Kempis and his *Imitation of Christ* (Bk. 4, ch. 11).

2. The Readings and the New List of Pericopes

The principal place in the liturgy of the word belongs to God's word itself, since in the readings Christ is present (cf. *CL*, no. 7). "In the readings the table of God's word is laid for the faithful, and the treasures of the Bible are opened to them" (*GI*, no. 34). Obedience is thus given to the instruction of the Council: "The treasures of the Bible are to be opened up more lavishly so that a richer fare may be provided for the faithful at the table of God's word. In this way a more representative part of the sacred scriptures will be read to the people in the course of a prescribed number of years" (*CL*, no. 51; Flannery, p. 17).

Justin Martyr informs us that as early as the year 150 there were already several readings from "the memoirs of the apostles" and "the writings of the prophets," or, as we would put it today, after the establishment of the canon of Scripture, sections or pericopes from the New and old Testaments.[1] The practice doubtless reflects the heritage of the synagogue with its several readings from "Moses and the prophets" (Luke 16:29).

The choice of readings, even at an early date, was not left simply to the

---

[1] *Apologia I*, 67.

pleasure of the presiding celebrant, but served the Church's desire to present, as far as possible, all the writings and all the truths of faith within a certain period of time. We may suppose that relatively long sections were read and that people took time to listen and "be available to God" (*vacare Deo*). The Scriptures were proclaimed in a "continuous reading" or "sequential reading" (*lectio continua*) — that is, on each successive occasion, the reader began where he had left off the last time.

The practice also began quite early of combining the various books of the Old and New Testaments according to a certain pattern. Even today, for example, the Chaldeans have four readings: two from the Old Testament (law and prophets) and two from the New (apostolic letters and Gospel). Constantinople and Milan followed the same practice for a time. In the early period Rome probably had three readings, at least on Sundays and feastdays: Old Testament, apostolic letters, Gospel. This is suggested by the fact, among others, that there were two differently structured kinds of song which were meant to be used between readings; but we do not have as much certainty on this matter as is sometimes claimed. The Syrians often have as many as six readings; the Copts have four from the New Testament alone.

It is to be noted that choosing the various readings in view of a single theme was not regarded as being of overriding importance. People were not interested in thematic ideas but in simply hearing the word of God and celebrating the mystery of God's speaking to men. For the liturgical year and certain feasts obligatory lists of readings came into use rather early. In the West these lists were often called a *comes* ("companion"). The Würzburg Comes, to which frequent reference is made in the histories of the liturgy, was compiled in England in the eighth century and reflects seventh-century Roman usage as taken over in the island kingdom. The Luxeuil Lectionary, on the other hand, reflects rather the usage of Gaul.

The assignment of readings to the various seasons and feasts shows at times the influence of catechetical ideas and concerns. The attempt to relate the two readings (Epistle and Gospel) to each other is especially noticeable in Lent, but the connection of the readings was later often frustrated by curtailments in which the key sentence might be omitted. For the Sundays after Pentecost, too, there seems to have been in the beginning an effort to relate the readings to one another, but, perhaps as early as the seventh century, this connection was likewise broken by a shift in the list of Gospel readings that left the Epistle always one Sunday ahead of the Gospel originally associated with it. In any case, the point is that some efforts at a thematic list had been made, but that thematic unity was not regarded as absolutely necessary.

The post-Tridentine Mass had a very curtailed and impoverished choice of readings. Important truths of revelation were in consequence omitted entirely from the proclamation. There was no longer a list of readings for ferias; on weekdays to which no feast was assigned, the readings of the previous Sunday were repeated, while on the feasts of the saints, which had gradually formed an overgrowth over the entire liturgical year, the same pericopes were read over and over again from the Common (formularies for various classes of saints). I still feel discomfited when I recall the years I spent in Rome. In the local calendar for the city of Rome, the memorial days of all pope-saints were feastdays, with the result that the celebrant read the same pericopes on more than half the days of the year. Even worse was the abusive practice in many parishes of using the formularies of Masses for the dead whenever the Mass was being offered for a deceased person.

The reform of the order of readings was thus long overdue. It has now been achieved, and the results are excellent. This is true, first of all, for the sheer quantitative increase in pericopes. A three-year cycle of readings for Sundays has the three Synoptic Gospels for its basis, with passages from the Gospel of St. John also being included, especially during the Easter season. In addition, every Sunday and more important feast has three readings instead of two as formerly.

For ferias, there is a two-year cycle. The readings from the Gospels are the same in both years, simply because of the limited extent of these four writings, but the readings from the Old Testament and the other parts of the New Testament vary in the two years, one group being used in uneven years, the other in the even years. In addition, the number of pericopes available for the feasts of the saints and in Masses for various needs and occasions has been increased; frequently several possible readings are provided. The possibilities of choice to meet a special pastoral need have likewise been greatly increased; the priest in the pastoral ministry now has a rich array of possible readings available to him. Of course, this kind of freedom is more demanding than the simple following of a strictly defined list. Each distinct Mass formulary requires careful preparation before the celebration; otherwise laziness will lead to a deadly monotony once again, or else the celebrant will settle for the first reading he comes across.

The basic norms for the choice of readings in the new list are given in articles 318–320 of the General Instruction. These articles are extracted from the *Ordo Lectionum* (Order of Readings) that was promulgated on May 25, 1969.

On Sundays and feastdays there are to be three readings: "Prophet," "Apostle," and "Gospel," that is, an Old Testament reading, a New Testament reading taken most frequently from the letters of St. Paul, and a reading from the Gospel.

The purpose of having an Old Testament reading is "to help the people grasp the continuity of the work of salvation as planned in a marvelous manner by God" (*GI*, no. 318). In the Apostolic Constitution with which he introduced the new Missal, Pope Paul VI emphasizes the same point: "In this way [by the addition of an Old Testament reading] the continuity of the mystery of salvation will be brought out more clearly in the revealed words of God himself."[2] This purpose is highlighted each Sunday inasmuch as an effort has been made to have each Old Testament reading be closely related to the Gospel of the day, frequently according to the pattern of prefiguration and fulfillment, or announcement of the theme and full orchestration of the same. Only during the Easter season is this approach changed, because, in keeping with ancient usage, the first readings are taken from the Acts of the Apostles.

The practice of having three readings on Sundays has drawn a great deal of criticism, as for example at the Synod of Bishops in 1967. According to many, it is too much to ask people to listen to three readings, especially if there is no direct thematic link between them. In this last case, the homilist is forced to explain only one reading (the Gospel) or at most two (the other being the usually thematically related Old Testament passage), while letting the middle reading (the passage from St. Paul, which is precisely the one in special need of explanation) be merely read or even omitted. Yet in the long run this last-named solution would create an unacceptable loss, since the letters of the Apostle are an essential part of the Church's proclamation. For this reason, the advice of the General Instruction is to be taken very much to heart:

> It is therefore very much to be desired that there be three readings. For pastoral reasons, however, and with the permission of the episcopal conference, the use of only two readings may be allowed. When a choice is thus to be made between the first two readings, the criteria set down in the lectionary are to be kept in mind, as well as the aim of leading the faithful to a more profound knowledge of the Scriptures; the mere fact that a text is shorter or easier should not enter into consideration (*GI*, no. 318).

There is no question but that this aspect of the reform of the readings must be approached and handled with a strong sense of responsibility.

On ferias there are special readings for every day of the two-year cycle. These are usually to be read on their assigned day unless a solemnity or feast occurs on that day. On the usual memorials of the saints, the readings of the feria should be preferred in most cases, when there are no solid pastoral reasons against such a course. If such reasons do occur, then an important reading which has been thereby eliminated can be

[2] Apostolic Constitution *Missale Romanum* (April 3, 1969).

integrated into the continuous reading being done on the other days of the week, either by substituting this reading for a less important one or by adding at least the essential verses from it to another reading.

In celebrations for particular groups (students; a family gathering; etc.), it is permissible to choose other readings that seem more suitable. For example, at a Mass with students, it might certainly be advisable to omit the story of the rescue of Susannah (though, precisely because it is the story of a rescue, it plays an important role in the writings of the Fathers and in the iconography of the catacombs), and to substitute something more appropriate. To counteract excessive whimsicality in the choice of readings, the General Instruction says:

> If a priest is celebrating with a congregation, he should consider chiefly the spiritual good of the faithful, and be on guard against imposing his own likes and dislikes on them. Let him take care especially not to omit too frequently, and without sufficient reason, the readings assigned for each day in the ferial lectionary, for the Church wants a more richly laden table of the word of God to be set before the faithful [cf. *CL*, no. 51].
> For the same reason, he should exercise restraint in using the formularies of Masses for the dead. After all, every Mass is celebrated for both the living and the dead, and the dead are commemorated in every Eucharistic prayer (*GI*, no. 316).

For Masses connected with the administration of the sacraments or sacramentals, special readings are provided that make the proclamation more suited to the occasion, and lead to a deeper understanding of the mystery. The readings thus serve as a mystagogy. In such cases it is always advisable to interrupt the weekly cycle and prefer the special readings, of which a large selection is offered. It is possible to disagree on the emphasis to be chosen for the liturgy of the word when a sacrament is to be administered (baptism, confirmation, matrimony, anointing of the sick): Should the sacrament be integrated into the liturgy of the word of the Mass, or should the administration of the sacrament, with its own special liturgy of the word, replace the normal liturgy of the word? The considerations involved are theoretical, but the application is eminently practical.

3. The Liturgy of the Word

a) The (first) reading

When the introductory rites have been completed, that is, when the prayer of the day has been said, the reader goes to the lectern for the (first) reading (*GI*, no. 89). Only by way of exception can the reading be done from the altar, as, for example, in a small chapel where little space is available. The General Instruction presupposes that the lectionary is already on the lectern (no. 80b). On the other hand, the Instruction also says that the reader may carry an evangeliary in the entrance procession and lay it on the altar after the greeting of the altar by the celebrant (no. 82d; 84). The lectionaries at present contain all the readings, including those from the Gospel, and evangeliaries in the proper sense are not being used. It follows that if the reader has placed the lectionary on the altar, he can now bring it from there to the lectern. The earlier ceremonial blessing of the lector has now been omitted.

The congregation sits for the reading. Sitting is in general the most relaxed and relaxing way to listen, and is the posture that most fosters alertness and understanding. It ought to be obvious to the congregation that all the members should adopt a given posture at the same time; the president may bid the congregation sit, if he deems this necessary, but he should not adopt the tone of a drill sergeant in doing so. "For all the participants to adopt the same posture is a sign of unity and community; it expresses the inner attitude and outlook of the participants, but also fosters the same" (*GI*, no. 20). The General Instruction has already spoken of "a conscious, active, and full participation of the faithful, a participation of mind and body" (no. 3).

When it is customary for the congregation to respond to the reading, the reader adds at the end the spoken or sung words, "This is the word of the Lord," and the congregation answers, "Thanks be to God." This custom does not exist everywhere, nor need it, since the real response to the reading is not so much the acclamation as the ensuing meditation in which the community assimilates the text. The acclamation can, however, make clear the transition to the responsorial psalm, especially in cases where there is no one to sing the psalm and the reader must also recite it from the lectern.

b) The responsorial psalm (Gradual)

"Then the psalmist, or cantor, says the psalm, and the people give the response" (Rubric).

> The first reading is followed by the responsorial psalm, or Gradual, which is an integral part of the liturgy of the word. The psalm is usually taken from the lectionary, since the texts there provided are closely related to the preceding reading; the choice of psalm depends, therefore, on the reading. However, to make it easier for the congregation to sing a response to the psalm, some texts of responses and psalms have been chosen for the various seasons of the year and the various categories of saints; these may be used instead of the texts that correspond to the readings, whenever the psalm is to be sung (*GI*, no. 36a).

In addition to the possible acclamation mentioned above, the responsorial psalm is the meditative response to the reading. By reason of its connection with the reading, its character is very different from that of the processional songs (entrance, bringing of gifts, Communion). It stimulates reflection on God's saving deeds in behalf of his people, and thus is in the tradition of the songs used between readings in the synagogue. A psalm that is chosen for use over a longer period of the liturgical year and that consequently pays less heed to the capabilities of the congregation is of course less suitable and further from the ideal.

"The singer of the psalm, or psalmist, utters the verses of the psalm from the lectern or some other suitable spot, while the entire congregation sits, listens, and usually participates by giving the response, unless the psalm is spoken or sung without interruption, that is, without a response" (*GI*, no. 36b). Accordingly, the response is not to be assigned to a schola, but belongs to the community. The manner of singing the psalm must be simple and not indulge in lengthy melismas, so that the psalm may be readily understood and may easily fulfill its spiritual function. It would not be helpful, therefore, to have the congregation sing the psalm in its entirety or even to have different groups sing alternate verses. If the congregation is to participate, it should be through the acclamatory response.

There are further possibilities if the text is to be sung in Latin. The gradual may be taken from the *Ordo Cantus Missae* or the *Graduale Romanum*, or a responsorial psalm or Alleluia psalm may be taken from the *Graduale Simplex*.

There is no mention of organ music being used without any singing of the psalm. Yet this should doubtless be at least considered in some cases, since it could easily create a space for meditation on the reading. Even more promising would be a charged silence, although this is likely to occur only in smaller groups. Experience shows that training is needed if people are to comprehend silence as a form of response.

If a second reading follows, it too is done from the lectern, and is concluded in the same manner as the first reading.

c) *Second song, before the Gospel*

"The second reading is followed by the Alleluia or other song, as the liturgical season requires" (*GI*, no. 37).

This second song is structurally related to the Gospel that will follow. It is less a meditation than an acclamation of the Lord who is present in his word. For this reason, the verse is always taken from the Gospels; the acclamation of the community, except in the penitential season before Easter, is always the Alleluia. According to the Instruction that accompanies the *Ordo Lectionum* of 1969, during Lent one of several other acclamations may be used: for example, "Praise to you, Lord Jesus Christ, king of endless glory" (no. 9) (ICEL).

Since the verse is already related to the Gospel, the congregation should really stand while it is sung or recited (as *GI*, no. 21b, provides). In practice, the congregation usually does not stand unless expressly told to do so, and such instructions are always awkward.

The Alleluia and verse have their proper place chiefly when two other readings precede the Gospel, so that two transitional songs are needed.

On ferias and Sundays that have only one reading (and therefore only one transition), the range of choices is extensive: responsorial song or Alleluia and verse or both, but in Lent only the responsorial psalm or the acclamation and verse. The responsorial psalm, however, always retains first place among the possibilities; it naturally deserves preference because it is meditative and relates to the reading, and consequently is best adapted to the structure of the liturgy of the word. This is why the General Instruction prescribes that if the responsorial psalm is not sung, it is to be recited, whereas if the Alleluia and verse before the Gospel are not sung, they are to be omitted.

A sequence is prescribed only on Easter and Pentecost; it is optional on the days of the octaves of these feasts, although it is desirable to use the sequence in solemn celebrations during the octave of Easter. The same is to be said of the other two feasts that still have a sequence (Corpus Christi and Our Lady of Sorrows). The *Dies irae* has now been dropped from Masses for the deceased.

Sequences have a close structural link with the Alleluia and verse: like the latter, the sequence looks ahead to the Gospel. Historically, moreover, sequences developed out of the melismas and tropes of the Alleluia melodies. Given this background, the *Dies irae* would really lack any function. It fits in poorly with the consoling Gospel pericopes of the Masses for the dead. In addition, it is very probable that this sequence was originally composed for the first Sunday of Advent with its Gospel concerning the end of the world and the general judgment. From a poetic viewpoint, it is admittedly very affecting; it is often regarded as the work of Thomas of Celano, who belonged to the circle of Francis of Assisi.

d) The Gospel

The Gospel is the high point of the liturgy of the word and since the fourth century has been read or sung by someone who is at least of diaconal rank.

> That the reading of the Gospel is to be surrounded by great veneration is clear from the liturgy itself, since it provides this reading with special marks of honor by comparison with the other readings. A minister is

assigned to proclaim it, and he prepares himself by a blessing or prayer. The faithful use acclamations to acknowledge and bear witness to Christ as present and speaking to them; they stand while listening to the reading. Finally, signs of respect are given to the book of the Gospels (*GI*, no. 35).

The high value set on the Gospels in comparison with the other books of Scripture has been based, since very early times, on the fact that the Gospels deal directly with the preaching and activity of Christ; they are, in an unqualified sense, the "good news" (*eu-aggelion*). Because of the authority of St. Jerome in matters biblical, the four evangelists have been associated with the "four living creatures" of the Apocalypse (4:6-9; 5:6, 8; especially 4:7), the association being mediated specifically through the beginning of each Gospel. Matthew is the "creature with the face of a man" (iconographically, the "man" is usually a manlike angel), because he begins his Gospel with the human genealogy of Jesus (1:1-17). Mark is the "creature like a lion," because he begins with John the Baptist crying in the wilderness (1:3). Luke is the "creature like an ox," because of the sacrifice offered by Zechariah (1:5). John, finally, is the "creature like a flying eagle," because of the intellectual heights he reaches in his Prologue (1:1-17).

The material book of the Gospels was always the object of great respect, and in earlier times was even expensively bound (this is why according to *Ordo Romanus I* it was handled like a treasure and sealed up in a casket after Mass[3]). It was adorned with precious stones and ivory, and the text was ornamented with miniatures and elaborate initials. In the juridical practice of both Church and civil society, oaths were often taken on the book of the Gospels, with the oath-taker laying his hand on it and thus confirming his oath: "So help me God and his holy Gospel which I touch with my hand." People seem to have liked to touch especially the beginning of St. John's Gospel, for many old manuscripts show clear signs of wear precisely at that point.

The Gospel stands for Christ himself, who through his word is present in his community. The honors paid to the book of the Gospels correspond accordingly to the honors paid to the altar: kiss, bow, use of incense, procession with lights, etc.

If incense is used, the celebrant silently places it in the censer during the Alleluia (we have seen that because of their content this acclamation and verse are already a part of the proclamation of the Gospel). Then, if the priest is to read the Gospel himself, he bows to the altar and says the preparatory prayer for purity of heart and lips. The prayer alludes to the seraph cleansing Isaiah's lips with a burning coal after the prophet has seen the Lord and before the Lord sends him on his mission (Is. 6:6-8).

[3] *Ordo Romanus I*, no. 65, in Andrieu, *op. cit.*, 2:89–90.

The prayer has now been shortened somewhat, and the explicit reference to Isaiah has been omitted.

If a deacon proclaims the Gospel, he asks in a low voice for the celebrant's blessing, and receives it. The formula of blessing simply puts into a deprecative form the preparatory prayer the celebrant would say if he were reading the Gospel himself.

The deacon (or priest) takes the book of the Gospels from the altar and goes to the lectern. Servers may accompany him with candles and incense (Rubric; cf. *GI*, no. 94).

> At the lectern the priest opens the book and says, "The Lord be with you," and then, "A reading from the holy Gospel . . . ," meanwhile making the sign of the cross on the book and on his own forehead, lips, and breast. If incense is used, he then incenses the book. After the acclamation of the congregation he proclaims the Gospel; when he has finished, he kisses the book and says quietly, "Through the words of the Gospel may our sins be wiped away." At the end of the Gospel, there is another acclamation by the congregation, according to regional custom (*GI*, no. 95).

The procession with the evangeliary has been in use since antiquity in almost all the liturgies of East and West. It is an especially solemn affair in the Liturgy of St. John Chrysostom and in the papal liturgy of *Ordo Romanus I*. The carrying of lights and incense in such processions is also an ancient tradition that has its roots in court ceremonial, as we pointed out earlier. Although ever since the Middle Ages the episcopal liturgy and the congregational Mass with assistants saw a great deal of simplification and elimination in other areas, the procession continued to be important. Even in the private read Mass, the Missal, which had by now absorbed the book of the Gospels, was carried by the servers from the "Epistle side" to the "Gospel side." This distinction between the sides of the altar reflected the ancient idea that the right side (as seen from the bishop's chair in the apse) was the more excellent side. The old custom of having book and celebrant turned diagonally toward the north at the reading of the Gospel also embodied the memory of the bishop's presence at the right. The medieval allegorical explanation of this slight turning to the north (the north is the place of darkness, but the Gospel brings the light of the world; cf. John 1:5) was secondary.

The exchange of greetings ("The Lord be with you," "And with your spirit") before the proclamation further highlights what is to follow. Such exchanges of greetings were more numerous in the old Mass. They now occur less frequently (at the beginning of Mass, where it is often paraphrased; at the beginning of the Gospel and the beginning of the Canon; and at the end of Mass), but the rarity only makes the exchange more significant, while also bringing out more clearly once again the parallelism in the honor given to word and sacrament.

The optative, "The Lord *be* with you," might well be changed into the indicative "The Lord *is* with you [in his word]," since the Latin, Greek, and Hebrew forms of the greeting have no copulative verb. The following proclamation of the Gospel would then become an exemplification of the presence of Christ in a particular pericope or passage of the Good News. The old introductory words, "A continuation of the holy Gospel according to . . . ," have been changed because they really supposed a strictly continuous reading. In the present formula ("A reading from the holy Gospel according to . . .") the word "holy" is optional; we tend today to be more reserved in using this adjective.

The sign of the cross on book, forehead, lips, and breast as a sealing of objects and persons reflects once again the theology and mysticism of the cross, of which we spoke earlier. This sign of the cross is paralleled by another during the liturgy of the Eucharist, since during the Eucharistic prayer there is a signing of the gifts (in the first Eucharistic prayer, or Roman Canon) or a large sign of the cross at the consecration-epiclesis (in the other three Eucharistic prayers). It is not prescribed that the congregation should likewise sign themselves before the reading of the Gospel, but this custom, still preserved in many places, is a meaningful one. The significance of the triple signing of forehead, lips, and breast (heart) is clear: man is to be dedicated entirely — thought, word, and action — to Christ.

If incense is used, the deacon (priest) now incenses the book. In the beginning, the censer was simply carried in the procession, but since the Middle Ages, the book of the Gospels, like the altar, has been incensed. We pointed out the meaning of the incensation when we were discussing the homage paid to the altar; the point is that the homage paid to the altar and the book of the Gospels is being paid to Christ himself. The use of incense is optional and depends on local preference, but it is a very meaningful action, and one that is intelligible even to the faithful of our day, as well as important from the ecumenical standpoint.

The congregation stands while listening to the Gospel (*GI*, no. 35). The significance of this posture is clear: standing connotes a greater alertness and readiness than does sitting. Far back, in the Book of Nehemiah, we read: "Ezra opened the book in the sight of all the people, for he was [standing] above all the people; and when he opened it all the people stood" (8:5).

The kissing of the book at the end of the reading is an act of devotion and veneration. It corresponds in meaning to the kiss given to the altar. According to the ancient *Ordo Romanus I*, after the reading one of the subdeacons held the evangeliary before his breast in veil-covered hands and carried it to all the clergy in the sanctuary so that they might kiss it.[4]

---

[4] *Ordo Romanus I*, no. 64, in Andrieu, *op. cit.*, 2:89.

In the congregational Mass with assistants, the subdeacon used to bring the book to the celebrating priest or bishop to be kissed, and even in a read Mass (except for requiem Masses) the celebrant kissed it. According to the new rubrics, only the reader now kisses the book, but he does so at every Mass.

In many places a ceremonial ending is customary. The deacon (or priest) adds, even if he has sung the Gospel, the words: "This is the gospel of the Lord," to which the congregation replies, "Praise to you, Lord Jesus Christ" (Rubric). In an earlier day, it was customary for the servers alone to give this response, but in the twenties and thirties, at the "congregational Mass" in Germany, the whole community made it their own.

The reader says quietly the words, "May the words of the gospel wipe away our sins." The power of the word of God to effect the forgiveness of sins is attested in Scripture: "Truly, truly, I say to you, he who hears my word and believes him who sent me, has eternal life; he does not come into judgment, but has passed from death to life" (John 5:24); "If you abide in me, and my words abide in you, ask whatever you will, and it shall be done for you" (John 15:7).

e) The homily

Since the early days of Christianity, and following the example of the synagogue, the homily has been an integral part of the Christian liturgy of the word. Its purpose is to actualize the proclamation, that is, to apply it and make it relevant to the concrete world of today. The quantitative increase in the number of Scripture readings, as well as the fact that they are now proclaimed in the vernacular, make it necessary today more than ever before that the proclaimer should provide a commentary and bring the message alive for his hearers. In the New Testament community, the word was not regarded as working magically any more than signs were: faith comes only through an intelligent hearing. This means that the word of God, originally spoken thousands of years ago in a different socio-cultural context, must be heard as something living and present now, something that sheds light on the meaning of life. "The ministry of the word, too — pastoral preaching, catechetics and all forms of Christian instruction, among which the liturgical homily should hold pride of place — is healthily nourished and thrives in holiness through the Word of Scripture" (*DV*, no. 24; Flannery, p. 764).

> The homily is part of the liturgy and is very much to be recommended, since it is a necessary food for Christian life. It is meant to be an explanation of some aspect of the readings from Sacred Scripture or of some other text from the Ordinary of the Mass or the Proper of the day. The explanation must take account of the mystery being celebrated or of the special needs of the hearers (*GI*, no. 41).

> On Sundays and holy days of obligation there is to be a homily at all
> Masses celebrated with a congregation; on other days a homily is re-
> commended, especially on the ferias of Advent, Lent, and the Easter
> season, as well as on other feasts and occasions when the people assem-
> ble in large numbers.
> As a rule, the celebrant is to give the homily (*GI*, no. 42).

The homily is thus a fixed part of the liturgy. The omission of the
homily, or at least some few words of interpretation, from a Mass celebrated with a congregation should be permitted only when unavoidable;
any priest should regard such a celebration as improverished. According
to the Dogmatic Constitution on Divine Revelation,

> all clerics, particularly priests of Christ and others who, as deacons or
> catechists, are officially engaged in the ministry of the Word, should
> immerse themselves in the Scriptures by constant sacred reading and
> diligent study. For it must not happen than anyone becomes ''an empty
> preacher of the Word of God to others, not being a hearer of the Word in
> his own heart'' [St. Augustine, *Sermo* 179.1], when he ought to be shar-
> ing the boundless riches of the divine Word with the faithful committed
> to his care, especially in the sacred liturgy (*DV*, no. 25; Flannery, p. 764).

''At those Masses which are celebrated on Sundays and holidays of obligation, with the people assisting, it [the homily] should not be omitted
except for a serious reason'' (*CL*, no. 52; Flannery, p. 18).

The explanation of the readings should ''take account of the mystery
being celebrated'' (*GI*, no. 41). To this end it is necessary to include in the
explanation the other special parts of the day's Mass (i.e., the Proper).
The reformers of the liturgy endeavored to make these texts harmonize,
but this was possible only to a certain degree, since there are several
cycles of readings. In the explanation, the unchanging parts of the Mass
(the Ordinary) should not be overlooked. This is to say that the parts of
the Mass being considered in the present book (which deals chiefly with
the Ordinary) are to be considered in the homily, so that the congregation
may be able to participate in the rites in an authentic way.

As a rule, the presiding celebrant of the Mass should give the homily. In
many cases, of course, one of the concelebrants can give it. Preaching by
the laity is being much discussed today, and instructions relative to it have
been issued by regional synods in the German-speaking lands. The whole
structure of the liturgy of the word shows that in principle the homily of
the Mass belongs to the president of the assembly, but in cases where the
professional competence of a layperson (an expert, for example in the
area of development; a mission Sister; etc.) is more to the point on a
certain question than the generalized competence of a cleric, the community should be able to profit by it. Thus, for example, the president of the
synagogue at Antioch in Pisidia asked Paul and Barnabas to speak:

"Brethren, if you have any word of exhortation for the people, say it" (Acts 13:15). In the early church, no on challenged the right of the charismatics to preach, that is, men who were not clerics but who had received special powers for building up the community. The prohibition against preaching by the laity came in only in the thirteenth century as a result of heretical movements..

"Dialogue homilies" can be quite profitable. They used to be common at one time in preaching to children. What is possible and meaningful for children may be quite appropriate for adults as well, provided that those who like to hear themselves talk are not the only ones to speak. This will depend, of course, on the spiritual self-discipline of the community. A suitable service of the word requires a degree of creativity to keep a homily from degenerating into wasted words.

The homily cannot replace all the other forms of Christian instruction. The community also needs catechetics, courses of sermons, conferences, adult religious instruction, etc., as part of a well-planned regimen. Here too the laity have their role. The homily, for its part, is a spiritual address and is, in a special and very specific sense, a proclamation by the Church.

f) *The profession of faith*

In the position it now has in the liturgy of the word, the profession of faith functions as an assent of the congregation to what "they have heard in the readings and homily" (*GI*, no. 43). The profession is a recall of the most essential truths of faith before the Eucharist begins.

The creed originally belonged in the rite of baptism, not in the Mass. In its formulation it is an expansion of the baptismal creed used at Jerusalem; as a kind of test, the candidate had to learn it by heart and recite it to the bishop (*traditio et redditio symboli*: the "presentation" of the creed to the candidates and their "return" of it to the bishop). Since it was a personal profession of faith, it was put in the first person singular; this alone is enough to show that it was not meant originally for recitation by a community at Mass.

Several variations of the creed are in use. Its elementary form is the "Apostles' Creed," which does not in fact date from apostolic times. This was expanded in the form of the Nicene Creed (named after the Council of Nicaea, 325 A.D.) and the Constantinopolitan Creed (after the Council of Constantinople, 381 A.D.). Other creeds — for example, the Athanasian and the Tridentine — are marked by theological rigor and precision, but are not used in the Eucharistic liturgy.

The Latin Missal uses the Constantinopolitan Creed for reciting or singing. The German Missal, however, allows the Apostles' Creed as well, and there are good reasons for so doing, inasmuch as the dogmatic expansions in the longer creed and the theological extract it contains from the Trinitarian disputes of the early Church do not have any great kerygmatic value, at least in this context. Yet it would certainly be meaningful if the community could sing the Constantinopolitan Creed in Latin and if they in fact sang it from time to time. The German Missal therefore adds this creed, and certainly not simply as a kind of apology for the fact that the rest of the Missal is now in the vernacular. At international congresses and pilgrimages and other gatherings, and on occasions when foreign migrant workers are attending Mass, the Latin creed would bring out the catholic unity of the faith in an impressive way.

The creed first entered the Latin Mass in Spain. At the Third Council of Toledo (587), the previously Arian Visigoths came over to the Catholic faith under King Recared, and since the Nicene Creed emphasized in an especially explicit way the unity of substance between Son and Father, its use at Mass by a previously Arian community was an obvious step. It was sung immediately before the Our Father; both texts were the ones every catechumen had to recite as a "short formula of the faith." A little earlier, under Emperor Justinian II (563–578), the creed had also become part of the Mass at Constantinople. In the seventh/eighth century it entered the Gaulish-Frankish Mass; the adoption was later explicitly approved by Pope Leo III (810), even though without the *Filioque*, i.e., the Latin word that teaches the procession of the Spirit from the Father *and* the Son, a point of grievous contention between the Western and Eastern Churches down to our day. Despite this dispute, this wording of the creed (one that had long been customary) was kept among the Franks. Rome adopted the Frankish-German custom of reciting the creed, but only because St. Henry II demanded it when he was crowned emperor at Rome in 1014.

The creed was sung at all Masses in the Eastern and Mozarabic liturgies, but the Roman liturgy used the creed only at certain Masses, especially when the mystery of the day was one mentioned in the creed. Consequently, the creed was prescribed at Christmas, Easter, the Annunciation, the feasts of the apostles and certain other saints (for example, the doctors of the Church), and on all Sundays. In the new Missal, the reduction in the number of prescribed days is quite noticeable. The creed is now sung or recited only on Sundays and solemnities, but it may also be used on especially festive occasions (cf. *GI*, nos. 44, 98), that is, when either the occasion as such or the greater participation of the people makes the Mass a special one. The rule is not a strict one.

By its nature the creed is one of the parts of the Mass that belong to the people. It is a response of faith from the entire community, even though it is spoken in the first person singular. The fact that the priest usually recites it along with the people only emphasizes its communal character. It is not prescribed that the priest be the one to start off the creed, but it is expected that he should introduce it by some such formula as "Let us recite our profession of faith."

The genuflection at the mention of the incarnation is now observed only on Christmas and the solemnity of the Annunciation, that is, the days on which the incarnation is the mystery being celebrated. On other occasions, all make a deep bow; this, unfortunately, is often omitted, but it should be insisted on. More than that, the theology of the incarnation, with all its implications for anthropology and the theology of the Church, should be more emphasized in preaching. Thus a one-sided paschal theology will be corrected by being placed within the full and explicitly Catholic profession of faith.

g) The general intercessions (prayer of the faithful)

This action, which ends the liturgy of the word, was reintroduced into the liturgy by the post-Vatican II reformers of the Mass, after the Council had explicitly wished it (CL, no. 53) because this prayer had "suffered loss through the ancients of history" (CL, no. 50; Flannery, p. 17).

As a matter of fact, the intercessions are one of the oldest parts of the Mass; Justin Martyr twice mentions them explicitly. He refers to them when speaking of the Eucharist that follows on a baptism: after receiving baptism, and after the community's liturgy of the word, the new Christian is brought in to the congregation, and all then "offer prayers in common for ourselves, for him who had just been enlightened, and for all men everywhere."[5] The intercessions are also a fixed part of the Sunday liturgy of the word: "Then [after the homily] we all stand and pray."[6]

From that point on, the usage of both East and West is well attested. The *Apostolic Constitutions* (ca. 380) bear witness for the East, and the tradition has continued down to the present day, when the intercessions take the form of a litany before the procession with the gifts. In the West we have the early witness of Hippolytus; later there were the solemn prayers in the specifically Roman liturgy, and although these were eliminated (except on Good Friday) from the time of Gelasius I, something of them remained in the Kyrie litany of the introduction to the Mass. Now the intercessions have been restored to their structurally correct place.

This prayer at the end of the liturgy of the word has always been regarded as an important element of the liturgy. Only the baptized and those in full communion with the Church took part in it, since it was expressly regarded as a prayer of the priestly people of God. Hippolytus explicitly mentions that the unbaptized were to pray apart from the baptized.[7] Justin had likewise made the point that only when a person was baptized could he share in the community's prayer. At the end of the

[5] *Apologia I*, 65.
[6] *Apologia I*, 67.
[7] *Traditio Apostolica*, 18 and 21, in Botte, *op. cit.*, pp. 41 and 55.

liturgy of the word, the Liturgy of St. John Chrysostom still has an extensive rite of prayer for the dismissal of catechumens, for penitents, and for possessed persons, even though such a rite has hardly any practical value now; only after this is the "prayer of the faithful" offered.

Because the range of the participants is thus limited, the intercessions have been known in the West too as the "prayer of the faithful." In relation to its content (prayer for the needs of the entire world), it is called the "universal prayer." From the viewpoint of its liturgical importance, it is a "solemn prayer." The General Instruction speaks of it as "universal prayer or prayer of the faithful" (*GI*, nos. 45 and 99; rubric). In English it is called "the general intercessions" or "prayer of the faithful." "In the universal prayer, or prayer of the faithful, the people exercise their priestly role and pray for all mankind. This prayer should be a regular part of every Mass celebrated with a congregation" (*GI*, no. 45).

The Scriptures expressly teach that the entire people of God, even though divided into ordained priests and laity, has a priestly character and office: "You are a chosen race, a royal priesthood, a holy nation" (1 Peter 2:9). The community is priestly only because it is united to Christ, whose mediatorship is interpreted as that of a high priest, especially in the Letter to the Hebrews, which develops the paradigm of the Old Testament high priest and his expiatory sacrifice. As head of the Church, Christ now works in and through his members, "every joint adding its own strength" (Eph. 4:16 JB). Jesus Christ is "the faithful witness, the firstborn of the dead. . . . To him who loves us and has freed us from our sins by his blood and made us a kingdom, priests to his God and Father, to him be glory and dominion" (Apoc. 1:5-6).

The people of God consciously exercises this priestly office on behalf of the entire world, since it prays "for holy Church, for those in authority over us, for those with various needs, and for all men and the salvation of all" (*GI*, no. 45). As such, the "priestly intercession" of the community leads over into the Eucharistic sacrifice; it links the liturgy of the word with the Eucharistic prayer. As a matter of fact, the intentions enunciated in the prayer of the faithful recur in the Eucharistic prayer. This connection with the Eucharistic liturgy is especially clear in the Liturgy of St. John Chrysostom, where the prayer of the faithful is closely linked to the "Great Entrance" (with the gifts for the sacrifice), and the intercessions already appear as a part of the preparation of the gifts. And yet, the whole liturgical tradition shows that the new Order of Mass in the Latin Missal is more correct: the great intercessions are, structurally, the final act in the liturgy of the word; with the preparation of the gifts something new and independent begins, namely the liturgy of the Eucharist. The Council was right in preaching the need of reintroducing this integral part of the Mass;

the Holy Father too explicitly mentions this restoration in the Apostolic Constitution with which he introduces the new Missal.

On theological grounds, then, the intercessions should be "a regular part of every Mass" (*GI*, no. 45; see nos. 33 and 39), and not merely of Sunday Mass. They are optional in a private Mass where there is no congregation (*GI*, no. 220); yet even then they may be said, "with the priest indicating the intentions and the server responding" (*ibid.*).

The content of the intercessions is the intentions of the Church; the intentions of rulers; the salvation of the world; the needs of those in difficulty; the local community. On special occasions such as a confirmation, a marriage, or a burial, the series of intentions can be adapted to the occasion (*GI*, no. 46).

As a priestly intervention by the people of God, the intercessions have a value in themselves and therefore are a self-sufficient part of the Mass. From the viewpoint of liturgical structure, however, they are the conclusion of the liturgy of the word, and consequently cannot simply pay no heed to the proclamation made in this section of the Mass. The petitions can and should take into account the section of which they are the conclusion; they should attend to the mystery being celebrated and should suggest petitions appropriate to it. On the other hand, the intercessions are not meant to be a kind of moralizing appendage to the homily or a repetition of the exhortation that is fittingly contained in the sermon. No, the intercessions are prayers, not proclamation or even a simple instruction in Christian living.

The special nature of the intercessions makes them a part of the liturgy that belongs to the people, and not a presidential prayer such as most of the prayers are that end a liturgical action or part of one (the prayer over the gifts at the end of the preparation of these; the concluding prayer after the sacrificial meal). There is no contradiction, however, in saying that the priest is the official leader of the prayer of the faithful. He too is a member of God's people; moreover, the shared character of the intercessions for the intentions of the Church and the world brings out in a very impressive way, more so than any other part of the service, the priesthood of the entire community, a priesthood that includes both the priesthood of the ordained and the general priesthood of all the baptized. Consequently, the prescriptions given in the General Instruction, no. 47, are more than a kind of stage directions:

> The role of the priest is to lead the prayer by briefly exhorting the faithful to pray and by concluding the intercessions with an oration. It is appropriate that a deacon or cantor or other person enunciate the intentions. The whole congregation then voices its own prayer either by an invocation repeated after each intention or by a silent prayer.

The intercessions are a revival of ancient Rome tradition inasmuch as they are once again being said at the end of the liturgy of the word. The ancient form, however, has not been restored. In antiquity the intercessions were in the form of the "solemn prayers" of Good Friday: the celebrant invited the congregation to prayer and stated the intention; the people then prayed in silence (on their knees during the penitential seasons); finally, the celebrant said a "collect" or "summarizing prayer." In the reformed liturgy, a simpler, litanic form is used: a deacon (or cantor or other person) states the intentions, and the people answer each with the same response (the response may vary from one Mass to another). The possibility of having a silent private prayer between intention and response should be carefully weighed; this would be a profitable expansion of the straight litanic form. It would combine the advantages of two types of prayer: the concise ectenie form of the Eastern Church and the more meditative "solemn prayer" of the Western Church.

3 THE LITURGY OF THE EUCHARIST

INTRODUCTION AND OVERVIEW

The liturgy of the Eucharist is the heart of the celebration of Mass. The other major part of the Mass, the liturgy of the word, came into existence only in early post-apostolic times to replace a regular meal; it contained elements of exhortation and prayer that were comparable to those found in the great model, that is, the meal instituted by Christ. However, Christ's command to repeat what he had done (Luke 22:19; 1 Cor. 11:24) referred in any direct way only to his actions with the bread and the cup. It is these that were to be repeated in his memory, and it is these that are the nucleus of the celebration of Mass.

As we saw in Part I, Christ's action was a thanksgiving (Greek, *eucharistia*; Hebrew, *berakah*) to God, and, in addition, a thanksgiving over the elements of a meal. In his interpretive words, Christ expressly declares these elements to be himself, his *body* and his *blood*; more than that, they are already his body that is *given* and his blood that is *poured out*, with the giving and the pouring out taking place later on in a real and non-symbolic form in the sacrifice of the cross. Such are the gifts Christ gives to his fellows at table for their nourishment. Thus, the memorial action which Christ orders the Church to repeat is the thanksgiving that turns the bread and wine into his body and blood by the power of the Spirit, as well as the reception of these gifts. In short, what Christ left us was a meal of a special kind, filled with meaning and reduced to essentials. Inasmuch as these gifts convey Christ as one sacrificed (his body given

155

and his blood poured out), the sacrifice of Christ is present in them unto salvation, that is, for our sake and the forgiveness of our sins.

Through, with, and in Christ the high priest the community enters by the power of the Spirit into Christ's sacrificial offering of his life to the Father: "Through him let us continually offer up a sacrifice of praise to God" (Heb. 13:15). The Eucharist is thus also the sacrifice of the Church — not a new sacrifice to be set alongside Christ's sacrifice on the cross, but a participation in Christ's sacrifice: "I appeal to you, therefore, brothers, by the mercies of God, to present your bodies as a living sacrifice, holy and acceptable to God" (Rom. 12:1). This cultic sacrifice of praise which Christ offers and to which the concrete community unites itself in each Mass is the summit and source of the Christian life of faith, hope, and love. It is the ideal center of all the human action by which the believer puts himself at God's disposal, lays hold of God's will, and serves the brothers with loving deeds. The Eucharist is thus open to the community and the world. In other words, Christians are to be clearly aware that liturgy is but one of the three self-actuations of the Church, and that it must be integrated with proclamation and service.

We may sum up all this by saying that the Eucharist is *essentially* both a meal and the sacrifice of Christ made present; that in *form* it is a prayer of thanksgiving over elements of food intended for eating; and that its *course* is an imitation of the model provided by Christ, who took bread and wine, gave thanks over them, and gave himself in them to those at table.

> At the Last Supper Christ instituted the sacrifice and paschal meal by means of which his sacrifice of the cross is made constantly present in the Church, whenever a priest, representing Christ the Lord, does what the Lord himself did and gave his disciples to do in his memory.
>
> For Christ took bread and the cup, gave thanks, broke and gave to his disciples, saying "Take, eat, drink; this is my body, this is the cup of my blood. Do this in memory of me." Therefore the Church has made the entire celebration of the Eucharistic liturgy to consist of the following parts which correspond to the words and actions of Christ.
>
> 1) At the preparation of the gifts, bread, wine, and water are brought to the altar; that is, the elements which Christ took in his hands;
>
> 2) In the Eucharistic prayer thanks are offered to God for the entire work of salvation, and the gifts offered become the body and blood of Christ;
>
> 3) The unity of the faithful is manifested by the breaking of the one bread, and in Communion the faithful receive the body and blood of the Lord just as the apostles did from the hand of Christ himself (*GI*, no. 48.)

A. The Preparation of the Gifts

1. SIGNIFICANCE OF THE PREPARATION OF THE GIFTS

In the ritual Jesus followed at the Supper, the taking of the gifts was still a very simple and unpretentious action. The food stood ready, since the disciples had made all preparations in advance (Matthew 26:19; Mark 14:16; Luke 22:13). At the Passover meal the memorial rite involved this much that was special: When the time for the symbolic explanation came, the head of the house took the bread and cup in his hands and raised them a little above the table as he spoke the words of praise and interpretation; he did this in order to direct the attention of the participants to what was being symbolized. Such an action was, of course, almost suggested by the very nature of what the master of the house was doing. The other items of food were simply left lying on the table as usual. The "taking" of the gifts, in the sense of raising them slightly above the table, was a specifically paschal ritual.

In the very early Christian community, the taking of the gifts by the celebrant must still have been a quite simple act. The preparation of the bread and wine, as well as the reception of them, was, however, the chief way in which the community of disciples contributed to the celebration. The meal was not only a sign of mutual brotherhood, but also a regular meal provided for the poor of the community. The frequent and generous giving away of what an individual often needed badly for his own sustenance must have been keenly felt as a "sacrifice"; in what he gave he gave himself, and the gift was in a sense the giver.

This, of course, is the basic religious experience that gives vitality and meaning to all the sacrifices of human history, namely, that in giving the necessities of life, the giver gives himself. Even once the feeding of the poor in the communal meal had been separated from the Eucharist, the collection of the "means of life" for the needy continued, and only a part was set aside for the cultic meal. It was natural, then, that at a very early time the preparation of the Eucharistic gifts should become a form of spiritual self-expression, an eloquent symbol of the incorporation of the gift of one's own life into the sacrifice of Christ, the one inherently effective sacrifice.

As communities grew larger, the giving of the gifts soon took the form of bringing them in a procession that was the symmetrical counterpart of the procession during which the transformed gifts were received back. To the extent that the community reflected on the actions by which it shared in the sacrifice, the preparation of the gifts underwent a ritual expansion.

Thus in Hippolytus (early third century) we already find the idea that he alone could bring gifts who was in communion with the Church and could therefore also receive the bread back when it had been changed.[1] Conversely, Cyprian criticizes those "who come without an offering but nonetheless [through Communion] take part of the sacrifice which the poor man has brought."[2] Statements of this kind are common in the Fathers.

A community in a procession is always glad to have singing as a help in lessening noise and distraction and in giving spiritual meaning to bodily action. Singing must have been introduced at a very early period; the singing of the psalms would have been appropriate, or the singing of a refrain in response to the singing of a schola or cantor.

Such processions with the gifts could easily lead to a misunderstanding of the Eucharistic sacrifice, at least in the popular mind. The man of the ancient world who embraced the faith was already familiar with "sacrificial processions" to the garlanded altars of the gods. What he carried with him or led after him in the form of animals for sacrifice was already the "sacrifice." It was and is important, therefore, in every age, to make fully clear the theological and spiritual meaning of an "offertory procession." This the revised rite for the preparation of gifts in the new Missal does. It also avoids the long customary name of "offertory" for this first part of the Eucharistic liturgy.

It is thus dangerous to say without qualification or to sing (in such songs at the preparation of the gifts as "We offer you these gifts, / the bread and flask of wine . . ."), that the Mass is "the offering of bread and wine." It is this only in the sense that the visible forms are those of bread and wine. These, in fact, signify and point to the true sacrifice they contain, namely, the body "given" and the blood "poured out." The Latin verb *offerre* basically means only "to bring, present, offer." (A misunderstanding on Luther's part led him to fear that the many Masses are new sacrifices alongside the once-for-all sacrifice of Christ and that they derogate from it as though Christ's sacrifice were insufficient.)

On the other hand, the preparation of the gifts is really the beginning of the Eucharistic sacrifice. When we say, in the prayers accompanying the preparation, that we present the bread and cup to God, we are erecting one pier of a bridge that connects the preparation with the formula of offering (the anamnesis) in the Eucharistic prayer. On both occasions, the Latin text has the same verb: *offerimus*, "we offer." We would fall short, then, were we to reduce the presentation at the preparation of the gifts to a simple "bringing in of the gifts"; theologically and spiritually this presentation is truly the beginning of the Church's Eucharistic sacrifice.

---

[1] *Traditio Apostolica*, 20, in Botte, *op. cit.*, p. 45. Cf. also the Council of Elvira, canon 28 (*PL* 84:305).

[2] *De opere et eleemosynis*, 15 (*PL* 4:636).

2. Altar and Eucharistic Gifts

At the beginning of the Eucharistic liturgy, the gifts that will become the body and blood of Christ are brought to the altar.

First of all, the altar, or table of the Lord, which is the center of the entire liturgy of the Eucharist, is prepared by setting on it the corporal, purificator, chalice, and Missal.

Next, the offerings are brought . . . (*GI*, no. 49).

The altar is "the center of the entire liturgy of the Eucharist," just as the lectern is the center of the liturgy of the word. In the architectural space of the sanctuary, lectern and altar are related as proclamation and sacrament are in the Mass. The shift of the center of attention in the celebration from lectern to altar makes it clear that something new is beginning.

The altar is the "Lord's table," a phrase that brings out in a striking way the nature and function of the altar. Articles 259–262 of the General Instruction go into greater detail on this point; we refer the reader to them. Article 259 especially has something to say that is to the point here: "The altar on which the sacrifice of the cross is made present under sacramental signs is also the table of the Lord in which the people of God are called together to participate during Mass; it is also the center of the thanksgiving service that is accomplished in the Eucharist." It is thus the special dignity of God's people that they "participate" in the table-altar; such participation is also the very content of their celebration.

"Participation" is a biblical term that was common in the Old Testament and then was taken over by St. Paul. He says in First Corinthians (10:16-22) that to participate in the altar is to share in the divinity; to participate in sacrifices to idols is to share in the idols; and to participate in the "cup of blessing" and the "one bread" is to share in the "body of Christ." This passage is perhaps the origin of the symbolic equation of altar and Christ; we spoke of in discussing the opening rites of the Mass.

The word "altar" expresses more the cultic aspect of the Eucharist and the presence of Christ's sacrifice, while the term "table of the Lord" expresses primarily the fact that Christ is present as food to nourish the faithful; it also points to the outward form of his presence. It would be misleading, therefore, in deciding on the form of the altar, to go back to pagan models. This is the case because the sacrament Christ instituted contains no ritual of sacrifice, but only a participation in the "bread" and the "cup of blessing." If we want to give symbolic visibility to the theological significance of the Mass as a sacrifice, the only means we have available is the cross that stands in the sanctuary. We cannot construct an altar of immolation, because the place where Christ gave his life in a physical death was not a pagan altar but the cross.

This is to say that the table is the only legitimate form the altar can take. In Christian antiquity the altar was for a long time movable and designed for utility. Later on, in order to assert its presence in the church, as it were, it became heavier and more massive in the vast basilicas and cathedrals. Under the influence of the law of orientation, which is not felt to be valid today, it was pushed back against the wall. Finally, it acquired extensive additions, and thus seemed smaller and less prominent, in the form of large retables, superstructures, and baroque altar-walls. Yet the name "altar table" continued to be used for the flat upper surface. Today there is a widespread return to simpler forms. The essential purpose of the altar is becoming more important and evident than the decorative additions, however well meant the latter were in their day.

Ideally, the altar should again be freestanding, so that it can be circled. "The altar is to be unattached to any wall, so that it can be easily circled and the celebration can be carried on facing the people. It is to be so positioned that it is truly the center to which the attention of the entire congregation will naturally be drawn" (*GI*, no. 262).

The Lord's table is covered with a cloth. "As a sign of reverence for the celebration of the Lord's memorial and of the banquet in which the body and blood of the Lord are given, at least one cloth is placed on the altar. The size, shape, and decoration of this cloth should be consonant with the structure of the altar" (*GI*, no. 268). Three cloths are no longer required, and especially not the bottommost one, the chrismal, which was oil-resistant and was meant especially for preventing oil left on the altar at its consecration from soaking through (oil was used in the consecration of altars since the Carolingian period). The number three first occurred in the Middle Ages and was inspired by allegorical considerations. A single cloth for a single table is common in contemporary experience; it is felt to be suitable, and allows the meal-character of the Mass to emerge more clearly.

Linen is not the only material now allowed, but there is no reason for changing the ancient practice. Linen cloths were long regarded as an allusion to Christ's sacrificial death and especially to his burial (cf. John 19:40). The shape of the cloth depends on the type of altar: it can reach to the floor when the altar rests only on legs; it can be attached to the corners of the altar when the altar is decorated (with an antependium or a relief, etc.). In any case, the ornamentation of the cloth should fit the character of the textile used and not make the cloth seem unnaturally stiff.

The preparation of the altar (according to *GI*, no. 49) supposes that it had previously been bare and not used as a storage place for all sorts of books and utensils (book of petitions, texts for introducing the pericopes, censer, incense boat, etc.). The custom of putting the cloth on the altar at this point is not simply to be rejected; after all, it was the custom in antiquity to remove the cloth after Mass, as is done on Good Friday. Such a preparation can be recommended occasionally for children's Masses and even in other circumstances.

On the altar cloth is to be laid a corporal, that is, a smaller (about 50 × 50 cm) linen cloth that can be folded; its name is derived from the fact that during and outside of Mass the body (*corpus*) of the Lord rests on it. The purificator, another and still smaller linen cloth, serves chiefly for cleansing (*purificare*, to purify) the chalice; it usually lies next to the corporal on the altar.

The Missal or sacramentary is now placed on the altar; the priest had previously been using it at his seat. The chalice is also placed on the altar if the priest himself is to mix the wine and water at the altar; in concelebrations and especially at a pontifical Mass, the mixing can be done at the credence. Nothing is now said of a special paten for the priest's large host; this is best put with the rest of the bread in the large dish which the celebrant takes, lifts up with a prayer, and sets down again.

In the Latin Rite, the bread for the Eucharist has been unleavened since the eighth century; that is, it is baked of flour and water without yeast. At the Last Supper, Christ probably took this kind of bread (*mazzah*), which was interpreted in the Passover memorial as a "bread of affliction," the bread of nomadic shepherds who had no homeland of their own. During the first millennium of Church history, however, it was the general custom in both East and West to use normal "daily bread," that is, leavened bread, for the Eucharist; the Eastern Churches still use it and usually have strict prohibitions against the use of unleavened bread (or "azymes"). The Latin Church, for its part, regards the question as of little importance, since at the Council of Florence, which sought to reunite East and West (1439), the difference in custom was simply acknowledged and accepted.[3]

Wheaten bread is now used by all the Rites; it is the "good" bread of the Mediterranean world. This universal practice by no means proves that Christ himself may not have used barley bread at the Supper (cf., e.g., John 6:9, 13). It is probably best to stay with the Latin custom and not make a theological issue out of the bread.

As for its shape, the bread brought to the altar in early times was beyond question a loaf: Christ broke the one bread; the rite of fraction, during which even in the West the Agnus Dei was sung from the seventh century on as an interpretive hymn, took a rather long time in the early Church. It is in the Carolingian period, at the earliest, that coin-sized, individually baked pieces of bread came into use for practical reasons. The symbolic power of the single loaf (1 Cor. 10:16-17) was doubtless lost

[3] Council of Florence, *Decree for the Greeks*, in *DS*, no. 1303.

sight of in the process. Today there is a return to the single large loaf or at least to several sizable loaves. Such a return is evidently legitimate, since the Agnus Dei "may be repeated as often as required to accompany the breaking of the bread" (*GI*, no. 56).

At the same time, however, this renewal of an ancient custom has undeniable practical disadvantages, to say nothing of the particles that are scattered about; these last are put into the chalice when it is being cleansed, but some of them are then ground into the purificator again. In a Mass for a small group, however, the symbolic value of the single loaf certainly outweighs the practical disadvantages. For decades now, it has been my practice at wedding Masses to give one and the same host, broken in halves, to the couple. As far back as the *Didache*, the one bread has been a symbol of the one Church: "Just as the bread broken was first scattered on the hills, then was gathered and became one, so let your Church be gathered from the ends of the earth into your kingdom" (9, 4).

The wine must be unadulterated "fruit of the vine" (Matthew 26:29; Mark 14:25; Luke 22:18). It was and is not always possible to assume that it is in fact unadulterated, and so the priest must see to it that it is pure. For the Jews of the Old Testament, wine was a sign not only of festive joy but also of the undisturbed possession of the land. To the medieval symbolists, wine was also a sign of the joy that is born of pain: only when crushed do the grapes yield grape juice and eventually wine.

In antiquity people usually drank their wine mixed with water; before and during the meal the two were poured into a bowl together, and the resultant mixture was drunk at table. Accounts of the liturgy since St. Justin's time show that this custom was carried over into the liturgy. We may well assume that it was also observed at the Last Supper. A symbolic interpretation readily suggested itself and has been current since the time of St. Cyprian of Carthage: "When wine is mixed with water in the chalice, the people are united to Christ. . . . If wine alone were to be offered, the blood of Christ would become present without us; if water alone were to be offered, the people would be there without Christ." [4]

This interpretation, or something close to it, has been taken into almost all the Liturgies (except the Monophysite, which emphasizes the divinity of Christ over his humanity), frequently with an added allusion to the blood and water that flowed from Christ's side when the soldier pierced it with his lance (John 19:34). The Council of Florence says that by Church law the priest mixes water with the wine being offered in the chalice, not only because Christ did the same but also because the blood which flowed from Christ's side was mixed with water (John 19:34); this mystery is renewed in the mingling of the two at Mass. Moreover, as the nations are called "waters" in the Apocalypse of St. John (17:1, 15), so here the

---

[4] *Epistula* 63: *Ad Caecilianum*, 13 (*PL* 4:395–96).

union of wine and water represents the union of the believing people with Christ the Head.[5]

These conciliar statements are not, of course, dogmatic truths of faith, but they do show the agreement of the Eastern and Western Churches on the symbolism. Luther, on the other hand, saw symbolized by the unmixed wine of his celebration of the Supper the redemption won by Christ alone without any contribution from man. It can be said that even in this contrary custom the same basic conception shows through.

The prayer now said at the mingling of the water and wine follows ancient liturgical tradition when it tells us that the union of wine and water symbolizes our participation in the divinity of Christ who assumed our human nature.

3. The Procession with the Gifts

The presentation of the gifts by the faithful is in no sense the "offering" (sacrifice) of the Mass, but it is indeed a symbolic expression of the fact that the people enter into the sacrifice of Christ. The form the procession takes has depended on the way the sacrificial character of the Mass has been conceived.

Justin Martyr (ca. 150) and Hippolytus of Rome (ca. 225) know of the procession. The procession is also attested at an early period in Africa, Milan, Spain, and elsewhere, where at the beginning of the preparation of the gifts a procession moved toward the altar, with the faithful carrying gifts of kind: bread and wine, oil, wax, flowers, etc. In the Antiochene Church, the custom seems to have been somewhat different: As they entered the church, the faithful deposited their gifts in a room near the entrance; deacons then chose a suitable amount of bread and wine and brought it to the altar. This custom probably became the preferred one in the Eastern Church and lived on in the Great Entrance of the Byzantine Liturgy, where it was accompanied by the solemn singing of the Cherubicon.

Rome, too, was familiar with a presentation made only by representatives of the people, inasmuch as deacons collected the gifts of the faithful and carried them forward.[6] But the custom of a procession of the people with their gifts is also well attested for Rome. In fact, Theodor Klauser thinks that the transepts of the Roman basilicas from the fourth century on owe their origin to this procession. As he sees it, the procession moved up through the nave to the altar. The faithful then laid their gifts on special oblation tables in the transept which was attached to the side of the

---

[5] Decree for the Armenians, in DS, no. 1320.

[6] See Ordo Romanus I (ca. 700), nos. 82–83, in Andrieu, op. cit., 2:93–94.

sanctuary precisely for this purpose; the people then returned to their places by the side aisles.

In the early Middle Ages, the procession with the gifts was generally dropped in the Western Church. The reason for this was that ordinary leavened bread was regarded as no longer suitable for the Eucharist. In addition, the number of communicants was becoming steadily smaller, so that both processions — the one with the gifts for the sacrifice and the one for receiving the consecrated gifts — gradually disappeared. The two disappearances were evidently connected: the ritual participation of the faithful in the Mass had become very limited and had even vanished entirely.

The procession with the gifts did not, however, disappear utterly, although with the shift from a barter economy to a money economy it changed into a giving of money. At Masses of consecration, an offering of candles is still common; at the consecration of a bishop, the newly consecrated bishop until recently brought a little flask of wine to the consecrating bishop. But apart from these occasions the custom has generally been to take up a collection of money in a basket, with the faithful remaining at their places.

The custom of a procession with the gifts has been restored in the new Missal. The General Instruction says:

> It is desirable that the faithful bring the bread and wine, which the priest or a deacon receives at a suitable spot and then places on the altar, to the accompaniment of prescribed prayers. Although the faithful of our day do not, as formerly, bring from their homes the bread and wine to be used in the liturgy, the rite of bringing these forward is nonetheless still expressive and retains its spiritual meaning (no. 49).

According to the rubric, "it is fitting that the faithful express their participation by an act of offering, bringing either the bread and wine for the Eucharistic celebration, or other gifts that meet the needs of the Church and the poor." The remark that follows in the German Missal is meaningful: "The money put into the collection is such a gift and is therefore to be deposited at a suitable place in the sanctuary. Care must be taken to finish the collection before the prayer over the gifts is said." Thus the custom followed in many places of placing the collection baskets near the altar is a reasonable one, since it brings out the connection between the Eucharist and care for the poor.

The collection, taken up by several people, is to be finished before the prayer over the gifts, partly to avoid disturbances during the Eucharistic prayer, but especially to keep the parts of the Mass clearly distinct. The prayer over the gifts ends the preparation for the sacrifice, and therefore all actions belonging to this period of preparation should be completed by that point.

The presentation and preparation of the gifts can be accompanied by an appropriate song or by organ playing, or can be done amid silence on the part of the congregation. Processional songs, usually psalms, are an ancient liturgical practice. We have already seen their purpose: negative, the avoidance of the restlessness that might otherwise be easily induced; and positive, the expression and interiorization of the action.

Article 50 of the General Instruction urges that the singing continue at least until the gifts have been placed on the altar. There is good reason for this. The singing is a structural part of the rite; it accompanies the presentation. In the days when the procession took some time, the singing was correspondingly extended. Usually a schola or cantor sang the song, and the people responded with an antiphon or other easily learned bit of song after every verse or every other verse. As the presentation of the gifts became a briefer rite, so did the singing become shorter, until in the Missal of Pius V nothing was left but the antiphon. This last must then have seemed rather pointless, and for this reason the General Instruction (no. 50) provides that if the antiphon is not sung it is omitted. It is also worth noting that the sacramentary contains, in smaller print, the verses for the introduction and the Communion but not for the preparation of the gifts. The verse is a meaningful accompaniment to a movement in the sanctuary, but it is not a necessary, constitutive part of the Mass.

The rubrics of the German Missal for the preparation of the gifts suggest for the accompanying song the corresponding texts in the *Ordo Cantus Missae* or the *Graduale Romanum* or the *Graduale Simplex*; they also suggest that songs be sung which are suited to the rite of preparing the gifts or to the general character of the day. Organ music or a "holy silence" are further possible alternatives.

4. THE PRAYERS AT THE PREPARATION OF THE GIFTS

In the first millennium, the preparation of the gifts at the altar was probably done in silence, since the procession with the gifts was an eloquent expression of the attitudes of the community and of the community's desire, through the mediation of the gifts which represented it, to enter into the sacrifice of Christ.

When the procession with the gifts was discontinued, understanding of the symbolism also waned, and ever since the Middle Ages prayers spoken quietly were used to give, to the priest at any rate, a spiritual interpretation of the action. Prayers of presentation were used for the purpose; they were very much like the prayers of the Canon, almost too much like them, so that people could with some reason speak of them as constituting a "Little Canon." The prayers included the *Suscipe, sancte Pater, . . .*

hanc immaculatam hostiam ("Receive, holy Father, . . . this spotless host") over the bread, the *Offerimus tibi, Domine, calicem salutaris* ("We offer you, Lord, the cup of salvation") over the chalice, the epicletic formula *Veni, sanctificator* ("Come, O Sanctifier"), and finally the *Suscipe, sancta Trinitas, hanc oblationem* ("Holy Trinity, receive this offering").

In this context, *offerre* and *oblatio* may be taken as meaning "to present" and "presentation," so that the expressions are still quite correct from a dogmatic viewpoint. Nor is the invocation of the Holy Spirit out of place at this point, since it is he who makes the people of God a holy people. On the other hand, the very same words carry a radically different meaning in the Canon, where *oblatio* is the true sacrifice of the Church.

To avoid possible misunderstanding, these prayers have been deliberately changed in the new Missal. Formulas of presentation have been replaced by prayers of praise modeled on Jewish prayers at table (the *berakot*, or "blessings"). The old interpretative meaning of the texts, however, has not been changed but fully preserved. Any claim to the contrary, such as traditionalists frequently make, is completely groundless, as a careful consideration of the prayers over the bread and wine will clearly show.

The prayers begin by praising God as the Creator of the world, who gives us these gifts. They are God's gift to us, but they are also the fruit of human toil and thus the possession of the human givers. The givers bring them as representatives of themselves before God (the Latin *offerre* has been deliberately kept!), so that by the transforming power of the Holy Spirit they may become the "bread of life" and the "cup of salvation," as they are called in the Second Eucharistic Prayer (prayer of offering, after the consecration). The prayers are new formulations of old teaching and are fully in the liturgical tradition of the Church.

We shall not discuss the possibility that the reformers of the liturgy might have omitted the prayers entirely, in response to the wishes of many. As things stand, the spiritual dimension of the preparation for the sacrifice is clearly shown and expressed. This is all to the profit of the prayer of offering in the Eucharistic prayer, because the latter can now be expressed with lapidary brevity and needs no paraphrastic lengthening or explanatory additions. The preparation of the gifts has not been conceived merely as a physical precondition for the sacrifice, but as a rite in which the faithful who wish to celebrate the sacrifice of Christ can prepare themselves spiritually and intensify their spirit of self-giving.

The mingling of the water and wine is accompanied by a prayer that explains the symbolism. The wine is a symbol of the divinity, and the water a symbol of humanity, while the mingling of the two symbolizes the incarnation of God in Christ and man's participation in the divinity of the

Redeemer. The prayer is only a remnant of an earlier prayer that is to be found in the oldest sacramentary (the "Leonine" or Verona Sacramentary), where it is a Christmas prayer according to which the birth of Christ is the necessary condition for a marvelous "exchange of lives."

Bread and wine, priest and people may now be incensed in silence. The incense that is consumed in the fire is itself an eloquent allegory of our self-giving to God and needs no accompanying words.

Two short prayers for purification emphasize the preparatory character of this part of the Mass. After the bread and wine have been prepared, the priest bows and says quietly: "Lord God, we ask you to receive us and be pleased with the sacrifice we offer you with humble and contrite hearts." Then, while he washes his hands, he says quietly: "Lord, wash away my iniquity; cleanse me from my sin" (cf. Ps. 51:4) (ICEL).

All these prayers for the preparation of the gifts are by their nature not official prayers of the priest, but private prayers that can therefore be said quietly. The rubrics tell us as much. If there is no singing or organ playing, the priest is allowed to say the prayers over the bread and wine in an audible voice; in this case, the community makes the prayers its own by means of an acclamation. When we reflect that the preceding liturgy of the word and the subsequent Eucharistic prayer are both done aloud, it can be recommended that the possibility offered of performing the preparatory rites in a "holy silence" be adopted, and that the two prayers over the bread and the wine not be said aloud. Silence is not a pause, but a structural element in the liturgy. It is necessary, of course, that the community be adequately instructed in sermons concerning the spirit and meaning of this part of the Mass; otherwise, they will be incapable of a "fruitful participation."

5. THE PRAYER OVER THE GIFTS

The prayer over the gifts marks the end of the preparation and of the first part of the liturgy of the Eucharist. This prayer sums up the content and meaning of the action (that is, the preparation of the gifts and the community), and acts as a transition to the Eucharistic prayer. In a theologically correct manner, it leads over to the Eucharistic prayer without any noticeable break.

The old name for the prayer was *secreta*, which was interpreted as meaning "silent (prayer)" (*oratio secreta*), because, although it was an official prayer of the priest who spoke it while in the posture of the orant, he spoke it in a low voice. This interpretation is evidently fairly recent, however, because the name occurs in the sacramentaries of the first millennium, but frequently in the fuller form of *oratio super (oblata) secre-*

ta — "prayer over the gifts that have been set apart," that is, over the portion of bread and wine that have been chosen for the Eucharist out of all the gifts brought by the faithful. Today this prayer is spoken as an official prayer and in a loud voice.

In the older Missal, the prayer over the gifts was preceded by an invitation by the celebrant to the clergy present, later to the entire congregation as well (*Orate, fratres*), that they would pray for him that his sacrifice might be acceptable to God. This invitation is the oldest of the additions made to the Roman *Ordo* in Frankish territory, and is attested first by Amalarius of Metz (d. 850). In its intention, this exchange (the invitation and response) fits in very well with the prayer over the gifts. Until the modern liturgical movement, the answer was given in a low voice by the servers or, if necessary, by the celebrant himself. Then, however, the answer was gladly taken up as an acclamatory prayer (one of the few available) and enjoyed great popularity.

As a presidential prayer of the celebrant, the prayer over the gifts shows the same structure as the prayer of the day and the prayer after Communion: invocation of God, praise of him, petition, and concluding formula. On the whole, however, the style of the prayer is less rigid than that of the other two. The content is usually a variation of one and the same idea, namely, the idea proper to the entire preparation: the gifts express the community's will to give itself, but this will needs to be stirred up anew so that the Eucharist may also be the Church's sacrifice in spirit and truth.

B. The Eucharistic Prayer

> "Now begins the Eucharistic prayer, which is the center and high point of the entire celebration. . . . In this prayer the whole congregation of the faithful unites with Christ in confessing the great deeds of God and offering sacrifice" (*GI*, no. 54).

As far as the history of the form is concerned, this part of the Mass, as we have already pointed out, goes back to the Jewish blessing at table, as expanded for the Passover meal. The type of prayer known as *berakah* ("blessing") occurs repeatedly in the Old Testament and is characteristic of the piety of the covenanted people. In it, God's manifestations of power or his gifts are recounted (see the psalms); he is praised as Lord, and he is asked, as the faithful God, to go on acting in the future as he has in the past. Such prayer links thanksgiving closely with confident petition.

The same spirit and approach are to be found in the songs of the Gospel: Mary's Magnificat (Luke 1:46-55), Zechariah's song of praise (Luke 1:67-79), and the song of the aged Simeon (Luke 2:29-32).

Christ himself followed this pattern of prayer when he instituted the Eucharist. He spoke the blessing over the gifts with which God had provided man, but in so doing he gave them new meaning and reality. Such a "thanking" (Hebrew *barak*; Greek *eucharistein* or *eulogein*; Latin *benedicere* or *gratias agere* — all these verbs mean the same thing) is thus not just any form of thanksgiving, but is precisely the "Eucharist" that Jesus and the apostolic community knew and used. In the Mass, this Eucharistic thanksgiving is now called the "Eucharistic prayer."

1. Scope and Name of the Eucharistic Prayer

The Eucharistic prayer, which in the Latin rite is interrupted by the Sanctus, extends from the dialogical introduction, through the preface, Sanctus, epiclesis, account of institution, prayer of offering, and intercessions, to the concluding praise of the Trinity and the Amen of the community. By this Amen the community makes the president's prayer its own and ratifies it. The Eucharistic prayer of Hippolytus, which we have already cited (Part I, Chapter 2, A 2), is a very early and impressive example of this unbroken flow of praise.

In the Latin Church, this part of the Mass was long known as the "Canon," but the term was frequently understood as not including the preface, which preceded the Sanctus. Such an exclusion was unjustified as the history of forms makes clear. "Canon" is a Greek word meaning the measuring rod which builders used; it consisted of a horizontal bar with a vertical plumb line hanging from it, and served to determine whether a wall was truly straight. As used in the Mass, "Canon" is short for *Canon actionis gratiarum*, that is, "Norm for the thanksgiving or Eucharist"; the words *actionis gratiarum* were an allusion to the "Let us *give thanks* to the Lord our God" in the dialogue before the preface, and *Canon actionis gratiarum* designated the traditional structure of the priest's Eucharistic prayer, a structure that was fixed at a relatively early date. The Latin Missal that was in use until recently still kept the old designation *Infra actionem* as a title for this prayer (*Infra actionem* is short for *Infra gratiarum actionem*).

The Greeks prefer the name "Anaphora" (a "lifting up" or "offering"), which was probably suggested by the *Sursum corda*, which in Greek is *anō tas kardias (anapherōmen)* — "let us *lift up* our hearts." In German, the Eucharistic prayer is called *Hochgebet*, or "High Prayer." Christ performed three actions in instituting the Eucharist: he took, gave thanks, and distributed. All three were to be the model for the later Eucharist, but the "giving thanks" was and is the heart and high point of the entire celebration.

2. THE ROMAN CANON

a) Origin

The Roman Canon, now known as the First Eucharistic Prayer, is over fifteen hundred years old. We may surmise that, at least in its essential lines, it had taken shape by the second half of the fourth century, possibly in the time of Pope Damasus I, a Spaniard who played an important part in giving the Roman liturgy its specifically Latin cast. It was also he who commissioned the official Latin translation of the Bible (the Vulgate, *ca.* 380) by Jerome. The reign of this Pope saw the end, at Rome, of the earlier Greek liturgy of which Hippolytus is our most important witness.

Unfortunately, we have no Roman witnesses for the Latin Canon in its earlier stages. St. Ambrose of Milan (339–397), however, has preserved the key passages of it in his *De sacramentis* (IV, 5, 21–6, 27). Evidently this Roman Eucharistic prayer was quickly taken as a model in other Latin-speaking areas. We do not find in Ambrose the various intercessions (with the lists of saints), but these are mentioned in various directives of Pope Innocent I (401–417), Boniface I (418–422), and Celestine I (422–432). The Canon must thus have acquired its present form soon after the year 400.

The foundations of the Latin liturgy were laid in the period of Pope Damasus. This new liturgy was not a word-for-word translation of the Greek liturgy earlier used at Rome; it was rather a new creation, dominated by the Roman spirit and style. This is especially clear from the orations or presidential prayers, which in this form had no prototype in the Greek liturgy. The same can be said of the Canon.

As compared with the anaphora of St. Hippolytus, the Roman Canon has two special characteristics. One is that the free and unbroken flow of language found in Hippolytus is interrupted by insertions of various kinds (cf. the next section on the "History of its form"). The other and more important is that the Canon develops in a symetrically stylized form around the central and unvarying words of institution and anamnesis (cf. section c, below).

b) History of its form

From the view point of the history of forms, this new Roman Eucharistic prayer derived originally from the anaphora of Hippolytus. In the latter, the praise takes the form of a series of relative clauses attached to "God," who is named at the beginning as the recipient of the thanksgiving; the prayer proceeds in an unbroken flow to the concluding doxology. The new Latin Canon was constructed quite differently, however, since it took more or less independent pieces of prose and strung them together, or, more accurately, arranged them like boxes within boxes, with the second half being a kind of mirror image of the first (see Chart 2 at the end of this book). The result was a highly artistic, even if somewhat artificial, creation. It allowed for almost no variation; if its clear structure were to be preserved, it had to be used as it stood. Time had filed and polished it, but only in order to make it a better embodiment of its structural principle. The Canon is as solidly built as a Roman arch; it is imposing, but also very rational and perhaps somewhat cold.

The Sanctus was the oldest of the insertions and the one most pregnant with consequences, not because of its origin but because of the extended form it gradually took. In the beginning, the Sanctus was simply a part of the praise of God's creation, and ultimately something inherited from the first part of the Jewish blessing after a meal (see above, Part I, Chapter 1, A 2). When the creation of the world, angels, and men was mentioned, the angels were thought of (in the Bible) as springing into action with praise of the thrice-holy God (cf. Is. 6:3). This citation from Scripture did not necessarily have to lead to the later division of the Eucharistic prayer into "preface" and "Canon," as we can see from the "Ambrosian Hymn," the Te Deum. In this hymn the threefold Sanctus is fully incorporated into the flow of the lines. Similarly, in the Old Gelasian Sacramentary and the Gothic Missal, preface and Canon are still undivided.

The Sanctus soon acquired, however, the character of an acclamation, because those listening knew the text and joined in the singing of it, possibly in a purely spontaneous way initially. Choral speaking is a risky undertaking. Singing is more beautiful, but it also takes longer, especially when meditative melismas are introduced. An impatient celebrant must have been easily prompted to continue the Eucharistic prayer in a low tone, raising his voice again when the singing stopped. At any rate, *Ordo Romanus I* (*ca.* 700) prescribes: "The bishop begins the Canon by himself,"[7] and the already Frankish *Ordo Romanus XV* says: "He continues in a low voice so that he can be heard only by those near the altar."[8] Thus, the longer the Sanctus lasted, the more parts of the Canon were read in a low voice.

Initially, this low-voiced reading had nothing to do with a "silence appropriate to the mysteries" or a "discipline of the secret" (*disciplina arcani*); the ancient mystery cults had long since been forgotten. In the France of the Merovingian period, moreover, the "stillness during the Canon" was not a problem, since the Germanic peoples could not understand Latin in any case. After a time, however, the stillness was strictly prescribed as the Canon came to be thought of only as an objec-

[7] *Ordo Romanus I*, no. 88, in Andrieu, *op. cit.*, 2:95.

[8] *Ordo Romanus XV*, no. 39, in Andrieu, *op. cit.*, 3:103.

tified "great mystery," and the words of consecration were regarded simply as the holiest of all possible words. In fact, because the words of consecration were effective, they were even viewed superstitiously and used for purposes of magic: "Hocus-pocus" is only a mispronounced form of "Hoc est corpus"! Pseudo-Germanus of Paris tells the story of children who heard the words of consecration in church and then mischievously repeated them outside — bears came and ate the children!

In the earliest editions of Anselm Schott's popular missal (1883ff.), the Canon, but not the words of consecration, was printed. In the hymnal used when I was young (the *Sursum Corda* of the Paderborn diocese), the following note was to be found on page 27: "Since these mysterious words [of consecration] have power and meaning only in the mouth of a duly ordained priest, they are omitted here out of reverence. Christian, prostrate yourself and adore your Savior present on the altar with faith, repentance, humility, and love."

As late as 1921, the Congregation of Rites completely failed to appreciate the structure and historical development of the Canon, and prescribed that the Benedictus, or second part of the Sanctus, was always to be sung only after the consecration. This meant that the Eucharistic prayer was now completely upstaged in every high Mass, just as it was already in polyphonic Masses.

A second group of insertions consisted of petitions for offering, blessing, and consecration. These, of course, are far lengthier than the Sanctus, but from the beginning they were integrated into the symmetrically constructed Canon. Therefore, unlike the increasingly luxuriant growth of the Sanctus, they always had their fixed place. In their entirety they represent a theological reflection on the Mass as the sacrifice of the Church.

Immediately after the Sanctus, the Canon begins with a prayer for acceptance, the *Te igitur*: "We humbly ask and beseech you, most merciful Father . . . to accept and bless these gifts, these offerings, this holy and spotless sacrifice." This opening prayer is matched in the second half of the Canon (which is like a mirror image of the first half) by the words of the concluding doxology: "Through whom you constantly create and sanctify, enliven and bless all these good things, and bestow them on us."

At the center of the Canon stands the consecration and anamnesis. Grouped around these are two petitions for acceptance and transformation; each of these petitions has two sections. Before the consecration there are the *Hanc igitur* and *Quam oblationem*; after the anamnesis come the *Supra quae* and *Supplices*. These various prayers together make up about half of the Canon.

The intercessions form two other large blocs of material: intercessions for the living (the Church, the pope, the local bishops, all the faithful, and certain of the faithful in particular) precede the first set of above-mentioned prayers for acceptance and transformation, while intercessions for the dead and for those present at the Eucharist follow upon the second set. To each group of intercessions was added a list of apostles and martyrs who were especially venerated at Rome and who were now being invoked as intercessors.

In the course of time the Canon was provided with ritual detail by the introduction of a number of signs of the cross (these too followed a symmetrical pattern). Three signs accompanied the opening prayer for acceptance (the *Te igitur*: *haec* ✝ *dona, haec* ✝ *munera, haec* ✝ *sancta sacrificia*), and three the closing doxology (*sancti* ✝ *ficas, vivi* ✝ *ficas, bene* ✝ *dicis*). Five accompanied the second preconsecration prayer for the transformation of the gifts (*bene* ✝ *dictam, adscrip* ✝ *tam, ra* ✝ *tam, ut nobis Cor* ✝ *pus et San* ✝ *guis fiat*), and five more the anamnesis after the consecration (*hostiam* ✝ *puram, hostiam* ✝ *sanctam, hostiam* ✝ *im-maculatam, Panem* ✝ *sanctum vitae aeternae et Calicem* ✝ *salutis perpetuae*). Five additional signs of the cross were made with the host over the chalice and between chalice and priest, just before the elevation during the final doxology.

These various signs of the cross were perhaps originally only a pointing with the right hand to the gifts on the altar; however, under the influence of the tendency to differentiate the sacramental signs into words and gestures ("form and matter"), they were changed into signs of blessing. It was a misunderstanding of the Latin word *benedicere* as "bless" that led to the signs of the cross being made over the bread and wine during the account of institution. The word *benedicere* here means, in fact, "to praise and thanks" (it represents the Greek *eucharistein* and Hebrew *barak*), and not "to bless" in the sense of making the sign of the cross over something.

Most of these signs of the cross have been eliminated in the new Missal. There is now but a single such sign, and it is made over the bread and wine together in the first prayer for acceptance at the very beginning of the Canon. The repeated *benedixit* in the account of institution has been correctly translated as "gave you praise and thanks"; thus the supposed basis for the two signs of the cross at this point was removed. In any event, Christ himself did not make any such signs at the Last Supper! From the High Middle Ages on, a further ritual parallelism was introduced into the account of institution by having a genuflection and elevation after each of the consecrations.

The artistic laws governing formal speech, especially juridical speech, in late antiquity showed their influence on the Canon in the use of two words (often synonyms) instead of one (*rogamus ac petimus; de tuis donis ac datis*; etc.), or three instead of one (*haec dona, haec munera,*

haec sancta sacrificia; hostiam puram, hostiam sanctam; hostiam im-
maculatam, etc.), or even five instead of one (*benedictam, adscriptam,*
ratam, rationabilem, acceptabilemque; creas, sanctificas, vivificas, bene-
dicis et praestas). Such a multiplication of words is also found in
Germanic and German juridical language, but it is not common elsewhere
and gives an impression of floridity. At the time when the Canon was
being composed, however, this style lent a special dignity and an aura of
the sacrosanct to what was being said.

c) Structure of the Canon

We have already mentioned the symmetry or mirror image character
that is shown in the structure of the Canon. This symmetry was perhaps
not so marked in the beginning, especially as far as the ritual elements
were concerned, since it presupposes the definite separation of preface
from Canon, and this separation occurred only at a somewhat later time.
It was only the Canon, and not the more independent and variable preface, that was subjected to this law of symmetry. Since the time of Gregory the Great, however (*ca.* 600), the text of the Canon, as we can see
from the various groups of sacramentaries, has changed only in very
minor ways.

For the following discussion the reader should have the text of the
Canon at hand; he should also refer to Chart II at the end of this book so
that he may more easily follow the analysis. Without the text and the chart
it will be difficult to understand the structure of the Canon.

The center of the Eucharistic prayer (A), and the axis on which the
whole symmetrical structure turns, is the bloc forming the "memorial,"
which in turn is built around the *memores offerimus* ("Mindful . . . we
offer"). In a memorial in which she repeats what the Lord did at the
Supper, a memorial which derives its content and meaning from the sacrifice of the cross and the resurrection, from "the prophecy which is the
cross, but a prophecy permeated by hope of the resurrection" (Heinz
Schürmann), the Church enters into the sacrifice of the Lord who is
present under the signs of bread and wine as "the body given" and "the
blood poured out" and who, in the reality-filled symbol of a meal, gives
himself to us as our food. This part of the Canon, then, contains both the
imitative memorial action (*memoria*) and the Church's participation in the
sacrifice of Christ thus made present (*offerimus*). The two aspects are
very intimately connected.

Around this center interpretive prayers are arranged like an elaborate
frame around a valuable picture. The frame is meant to draw our eye to
the essential thing, while also serving to bring out the preciousness of
what it contains (see Chart II, sections B, C, D).

The part closest to the center consists of the prayers of offering (B) which interpret the sacrifice. First (in B¹), the community, through the prayers of the celebrant, offers itself to God (*Hanc igitur*: "Be pleased, Lord, to accept"); it asks for God's gracious acceptance of the gifts which at their preparation had become a symbol of God's people in their self-giving. The community knows its own sinfulness, but it prays for eschatological peace, freedom from sin, and final fulfillment. On Easter and Pentecost this prayer is paraphrased and expanded a bit.

In the immediately following prayer (*Quam oblationem*: "O God, fully bless this offering"), which is closely connected with the preceding, the community asks, in a kind of consecratory epiclesis, that God would indeed accept this sacrifice, for he alone can take the community, represented by its gifts, into the sacrifice of Christ. "Epiclesis" means a "calling down," especially of the Holy Spirit. The Spirit is not expressly named here as he is in the Liturgy of the Byzantine Rite; nonetheless, it is always the Spirit "who proceeds from the Father" that sanctifies us.

After the memorial of what the Lord did, the community again prays (B²) for the acceptance of the sacrifice (*Supra quae*: "Look with eyes of mercy"): May God accept the congregation in its gifts. In fidelity to the prayer tradition of the old covenant, the Church appeals to God's fidelity and manner of acting with the patriarchs, Abel, Abraham, and Melchizedek, when they offered him sacrifices which he found pleasing because they represented an unconditional self-dedication. Here, however, there is something more than in the old covenant: This sacrifice is the sacrifice, sure to be accepted, of the Christ whose "blood speaks more graciously than the blood of Abel" (Heb. 12:24).

This second prayer for acceptance, like the one before the consecration, is closely connected with a petition for God's effective action. The latter petition can be called a "communion epiclesis" such as we have in the new Eucharistic prayers, and had long ago in the anaphora of Hippolytus. Only if God accepts the sacrifice will it become fruitful for those who receive the body and blood of Christ: They will be "filled with every heavenly blessing and grace." Of itself an epiclesis or "calling down" supposes a movement from above, from God to the sacrifice on earth. Here, however, the representation is reversed: The angel establishes a unity with the heavenly liturgy, and this, as it were, ratifies the sacrifice as one acceptable to God.

It is possible that this "angel" is *Christos angelos*, that is, Christ who is the "messenger" of the Father in word and sacrament. If so, then the consecratory epiclesis (in the *Quam oblationem*) and the communion epiclesis (in the *Supra quae*) of the Roman Canon gave expression to the dialogical movement inherent in our redemption: from the Father through Christ to men, and from the faithful through Christ back to the Father. It is noteworthy, here again, that the Spirit is not named, as he is in the Greek Liturgies. We may, therefore, legitimately speak of a "Logos epiclesis" as distinct from a "Spirit epiclesis." In the last analysis, however, the meaning of both is the same.

Around this first inclusion (B^1 and B^2) stands another (C^1 and C^2). The intercessions tell us for whom the Mass is being offered insofar as it is a sacrifice of expiation. In both intercessions the naming of the various groups is followed by a list of saints especially venerated at Rome; these are invoked as intercessors who plead for men before God's throne. Here we have a fine expression of the unity that binds the pilgrim Church with the heavenly Church that has already reached the goal. In the first inclusion (B^1 and B^2), the sacrifice of Christ was interpreted (in the anamnesis) more as a sacrifice of praise to the Father. In the manifold intercessions (C^1 and C^2), the emphasis is on the sacrifice of expiation for the community.

First (C^1), the Church as hierarchically organized under pope and bishops is named. This petition is closely connected, through a relative clause, with the opening prayer of the Canon, namely, the *Te igitur*: "We humbly ask and beseech you, most merciful Father . . . to accept and bless these gifts. . . . which we offer you first of all for your holy Catholic Church." There immediately follows the mention of those whom the Church wishes especially to commend to God, either by reason of their office (in earlier times, other patriarchs were also named, as were the emperor and others) or because of special services they have provided to the community or to the sacrifice now being celebrated. In earlier times, the names of these various individuals were written on folding tablets, or "diptychs," and were read out during the Eucharistic prayer.

The naming and commendation of this group of persons is followed by the naming of the saints who are asked to intercede (*Communicantes*: "In communion with"). The community realizes that these saints belong to the entire people of God, and it celebrates their memory (*memoria*). On important feasts (Christmas, Epiphany, Easter, Ascension, and Pentecost), mention is also made here of the mystery being celebrated; it is this, even more than the saints, which guarantees that the Church's prayer will be heard. After the Mother of God (St. Joseph was added only recently by Pope John XXIII), the apostles are named first. Then come the early bishops of Rome: Linus, Cletus, Clement, Sixtus II, and Cornelius. Finally, other martyrs are named: Cyprian, bishop of Carthage (d. 258), who was venerated at Rome from a very early date; Lawrence the deacon (d. 251); and five laymen: Chrysogonus of Aquileia (d. 304); John and Paul (d. 362), who were officials at the court of Emperor Julian; and Cosmas and Damian, Persian doctors, known as the *Anargyroi* (those who healed without asking for payment), who died at Rome and were invoked by the Romans in all sorts of bodily and spiritual needs.

To this bloc of intercessions corresponds another (C^2) after the communion epiclesis. It follows on nicely from the preceding prayer (the *Supplices*), in which petition had been made for the grace and blessing of heaven. In this new set of intercessions, the deceased are named first (*Memento etiam*: "Lord, remember also"): those who should be remembered because of their services to the community or because of a special gift from their relatives, and all who sleep in Christ. This remembrance is followed by a commendation of the entire congregation present. The congregation is aware that it is a Church of sinners, but it knows too that it is the Church of the promise.

As after the intercessions prior to the consecration, so here after the second set of intercessions there follows a list of heavenly intercessors, all of them martyrs. John the Baptist heads the list. After him come seven men and seven women. The men are: Stephen, the deacon at Jerusalem (Acts 7:58); Matthias, who took Judas's place as an apostle (Acts 1:26); Barnabas, Paul's companion (Acts 4:36; 9:27; 11:22; etc.; 1 Cor. 9:6; Gal. 2:1, 9, 13); Ignatius of Antioch, a bishop martyred at Rome in 107; Pope Alexander (d. 119; honored at Santa Sabina on the Aventine); Marcellinus, a Roman priest (d. 304); and Peter, an exorcist, whose name is usually joined to that of Marcellinus. The women are: Felicity and Perpetua, martyred at Carthage in 202; Agatha (251?) and Lucy (304?), both from Sicily; and Agnes, Cecilia (177 or 203), and Anastasia, all Romans.

Two relatively short transitional formulas (D) connect the body of the Eucharistic prayer with the two great acts of praise at the beginning and the end of the Canon. The first (D^1) is a prayer for acceptance (*Te igitur*) after the preface; the second (D^2) is a final blessing of the gifts before the closing doxology. It was frequently the custom at this latter point to bless also the first fruits (beans, grapes, etc.) or special devotional gifts (for example, the "St. John's wine" that was to be blessed on December 27; small loaves of bread; etc.), which were then taken home as *eulogiae* (literally, "blessings").

The body of the Roman Canon contains no strict elements of praise, but it is framed within two very impressive prayers of praise (E): the preface (E^1) at the beginning, and the great Trinitarian doxology (E^2) at the end. A comparable doxology is already to be found in the anaphora of St. Hippolytus at the beginning of the third century.

The "Amen" of the congregation is an essential part of the Canon; it expresses the ratification of the people, who thus explicitly make the praise of God their own. In the earliest account we have of the Mass, in St. Justin's *First Apology*, there are two references to the "Amen":

"When the prayer of thanksgiving is ended, all the people present give their assent with an 'Amen' ('Amen' in Hebrew means 'So be it')'' (65, 3-4); "The president offers prayers of thanksgiving, according to his ability, and the people give their assent with an 'Amen'" (67, 5).

d) The preface

Of all the parts of the old Roman Eucharistic prayer, the preface (E[1]) most fully retains the character of the early Eucharist. In it the model given by Hippolytus lives on, as does, ultimately, the *berakah*, or "blessing," of the apostolic community and the kind of prayer used by Christ himself. The introduction, in the form of a dialogue, is followed by praise of God for his saving deeds past and present, and by the concluding angelic acclamation of the thrice-holy God. The preface thus has three parts: dialogue, praise, and Sanctus.

In its structure (rather than in its present wording) the dialogue is descended from Jewish models; the point was to gain the participants' attention and invite them to prayer. Such formulas were especially desirable when the time came for the blessing after meals; they served as a transition from eating to praying. The opening wish for God's blessing (in the Christian form of the dialogue), together with its answer, was modeled on Jewish good wishes of peace. The *Sursum corda*, or "Lift up your hearts," is an Old Testament phrase. We read there, for example: "Let us lift up our hearts and hands to God in heaven" (Lam. 3:41). Paul exhorts his readers: "Seek the things that are above. . . . Set your minds on things that are above" (Col. 3:1-2). Hippolytus of Rome, in the early third century, had already inserted this "Lift up your hearts" in the dialogue which opens his anaphora, and Cyprian, writing later on in Africa, comments: "For this reason, when the time comes for the preface before the [Eucharistic] prayer, the priest prepares the minds of the brethren by saying 'Lift up your hearts,' and the people reply 'We have lifted them up to the Lord.' They are thus admonished that their thoughts should be only of the Lord." [9]

The *Gratias agamus* ("Let us give thanks") was probably taken over from Judaism and is meant to tell the hearers that they are about to offer not just any kind of thanksgiving but the special praise contained in the *berakah* — *eucharistia* ("blessing"). This point is even clearer in the Greek *eucharistēsomen* of the Byzantine Liturgy of St. John Chrysostom. The response *Dignum et iustum est* ("It is right and fitting"), on the other hand, has a Hellenistic origin. In the civic assemblies of the Greek polis, *axios* ("worthy, right") was the acclamation of agreement.

The meaning and purpose of the dialogue that begins the preface is to

---

[9] *De oratione dominica*, 31 (*PL* 4:557).

make the congregation conscious of its communion with its president and official spokesman. In this sense, the *Dignum et iustum est* at the beginning of the preface and the *Amen* at the end of the Canon are closely connected, since both manifest the fraternal communion and ecclesial unity of all who are praying together.

The second part, the praise of God, flows out of the dialogue. In fact, it begins with the priest picking up the *Dignum et iustum est* of the congregation and using it to launch into his praise: Yes, God is always and everywhere worthy of praise! He is the "Lord"; to his people he is the "holy Father"; by his very being he is the "almighty, everlasting God." This opening address is found in all the prefaces. It is followed by a statement of the special reason for praise at this particular moment; this reason may be drawn from the mystery being celebrated or from God's saving acts generally. The language is usually concise and pregnant, Roman in its lapidary quality, and free of verbosity. The prefaces, like the orations, are among the most impressive prayer formulas of the Roman Church.

The naming of God's redemptive actions is followed, in the third part of the preface, by the conclusion of the praise. Here emphasis is laid on the unity of the earthly and the heavenly liturgy, and a transition is made to the song of the seraphim (cf. Is. 6:2-4), the threefold *Sanctus*. This hymnic part of the preface is very old, but perhaps not original. Hippolytus, for example, does not have the Sanctus in his anaphora. Clement of Rome, on the other hand, knows of the Sanctus (before 100), possibly as part of a Eucharistic prayer. The Sanctus has already been integrated into the Eucharistic prayer in Book VIII (12, 27) of the *Constitutiones Apostolorum* (end of the fourth century), as well as into the ancient Eastern Liturgies of Jerusalem (Liturgy of St. James), Constantinople (Liturgy of St. Basil), and Armenia.

The Sanctus resembles the Gloria in that it too begins with praise of God that is drawn from the Bible (in this instance, from Is. 6:3); then, however, it takes various liturgical acclamations and combines them into a hymn. The mention of "heaven" as joining earth in the song of praise is already an addition to the biblical text, although one that is readily suggested by the context in the Book of Isaiah, since it is the angels who cry the words "Holy, holy, holy!" This expansion was current in Judaism and is found in all the Liturgies. The praise of God's "glory," as in Isaiah 6:3, carries with it the idea of transcendence, since this "glory" (Hebrew *kabod*; Greek *doxa*) is a predicate reserved to God throughout the Old Testament. God alone possesses glory.

Hosanna is the Greek form of the Hebrew *hosian-na* and means originally "Rescue us! Help us!" (cf. Ps. 118:25: "Save us, we beseech thee, O Lord! O Lord, we beseech thee, give us success!"). In the synagogal liturgy, however, the petition had already been turned into praise of the Helper, as can be seen from the shouts of the people as Jesus entered Jerusalem: "Hosanna to the Son of David!" (Matthew 21:9). It is clear that our Sanctus has taken the sentence from Matthew, along with the words that follow it in the Gospel: "Blessed is he who comes in the name of the Lord!" In the context of the Eucharistic prayer, the "coming" evidently looks ahead to the awaited presence of the Lord in the Eucharistic gifts.

The second part of the Sanctus, which begins with the *Benedictus*, is acclamatory in nature. The very word *benedictus* (Hebrew *baruch*) shows that we have here an echo of Jewish prayer in which the praise offered by the president was always followed by this kind of agreement on the part of the people. (See, too, the new prayers accompanying the presentation of the gifts of bread and wine.) Similarly, in the Letter to the Romans, the mention of God's name impels Paul, a Jew, to follow synagogal custom and immediately add: "(May he) be blessed for ever. Amen" (9:5).

3) Defects of the Roman Canon; its reform

The Roman Canon is undoubtedly a very venerable liturgical prayer of the Church. It deserves esteem not only because of its age, but because of the witness it bears to Eucharistic doctrine. And yet a certain artificiality of structure made it difficult for the praying community to comprehend it fully, and this was probably so from the beginning.

A parallel will help bring home the point I am making. Even a professional archeologist, when examining a great symmetrically built complex of baths that have been excavated, finds it difficult to grasp every shift in the line of the walls unless he has first gotten the ground plan clear in his mind and keeps it there or in his hand. This is all the more the case when a number of later strata are imposed each upon the preceding, so that they further obscure the outline of an originally complicated structure. The cleverness of the architect is certainly admirable, but an untrained observer easily becomes confused; only with great difficulty will he get an overall view, no matter how ingenious the plan is. He feels much more at home with a building whose plan is easily grasped, for example an ordinary house; he always knows where he is and what the function of each part is.

The Canon in its final form before the recent reform resembled the complex of baths in the example given. For far too long it had become something wholly objectified. It was considered to be as immutable as the word of God, but as a matter of fact it had gotten disarranged through insertions and obscured by allegorizing additions. For the simple worshiper whom the liturgical movement was urging to become once again an active participant in the liturgy, the Canon contained too many obstacles for him to see in it an expression of the praise of God which he, at the end, could authentically call his own by his "Amen."

The defects of the Canon were many. The most striking was the absence of prayers of praise — in other words, its poverty of content. The preface did, of course, contain such praises, but on more than half the days of the year the Common Preface was used, and this consisted of a framework for praise, with a stereotyped opening and conclusion, but without any content. In the fullest sense of the term, it was an empty formula without any substance. Only on feast days was a "proper" preface used. Within the Canon, too, a special or "proper" insert was used on only a few feastdays, and the effect of this was more didactic than devotional. On most Sundays the Preface of the Trinity was used, but this was simply a slightly adapted bit of dogmatic theology, couched in a Christological vocabulary out of the past.

The intercessions took up far too much space in the Eucharistic prayer; they were regarded as essential precisely because a stipend had been paid for them. The lists of saints were utterly uninspiring. Did anyone call upon Linus, Cletus, Clement, Sixtus, Cornelius, or Cyprian as intercessors in his daily needs? Local saints, saints more fervently venerated in this or that place, and whose image was more familiar from history, art, and legend, had only "paraliturgical" significance, that is, they were venerated only outside the Mass. No wonder, then, that this veneration became heavily folkloric or even superstitious.

The epicletic elements were much too vague or even unspoken; certainly they did not emerge in the Canon as strongly as they did in the *Veni sanctificator* during the preparation of the gifts. This last-named prayer was very much open to misunderstanding in that context, while the Holy Spirit, the soul of God's people and Church, went practically unnamed in the Canon! A well-known churchman from an Eastern Rite said to me a while back that this odd state of affairs was a sign that "the Latin Church is notably allergic to the Holy Spirit." He spoke in sadness, not in malice, and who can say he was completely mistaken?

Also completely lacking was the eschatological dimension proper to the assembly of a community which awaits the Lord "until he comes again." Yet this dimension certainly is essential in St. Paul's account of the Lord's Supper (1 Cor. 11:26).

Even stylistically the Canon was so fragmented by the many insertions and the numerous "Amens" which chopped up the Eucharistic prayer into a series of separated prayers that the grammatical connections and relationships were often broken. The *Communicantes* is an example of this, as is the account of institution. Then there is the quite misleading *pro ecclesia tua quam . . . regere digneris toto orbe terrarum, una cum famulo tuo Papa nostro N. et antistite nostro N.*, as though in his governance of the world God were arranging things with the pope and each local bishop, even though the latter might have only a little Italian town for his domain. Everything was mixed up. The early Canon may have deserved praise for resembling a carefully made Roman arch in which every stone fitted neatly, but later the stones got moved about as though an earthquake had shaken the arch. The stones no longer fitted together. The many signs of the cross became insufferable, especially when the celebrant observed the rubrics without asking what he was really doing, and made the signs of the cross in such rapid succession that he seemed to be chopping at something with his hand!

The complaints are now quite unnecessary, because the reform has introduced many improvements. The prayers of praise have been increased by the many prefaces that are geared to the feast or the season of the liturgical year; the empty Common Preface has disappeared. The many new expansions of the text of the Canon (in translation) so as to adapt it to the concrete situation are a real help to the person praying it; they stimulate thought and suggest ways of celebrating the feast so that it fits the real situation. The intercessions have regained their proper proportion in the relation to the whole. The lists of the saints have been shortened and can readily be varied according to the need and spiritual profit of the participants. The two epicleses — the consecratory and communion invocations of the Holy Spirit — are now clearer in their meaning, in the vernacular translations. Generally speaking, it has been easier to alter the Canon in translation than in the original; with regard to the latter, there was a quite understandable desire, inspired by reverence, to change the wording as little as possible.

Expectation of the Lord's coming has been accentuated in the bloc forming the "memorial" (consecration and anamnesis), that is, at the very heart of the sacrifice, by the new acclamations of the congregation. The use of these acclamations has great advantages. The earlier, superfluous *Mysterium fidei* has been removed from the words of consecration and turned into an exclamation that brings a response from the people. The response in turn expresses an essential aspect of the Eucharist. The acclamations are also a good substitute for the "Amens" that have been eliminated; the latter never really signified an authentic ratification by the people but simply broke up the priest's prayer in an unsatisfactory way. No one will look back nostalgically to the old ritual garnishings: for example, the twenty-one signs of the cross, instead of the single meaningful one that has been retained; the kissings of the altar, and so on. And if any one does, he will not find the liturgy sympathizing with him! The reform has not brought any real loss or curtailment, either in doctrine or in the range of celebrations now possible or in the spiritual dimension of the authentic participation. On the contrary, the reform has meant that the ancient and venerable Canon now has a chance of surviving.

3. THE NEW EUCHARISTIC PRAYERS

Only a few months after the publication of Vatican II's Constitution on the Sacred Liturgy in April 1964, a liturgical commission was established at Rome for the execution of the conciliar decisions. This commission in turn appointed a special committee to study the Eucharistic prayer. Its task was one of the most sensitive the liturgical reform had to face, for many bishops and liturgiologists were convinced that such a liturgical monument as the Canon must be regarded as incapable of further development and therefore beyond the reach of reform, except perhaps for some very minor alterations.

The majority of bishops preferred that new Eucharistic prayers be introduced which would have equal standing with the Roman Canon. Those commissioned to produce these new prayers were told, however, that any new Eucharistic prayer must "be attuned to the genius of the Roman liturgy" and "be consistent with the traditional liturgy of the Mass." "Genius of the Roman liturgy" meant, in terms of form, the old style: concise and not verbose; neither hymnic chant nor dogmatic treatise. In terms of structure, it meant keeping, and greatly increasing, the variety of prefaces. The anaphoras of the Eastern Churches tended to list as many as possible of God's saving deeds in a single Eucharistic prayer, but from the beginning the custom in the West had been to suit the praise of God in the preface to the feast or liturgical season as far as possible, while the Eucharistic prayer proper lay greater emphasis on the sacrificial action (prayers presenting the sacrifice of the Church; the epicletic elements; the intercessions).

In addition, the single epiclesis which came *after* the account of institution in the Eastern Liturgies was in the West broken up into its essential components: a prayer for transformation of the elements before the anamnesis (or memorial bloc, regarded as the point of the transformation) and a communion epiclesis that came after the consecration and functioned to some extent as a transition to the later reception of the Eucharist. These prescriptions given to the committee on the Eucharistic prayer did in fact reflect the Latin tradition and were thus well founded.

The committee went to work immediately and was able to present the results of its labor to the full liturgical commission in April 1967. The committee suggested, first, that the ancient, slightly emended Canon be henceforth known as the First Eucharistic Prayer. It proposed, second, that there be four more Eucharistic prayers. The first would be fairly short; it would be composed of materials from the anaphora of Hippolytus, but these materials would be shifted around so that a (variable) preface would, according to the Latin custom, name the saving deeds of God and end with a Sanctus, while the Eucharistic prayer proper would correspond more to the material contents of the Roman Canon. A second, newly composed Eucharistic prayer would contain chiefly elements of the old Canon, but these would be arranged to give a more readily intelligible structure and a logical development. A third Eucharistic prayer would draw upon the prayer treasures of the Antiochene tradition, especially Book VIII of the *Constitutiones Apostolorum*; it would be less Roman in character, since the praise of God would not be limited to the preface but would resume after the Sanctus in the first part of the Canon. Such a Eucharistic prayer would by its nature have a single unvarying preface. A fourth Eucharistic prayer would be an anaphora adapted from the Alexandrian Liturgy of St. Basil.

In all these Eucharistic prayers the words of institution from the account of the Supper, though not the language framing these words, would be completely identical and also concordant with the words of consecration in the old Roman Canon. This would insure that the consecration was the same in all the Eucharistic prayers and would keep the celebrant from having to look in the Missal each time for a different form of consecration. The words over the bread, however, would now have the relative clause found in the Gospel of Luke: "which is given for you" (22:19). Surprisingly, the Roman Canon, despite its great emphasis on the sacrificial aspect of the Eucharist, had never incorporated this clause.

After lengthy discussion and no little opposition from various individuals, the Feast of the Ascension 1968 saw the publication of the Roman Canon, reformed in the way already described, together with three other Eucharistic prayers and eight prefaces (more prefaces would follow). The suggested fifth Eucharistic prayer, adapted from the Liturgy of St. Basil, was not accepted. The four Eucharistic prayers were later incorporated into the new Missal.

Amid all the differences, the three new Eucharistic prayers are at one in the sequence of their contents: dialogue and preface with Sanctus; a more or less lengthy praise that leads into the consecratory epiclesis; the sacrificial prayers (account of institution, acclamation of the people, prayer of offering); the communion epiclesis, which leads naturally into the various intercessions; and the traditional, immutable closing doxology, followed by the "Amen" of the community. Here is the structure in schematic form:

EUCHARISTIC PRAYERS II and III   EUCHARISTIC PRAYER IV
   Dialogue   Dialogue
   Preface   Praise I: God, creation,
                                                 angels
   Sanctus   Sanctus
   Transition   Praise II: Saving deeds
                                       of Old and New Testa-
                                     ments

           Consecratory epiclesis
           Anamnesis/Consecration:
              Account of institution/Double consecration
              Acclamation of people
              Anamnesis prayer of priest
           Communion epiclesis
           Intercessions: Church—Pope—Bishop—People of God
                             Deceased
                             The community itself
           Closing doxology and Amen of the community

a) The Second Eucharistic Prayer

As we have already said, much of the material for this prayer comes from the anaphora of Hippolytus. The sentences have, however, in part been reordered in accordance with the schema just given or else brought into closer accord with "the spirit of the Roman liturgy." Thus, Hippolytus's listing of God's saving deeds in creation and in the slightly condensed Christological history of salvation down to Jesus' death and resurrection now form the preface; the Sanctus has been added. After a transition that is almost too short (the new Missal therefore provides insertions for Sundays and solemnities), the first part of Hippolytus's epiclesis is brought forward as a consecratory epiclesis; it is followed by the account of institution, the acclamation of the people, and the prayer of offering, and then, as in the Roman Canon, by a petition, in a communion epiclesis, for a share in the body and blood of Christ. The intercessions (for Church and hierarchy; for recipients of a baptism, confirmation, or marriage that takes place within the Mass; for the dead and for all present) come in suitably at this point; only the Mother of God and the apostles are named as intercessors. The prayer ends with the great doxology and the Amen of the community. (It will be worth the reader's while to go back to the text of Hippolytus as translated in Part I, Chapter 2 A 2, and to compare it in structure with the new Second Eucharistic Prayer, as outlined in Chart III at the end of this book.)

It can be said that the new prayer makes good use of Hippolytus's model, but also that it is somewhat heavy-handed in the rearrangements it introduces. For example, in Hippolytus's prayer the Father, working in Christ, is on the scene throughout. The new preface retains this theology, but then it is dropped after the Sanctus. The formula of offering corresponds both to Hippolytus and to the Roman Canon, but after that the structure of the Roman Canon becomes almost the sole norm. On the other hand, this last choice is quite meaningful and logical, especially since it allows the entire Church and not just the immediate community to be brought into the intercessions. The Mass, after all, is not only a communion of the individual with Christ but a communion with the entire Church as well.

The preface of this Eucharistic prayer is variable. In itself the preface seems somewhat un-Roman, inasmuch as it does not give preference to the single mystery of the feast but reports the entire history of salvation from creation forward, although it does this very concisely and has eliminated some decorative passages of the original. Evidently the reformers were inclined not to have a preface that would much exceed a normal Roman preface in length.

The providential guidance of God in the Old Testament, which is extensively included in Eucharistic Prayer III and especially in Eucharistic Prayer IV, is lacking here as it is in the model. The preface thus becomes a "Short Formula of the Faith" of the New Testament community and is materially quite like the creed recited during the liturgy of the word. It would therefore make sense not to use this Eucharistic prayer, or at least the preface, in a Mass with a creed, so as to avoid unnecessary duplication within the overall structure.

b) The Third Eucharistic Prayer

This prayer follows for the most part the general lines of the traditional Roman Canon. Thus it contains no preface of its own for feria or feast, and many of its formulations are taken from its Roman model. Simplifying a great deal, we might say that in it the old Canon has been rearranged according to new structural laws and enriched with many formulas from other liturgical traditions.

Connection is neatly made with the preceding, variable preface and especially with the Sanctus by the opening words: *Vere sanctus* ("Holy indeed"). The saving deeds of God which had been named in the preface are briefly summarized. In the summary the Church is seen as the culminating fruit of God's saving will and as the offerer of the "pure offering . . . from the rising of the sun to its setting" which the prophet Malachi had foretold (1:11). The inserts provided for Sundays and feastdays are of the kind already used in the Roman Canon and are a further structural link with the great praise of the preface; they reinforce the unity of the entire Eucharistic prayer.

The epiclesis, too, is neatly worked in, for it flows directly from

Malachi's prophecy of the pure sacrifice and asks that the Spirit be sent on these gifts so that the Church may offer her memorial sacrifice. The text then moves on without a break into the account of institution and the anamnesis. The latter, recalling the death, resurrection, and ascension of Christ, as did the Roman Canon, picks up the eschatological aspect of the immediately preceding acclamation of the people. The communion epiclesis is a good example of theology at prayer. It tells us that the victim sacrificed, by which God wills us to be reconciled to him, is the gift of his Church; the fruit of this sacrifice of Christ is the gift of the Spirit and our unity in Christ; this unity is to find its eloquent expression in our sharing of the same bread. The community, too, is to enter into this offering: the Spirit first makes Christians into a gift pleasing to the Father.

Here again the epiclesis flows smoothly into the following intercessions, for the prayer for receiving the promised inheritance turns our gaze vertically to our fulfillment in heaven, and horizontally to the entire people of the redeemed, including "all your scattered children everywhere." In these lines God's universal salvific will (1 Tim. 2:4) and the priestly intercession of God's people for all mankind (1 Tim. 2:1) meet and merge. Next, those who have departed from this world are included in the intercessions. Finally, the horizon is broadened still further or, more accurately, is transcended entirely as we look forward to the heavenly liturgy of eternity when Christ comes and we share his glory. The old prayer of the Canon for the blessing of the gifts of nature is briefly summarized; it leads into, and motivates, the unvarying final doxology.

If we frequently meditate on this new Canon and use it for our prayer, we will see clearly how the rich treasure of prayer which the Roman Church has inherited has been taken up, broadened, and so shaped that it combines the dynamic flow of the Greek anaphoras with the firm structure and close relationship of the parts to each other that are characteristic of the Roman tradition.

c) The Fourth Eucharistic Prayer

The Second Eucharistic Prayer took its components from the anaphora of Hippolytus, and the third chiefly from the Roman Canon. The fourth new prayer draws its substance from the Antiochene *Constitutiones Apostolorum*. This prayer might be called the most ecumenical, since it has a notably Eastern structure, especially inasmuch as the Sanctus does not really divide the preface from the Eucharistic prayer but is itself part of the praise, the latter being continued after the Sanctus.

In structure, this prayer too derives from the Jewish prayer after meals, and presupposes the prayer of Hippolytus. It begins with praise of God himself and of his creation of the visible world and the universe of the angels who sing "Holy." It moves on to praise God for creating man in his image — man who lost God's friendship through disobedience and fell under the power of death, but who was not abandoned by God but received a covenant from him and was taught by the prophets to look forward to salvation in Christ. Next comes a prayer of thanksgiving for God's saving action in the New Testament, an action that climaxes in the death and resurrection of Christ and the sending of the Spirit, and is prolonged and brought to completion in the Church, which is Christ continued in the world. The mention of the sending of the Spirit leads into the consecratory epiclesis and the usual sacrificial section made up of the account of institution, the acclamation of the people, and the anamnesis of the death of Christ, his descent among the fathers, his resurrection and ascension, and his second coming which we await.

This objective and real memorial also contains the presence of the sacrificed Lord and introduces the community into that sacrifice, in which it shares through the one bread and the one cup, so as to become one body in the Holy Spirit and one living sacrificial gift in Christ. The Spirit is the one who effects the communion of pope and bishops, priests and deacons, the givers of the gifts and the whole congregation, the entire people and all who seek God with a pure heart, those who have died in the peace of Christ and all the deceased, whose faith only God knows. These final lines have a new ring; they embody the optimism about salvation that has been familiar to us since Pope John XXIII. The recall of those who have reached the goal — Mary, the apostles, and all the saints — leads us further, to expectation of the final coming of God's kingdom and to the concluding doxology and the community's Amen.

This composition has many good points. Viewed in purely external terms, it is not unlike the Latin liturgy, since it has a preface, Sanctus, and Canon. However, the fact that the preface is not variable but is an integral part of an unbroken Eucharistic prayer is rather a Greek trait. Also a Greek characteristic is the fact that the Eucharistic prayer looks less to an individual festal mystery than to the entire saving action in which the Father is the one who disposes and acts. His action runs from the creation of the visible and invisible worlds through the providential guidance of our fathers in faith, the redemption wrought by Christ, and its continuation in the Church to the ultimate fulfillment of the world at Christ's return. The central proclamation made in the account of institution is thus fully integrated into the presentation of the entire work of salvation in Christ, as we see it in the liturgical tradition of the early Church. This Fourth Eucharistic Prayer thus becomes a real ecumenical bridge, since East and West meet in it and embrace.

C. The Communion

In the memorial representation of what Christ did at the Last Supper, the Communion corresponds to the last of the three actions of "taking, thanking, and distributing." "In the breaking of the one bread the unity of the faithful is manifested, and through Communion the faithful receive the body and blood of the Lord just as the apostles did from the hands of Christ himself" (*GI*, no. 48. 3). With regard to the carrying out of this action as part of the Mass, the General Instruction says: "Since the Eucharistic celebration is a paschal meal, the faithful shall, with suitable preparation, receive the body and blood of the Lord as spiritual food, in accordance with his commandment" (no. 56).

In the very earliest days, the distribution of the consecrated bread probably took place without ceremonial, as indeed it still did in the time of Justin Martyr. It is also likely, however, that the celebrant's prayer of praise and thanksgiving contained at an early date a petition for the fruitful reception of the gifts by the power of the Holy Spirit. This is what we find, in the form of a communion epiclesis, as early as Hippolytus. The breaking of the bread into as many pieces as there were communicants was already part of Christ's action; it was, of course, a functional necessity. We find Paul soon reflecting on the spiritual meaning of the action: "The bread which we break, is it not a participation in the body of Christ? Because there is *one* bread, we who are many are *one* body, because we all partake of the *one* bread" (1 Cor. 11:16-17).

The unity of the many and the mutual love within the community that are expressed in the breaking of the one bread which is made from many grains is formulated in the very oldest Eucharistic prayers we have, as, for example, in the *Didache*: "Just as the bread broken was first scattered on the hills, then was gathered and became one, so let your Church be gathered from the ends of the earth into your kingdom, for yours is glory and power through all ages" (9, 4).

In addition to the concern for unity, there was a concern for worthiness. "Let a man examine himself, and so eat of the bread and drink of the cup" (1 Cor. 11:28). The *Didache* warns, in keeping with Matthew 7:6, "Do not give what is holy to dogs" (9, 5). Prayer for right dispositions occurs frequently in the Mass, from the communion epiclesis in the Eucharistic prayer on through the final petitions of the Our Father with its embolism, the Agnus Dei, and the low-voiced prayer of preparation, to the acclamation, "Lord, I am not worthy."

In the course of time, expressive ceremonial and preparatory prayers were added to the originally very simple action of breaking and distributing the Eucharistic bread. We now have

1. the Our Father as a prayer before a meal;

2. the prayer for peace and the sign of peace;

3. texts interpreting the breaking of the bread;

4. the song for creating the proper mood during the Communion procession, and the interpretive formulas accompanying the giving of communion;

5. the concluding prayer.

1. THE LORD'S PRAYER

The Lord's Prayer (Matthew 6:9-13; cf. Luke 11:2-4) begins the third part of the Eucharistic liturgy in the Latin Rite. It functions as a prayer before meals for the communicants, especially because of the fourth petition: "Give us this day our daily bread." As early as Cyprian and Augustine, this petition was given a Eucharistic interpretation. The fifth petition: "And forgive us our trespasses as we forgive those who trespass against us" sounds the note of unity and peace and at the same time introduces the note of concern for worthiness in receiving the Eucharist, which is explicit in the sixth and seventh petitions for freedom from temptation and evil. An embolism, or "insertion," paraphrases these final petitions, gives them an eschatological reference, and leads into a doxological acclamation which turns attention back to the beginning of the Lord's Prayer and the expectation of the full breakthrough of God's reign. In its petitions for bread, unity, and worthiness of the communicants, the Lord's Prayer already voices all the chief concerns of the communion celebration.

The Our Father has certainly been part of the Mass since the late fourth century. Jerome,[10] Ambrose,[11] and Augustine[12] attest it for the West, Cyril of Jerusalem for the East.[13] In the Eastern Liturgies, the prayer is usually said after the breaking of the bread and immediately before Communion; the Latins have been saying it before the breaking of the bread, at least since the time of Gregory the Great, who regarded it even as part of the Eucharistic prayer.

The Our Father is the prayer of priest and people alike. From the Carolingian period on, and until quite recently, it was in fact said only by the priest, except for the concluding petition, even though the plural verb of the introduction, "we dare to say," could only refer to the entire community. The acclamatory "Amen" of the community that used to

---

[10] *Dialogus adversus Pelagianos*, III, 15 (*PL* 23:612–13).

[11] *De sacramentis*, VI, 5, 24 (*SC* 25bis:150–52).

[12] *Epistula* 149, 16 (*PL* 33:636).

[13] *Catecheses mystagogicae*, V, 11–18 (*SC* 126:160–68).

follow the prayer when the latter was said by the priest has been dropped now that the community is once again exercising the role proper to it.

In the Mass the Lord's Prayer has an introduction and is followed by an embolism and a concluding acclamation. The invitation to prayer used to have but a single form.[14] Today there are several possible forms in which the usual "Let us pray" is thematically expanded. It should be noted, however, that "Let us pray" usually introduces a pause before the prayer itself, while here, in its expanded form, its aim is to assure a concerted entry into prayer; everyone together addresses God, for it is an address proper to the entire community.

In prayers that thus belong to the community, it is out of place for the celebrant to intone or say the opening words of the prayer ("Glory to God in the highest" or "I believe in God") and for the people only then to join in. The congregation should recite the entire prayer. The situation has been rectified for the creed, because the priest now invites the people to recite the creed, which all then begin together. The situation with the Gloria is still unsatisfactory.

The Lord's Prayer is once again a prayer of the congregation as it used to be in early times, and not a special prayer of the celebrant, even though the latter continues to adopt the posture of the orant, that is, with hands raised and extended. A festive singing of the prayer is, of course, more beautiful and meaningful than a simple recitation of it.

The embolism, or "insertion" (the *Libera*: "Deliver us"), is of later origin. Until recently the priest said it quietly; now he prays it aloud. It is not a prayer meant to be said by the people. It is now more concise than it used to be, since heterogeneous petitions introduced at various periods have been eliminated. In content it expands upon the final petition of the Lord's Prayer and sounds the idea of peace.

The new text of the *Libera* ends with the expectation of the eschatological coming of the Redeemer (cf. Titus 2:13). This provides a good transition to the people's acclamation: "For the kingdom, the power, and the glory are yours, now and for ever." This acclamation was part of the liturgy at a very early period, so early that it even crept into many manuscripts of St. Matthew's Gospel (after 6:13) as a gloss. It is also found in the *Didache* (9, 4) and in many Eastern Liturgies. Especially, however, did it become a mark of the "evangelical Our Father" in the Churches of the Reformation, although without the embolism. The force of the ecumenical gesture of adding the words "For the kingdom . . ." is somewhat lessened by the embolism; the embolism is also customary, however, in the Liturgies of St. James and St. Mark.

[14] Cf. Cyprian, *De oratione dominica*, 2 (*PL* 4:532).

2. THE GREETING OF PEACE

In the old Missal, the breaking of bread and the prayer for peace had in the course of time gotten intermingled and confused. The reform of the Missal has restored the proper order.

According to Justin, the people exchanged the kiss of peace at the beginning of the Mass of the faithful, that is, after the catechumens had been dismissed. He says that "when we finish praying [the general intercessions or prayer of the faithful], we greet one another with a kiss" (*Apologia I*, 65, 2). Hippolytus[15] and the *Constitutiones Apostolorum*[16] attest a similar practice, as do most of the Eastern Rites. This practice seems to have been followed at Rome and Milan in the early centuries, though not in North Africa; it was from the latter that Rome in the fourth century took over the practice of having the greeting of peace take place only before Communion. The greeting is a meaningful action at either of these two points in the Mass.

The practice of all the faithful receiving Communion at every Mass ceased only in late antiquity. When it did, the continued presence of non-communicants during the time of Communion was soon felt to be unsuitable, and the non-communicants departed before the Communion. To avoid a helter-skelter departure, a dismissal-blessing was given to them; this was even regarded as a kind of substitute for Communion. Augustine attests the existence of such a blessing.[17] Caesarius of Arles, in the early sixth century, requires that everyone remain in the church "until the Lord's Prayer is said and the blessing is given to the people."[18] Gregory of Tours expressly says that the Communion of the people begins only after this dismissal of non-communicants.[19] At Rome we find the announcement of the next station for the Eucharist being made before Communion; this certainly means that a large number of the faithful left at this point.[20]

Such a dismissal of the non-communicants and the resultant interference with the course of the celebration led in time to a good deal of confusion in this part of the Mass. Thus in the Missal of Pius V the breaking of the bread occurred during the praying of the embolism; the placing of a part of the host in the chalice to the accompaniment of three signs of the cross, which originally were probably part of the dismissal-blessing mentioned above, took place during the greeting of peace. Only

[15] *Traditio Apostolica*, 21, in Botte, *op. cit.*, p. 55.

[16] Book VIII, 1, 9.

[17] *Epistula* 149, 16 (*PL* 33:637).

[18] *Sermo* 73, 2 (*CCL* 103:307).

[19] *De miraculis sancti Martini*, II, 47 (*PL* 71:963).

[20] Cf. *Ordo Romanus I*, no. 108, in Andrieu, *op. cit.*, 2:102, and L. C. Mohlberg (ed.), *Liber sacramentorum Romanae Aeclesiae ordinis anni circuli (Sacramentarium Gelasianum)* (Rerum ecclesiasticarum documenta, Series maior, Fontes 4; Rome, 1968), no. 186.

then came the Agnus Dei, the real function of which was to accompany the breaking of the bread, while the kiss of peace (exchanged only by the clergy, and then only at a Mass with a deacon) took place after the first silent prayer of preparation and petition for peace. As a result of the recent reform, the wish for peace and the greeting of peace are placed together, as are the Agnus Dei and the breaking of the bread.

The ceremony of the greeting of peace now has three parts: the priest's prayer for peace; the priest's wish for peace in the community, together with the community's answer; and the gesture of peace between all who are participating in the Mass.

The introductory prayer for peace in the new Latin Missal is the first of the former three preparatory prayers before Communion; now, however, it is said in the plural number. In the early Middle Ages, this prayer came into the Mass from a collection of private prayers. It picked up the third petition ("Grant us peace") of the Agnus Dei and motivated the subsequent exchange of the kiss of peace by the clergy in the sanctuary. As a private prayer of the priest, it was in the singular, had no introductory "Let us pray," and was addressed not to the Father but to Christ. Now it has become an official prayer of the priest, although its style still militates against this. The rubric bids the priest offer this prayer with extended hands.

The wish for peace, with the congregation's answer, is a very old liturgical formula, and corresponds to that of the bishop at the beginning of Mass. The description of the peace in question as "the peace of the Lord" shows its Christological and ecclesial dimensions; it is a different and greater peace than any that the world can give (cf. John 14:27). The wish for peace comes originally from the secular sphere and is especially widespread in the Semitic world (Hebrew *shalom alechem*; Arabic *salaam aleikum*). The Pauline letters usually begin and end with such wishes for peace, peace being an element in eschatological salvation and a fruit of the communion proper to the Church. The gesture of extending the hands during the wish was originally a kind of collective embrace; as such, it differs from the similar gesture made during the invitation to prayer ("Let us pray") and from the orant posture which the celebrant adopts during his presidential prayers.

The rubric for the gesture or greeting of peace says: "All give one another a sign of peace and love, in accordance with the customs of their locality." The General Instruction tells us that the manner of giving the sign of peace is to be determined by the episcopal conferences, which will take into account the character and customs of their peoples (no. 56b). The embrace, the accolade of the Latin countries, or the kiss on the cheek are not widespread in our country, but the handshake has a similar function, since, while it can be a simple formality, it is also capable of expressing the warmth and closeness of friendship. This is something on which we should reflect, since gestures are more expressive than words alone.

3. THE BREAKING OF THE BREAD

"He [the priest] then takes the host, breaks it over the paten, and puts a piece of it in the chalice, saying in a low voice . . ." (Rubric).

a) The rite

The breaking of the bread was a necessity as long as one loaf was consecrated and then had to be broken into as many pieces as there were communicants. The introduction of small, coin-sized hosts should of itself have made the breaking of the bread unnecessary. According to the old Missal, only the priest's host was now broken; it was divided in two, and a small piece was then broken from one half and placed in the chalice at the "commingling." This last-named rite, however, had a different origin and meaning than the original breaking of the bread (cf. 3c, below).

The breaking of the one loaf was not only a functional necessity but had, in addition, a symbolic meaning that is already implicit in the accounts of institution: the one bread is Christ who by way of the broken bread gives us a share in his life. "The action of breaking which Christ performed at the Last Supper provided the name for the entire Eucharistic celebration in apostolic times. The rite is not only a practical one; it also signifies that we who are many become one body through communion in the one bread of life which is Christ (1 Cor. 10:17)" (*GI*, no. 56c).

It is not quite certain that the "breaking of bread" in apostolic times (Acts 2:42) is a reference to the Eucharist, as this article of the General Instruction claims. It could also refer to an ordinary meal, since in Jewish idiom it meant simply the blessing over bread before a meal and was therefore essentially different from Christ's dividing of the one piece of bread (Matthew 26:26; Mark 14:22; Luke 22:19; 1 Cor. 11:24). Christ's action is probably related to an aspect of the Passover ritual that is here being given a New Testament meaning. It was a Jewish conviction that if a person ate a bit of the Passover lamb no bigger than an olive, he shared in the entire Passover blessing. So here, the bread we break brings a participation in the body of Christ (1 Cor. 10:16), who is our slain Passover lamb (1 Cor. 5:7).

The ritual of bread-breaking is full of meaning and therefore should be highly regarded even today. The practical difficulties we mentioned earlier — scattering of particles; difficulties connected with the reception; etc. — should not cause us to minimize it. The General Instruction (no.

195) therefore assumes the regular use of large hosts that can be broken into several pieces, although the use of smaller hosts as well is not to be entirely excluded. We should keep no. 283 of the General Instruction in mind:

> The fact that the Eucharist is a sign requires that the material used in its celebration should have the appearance of real bread. The Eucharistic bread, therefore, although unleavened and in the traditional form, should be so made that at a Mass with a congregation the priest can really break it into several pieces and distribute these to at least some of the faithful. Small hosts are by no means excluded, however, when the number of communicants or other pastoral reasons urge their use. But the breaking of the bread — a designation for the Eucharistic celebration in apostolic times — will more clearly bring out the force and importance of the Eucharist as a sign of unity, since all the faithful share in the one bread, and as a sign of love, since the one bread is distributed to the brethren.

Especially in wedding Masses, Eucharistic celebrations in small groups, concelebrations, and so on, it is desirable that this breaking of the bread be done in such a way that its symbolism comes home to the participants. In addition, it is no longer prescribed that the priest alone consume the large host. He may therefore share it with the lectors and servers, for example. In any case, it is important and helpful that if all do not share in the one piece of bread, they at least receive hosts taken from a single ciborium or dish. The General Instruction is explicit on this point: "For the consecration of the hosts a single large dish may suitably be used on which the bread for the servers and the faithful as well as for the celebrant can be placed" (no. 293). The customary small paten that was formerly used for the priest's host is thus no longer required. The breaking of the hosts is now done over the dish, not over the chalice as formerly (cf. Rubric).

"It is very much to be desired that the faithful receive the Lord's body in hosts consecrated at that Mass" (*GI*, no. 56h). The distribution of hosts stored in the tabernacle should therefore be an exception. Unfortunately, the reverse is often true in practice. Sometimes this is due to thoughtlessness, but often it is due to practical considerations. And yet the community should not be deprived of the sign of the *one* bread from the *one* altar, in accordance with a wish that the Church has often repeated since Pope Pius XII's encyclical on the liturgy (*Mediator Dei*) of 1947. In addition, whenever the bread for the Mass is supplied by members of the community, *that* bread should be given back to the faithful as a consecrated gift.

It is difficult, of course, to know just how many communicants there will be. It would be tactless, as well as a cause of disturbance, to ask before the Mass how many will be receiving Communion. Many communities have adopted the practice of having communicants place a host in the dish before Mass. It will then, of course, often be necessary to put the leftover hosts into the tabernacle for distribution at a later Mass.

b) The commingling

"The celebrant places a piece of the host in the chalice [after the breaking of the bread]" (*GI*, no. 56d).

This ritual has a confused and complicated tradition behind it. The reasons for continuing it were in all probability chiefly ecumenical, although explanations will be required if today's faithful are to understand it. Surprisingly, the General Instruction offers no such explanations.

The custom probably originated in the Communions at home in the early period. The faithful took the sacred species home with them, or, in case of necessity, a deacon brought them.[21] Now, leavened bread keeps for a long time under certain conditions, but it also becomes hard very quickly. When the time came to eat it, it was therefore dipped and softened in wine or water. There was even a widespread belief that the wine was "consecrated" by this contact with the body of Christ. In the Masses of the Presanctified (that is, Masses in which there was no consecration but gifts consecrated at a previous Mass were consumed) that have been celebrated on the weekdays of Lent in the Eastern Church ever since the sixth century but in the Latin Church only on Good Friday, the practice of softening the consecrated bread by commingling was an obvious solution. The practice in the Eastern Church of distributing Communion by placing the bread in the consecrated chalice and then giving the dampened piece to the communicant on a small spoon probably goes back to similar customs and circumstances.

Especially in Syria, though elsewhere too, the custom of commingling was given a symbolic meaning: Just as the separate consecrations of the bread and wine represent a "fatal" separation of flesh and blood and thus symbolize Christ's death, so the mingling and reuniting of what had been separated symbolize Christ's resurrection and return to life. With the help of this symbolism, people were able to understand the Mass as "the memorial of death and resurrection" and to have an experience of it.

Two specifically Roman customs also exercised a great influence on the commingling. In order to bring out the historico-vertical uniqueness of the one sacrifice of Christ, a piece of the host from a previous Mass (the piece was called the *sancta*) was put into the chalice before the Communion of the next Mass. This custom was followed especially in the papal Mass, as *Ordo Romanus I* tells us.[22]

A further custom brought out the local-horizontal uniqueness of the one

---

[21] Cf. Justin, *Apologia I*, 65 and 67.   [22] *Ordo Romanus I*, no. 95, in Andrieu, *op. cit.*, 2:98.

sacrifice in the many Masses. The pope sent a small piece of his consecrated host (the piece was called the *fermentum* or "leaven") to the
priests in the titular churches of Rome, and they added it to the chalice at
their community Masses. The custom became a fine symbol of the unity of
the Roman presbytery, and each community was thereby able to experience its unity with the other churches of the diocese in a sensible way.

All the customs of which we have been speaking had different origins
and different histories, although the softening of the hardened bread is the
ultimate source of them all; customs that were one in their root had
different symbolic meanings. These varied historical backgrounds can
usefully be explained to the faithful so that the commingling will not seem
to be a meaningless insertion into the Mass.

In the new Missal, there is evidently an intention not to call any special
attention to the rite of commingling. This is a justifiable attitude, especially since not all rituals that have been introduced in the course of time
are necessarily to be kept when they are no longer meaningful. The community, after all, is not an assembly of historians. Strictly speaking, it
makes sense to keep the rite of commingling only when it is permitted to
follow the Byzantine custom and distribute Communion by giving each
communicant a piece of the host soaked in the precious blood on a spoon.
This is a custom that might be desirable in areas where Roman Rite
Christians live near or are intermingled with Eastern Rite Christians, but
that will hardly be the case among us. For us, therefore, the commingling
will continue to be rather meaningless, a simple relict of a historical development and symbolism that were important in their day but have now
disappeared, leaving a custom that has no purpose.

c) The singing of the Agnus Dei

The Agnus Dei is now a song to accompany the breaking of the bread.
The text is based on the words which John the Baptist spoke when he
pointed Jesus out to some of his disciples (John 1:29, 36), but the words
are read in the context of the Book of Revelation 5:6 and 13:8. The "Lamb
slain" is the one abiding expiatory sacrifice for mankind. This saving deed
gives rise to the cry for mercy and eschatological peace. In the old Missal
the acclamation was changed, in Mass for the dead, to "Give them (eternal) rest"; this change has now been eliminated.

In the Middle Ages it was often customary to sing the Agnus Dei *before*
the breaking of the bread (at Lyons; in the Dominican Rite and the Carthu-
sian Rite). The purpose may have been to emphasize the importance of
the Lamb for our salvation, while at the same time not contradicting the
statement in the Gospel of John (19:33) that when the soldiers saw that
Jesus was already dead, they did not break his legs, a fact which the

evangelist interprets as the fulfillment of Old Testament prophecies (Ezek. 12:46; Ps. 34:21).

The song is of Greco-Syrian origin and was introduced into the Latin Mass by Pope Sergius I (687–701), a Syrian born at Palermo. Many of our acclamatory and hymnic compositions (the Gloria, the Kyrie, etc.) are an inheritance from the Eastern Church in which there have been no language barriers to the participation of the people and the people have in fact always participated actively.

Since the twelfth century it has been customary to say or sing the Agnus Dei three times, and at the third to change the cry for mercy (which is comparable to the Kyrie) into a cry for peace. The new Missal permits but does not prescribe this custom. It is now possible (as in the Liturgy of St. James) to repeat the Agnus Dei as often as is required for the breaking of the bread (Rubric). "During the breaking of the bread and the commingling, a schola or a cantor sings the Agnus Dei or recites it in a loud voice, and the people respond. The invocation can be repeated as often as is necessary until the breaking of the bread is completed. The final invocation ends with the words 'Grant us peace'" (*GI*, no. 56e). The Agnus Dei is a prayer of the people; the priest should not intone it or even sing or recite it with the people.

It was long customary to strike the breast at the petitions of the Agnus Dei. Neither the General Instruction nor the Rubrics mention this practice, but it is not therefore to be unconditionally discouraged, since symbolic gestures long customary among the people can be very meaningful. Originally, this striking of the breast was probably only a gesture to emphasize the "us" of the petitions; it later became a sign of repentance.

4. THE RECEPTION OF THE EUCHARISTIC GIFTS

a) Preparation

"In order that he may receive the body and blood of Christ in a fruitful manner, the priest prepares himself by a prayer said in a low voice. The faithful likewise prepare themselves by silent prayer" (*GI*, no. 56f).

Of the three prayers of preparation that used to be said, only the second and third have been kept, and the priest chooses one of these. The former first prayer now introduces the greeting of peace between the clergy; the restoration of a clear order among the rites of preparation for Communion has thus removed that prayer from its old position.

As the style shows, these are private prayers: there is no invitation to pray; they are addressed to Christ; they are said with joined hands; and there is no acclamatory Amen at the end. They have been recited in this manner since the eleventh century, when they were introduced because of the Church's concern that her priests should receive Communion in a conscious and recollected way. The fact that they are private prayers is, of course, no criticism of their value and meaningfulness. The first of the two presently in use is attested as early as the ninth century in the Carolingian Sacramentary of Amiens; this was the only one of the three (now two) prayers that the Carthusians and Dominicans used.

The rubric tells the priest to say the prayer in a low voice. The community should likewise pray silently for a short space, and the celebrant may urge them to do so, if such urging seems helpful. A reflective silence, which during worship is not a period of idleness or emptiness but a "part of the celebration" (*GI*, no. 23), will certainly be felt as beneficial by the participants, especially when preceded by a special greeting of peace and the singing of the Agnus Dei.

b) Invitation

"The priest shows the faithful the Eucharistic bread they are to receive in Communion, and invites them to the banquet of Christ. Along with the faithful he makes an act of humility with the help of the words from the Gospel" (*GI*, no. 56g).

The ritual of showing the Eucharist is interpreted, first, by another repetition of John the Baptist's words as he pointed Jesus out (John 1:29). The the priest and community together recite the humble, confident words of the centurion at Capernaum: "Lord, I am not worthy . . ." (Matthew 8:8). The somewhat old-fashioned phrase "under my roof" has legitimately been kept (in the Latin text) because it has long been customary. The change of "my servant" to "my soul" (in the Latin text; "I" in the English text) adapts the words of Scripture to a different situation. It is good that this ancient formula has not been altered in the reformed liturgy. On the other hand, the single recitation of it, as opposed to the triple recitation of earlier years, suits our sensibilities, since we do not usually find that a stereotyped repetition of an identical formula intensifies our participation or response.

The fact that priest and people recite the formula together shows that all form a single community sharing one and the same meal. Formerly, the priest recited the formula three times, and then if the people were going to receive Communion, they too recited it three times; between the two recitations came the Confiteor and the formulas of absolution. This practice was the same as in the ritual for Communion of the sick and shows how far the reception of the Lord's body had become separated from the Mass and how reception during Mass was regarded as exceptional.

After the words "Behold the Lamb of God . . ." and before the words

"Lord, I am not worthy . . . ," the priest adds the verse: "Happy they who are called to the supper of the Lamb." The words are from the Book of Revelation (19:9) and remind us of the eschatological dimension of the Eucharist and the liturgy of heaven. They are perhaps not easily understood by everyone, but presuppose a congregation that is relatively familiar with the Scriptures.

c) Distribution of Communion

After the breaking of the bread and the invitation to the Lord's table, the meal is now ready for the community. Christ himself "is present . . . in the person of his minister" (CL, no. 7; Flannery, p. 4). He "gives the bread" and "extends the cup" (Matthew 26:26-27; Mark 14:22-23; Luke 22:19; 1 Cor. 11:24) through the celebrant of the liturgy, who is helped by deacon, servers, or ministers of the Eucharist when the congregation is large. If the congregation is not too large, both the symbolism and the distinction of liturgical roles make it preferable that the celebrant alone distribute Christ's body and blood to the participants.

In all Rites, the rule has been that the priest receives first, then the community. Since Christ is the real president of the celebration, the visible celebrant is the first to share in the meal. This precedence is due not so much to him as an individual but to his office. On the other hand, our contemporary sensibility may lead us to think that the officeholder should first serve the community and only then receive the Eucharist himself, especially since he can then consume the remaining hosts and the rest of the precious blood instead of having to "communicate again" after the Communion of the congregation. Perhaps we should consider such an adaptation to contemporary sensibilities. In smaller liturgical gatherings — at a home Mass, for example — it is certainly possible to imitate what is done at concelebrations (GI, nos. 197–199), where the celebrant gives the Eucharistic bread to all, or lets all take it, and then all consume it simultaneously.

The celebrant receives the Lord's body after saying quietly the prayer (substantially the same as in the old Missal): "May the body (blood) of Christ preserve me for everlasting life." The older, hebraizing "my soul" has here been changed to "me," and rightly so, for this formula, unlike the "Lord, I am not worthy . . . ," does not represent something familiar to and customary in the community.

Then the celebrant distributes the Lord's body to the community. He shows the host to each person by raising it a little above the dish, and says: "The body of Christ." The communicant answers "Amen" and receives the bread. A deacon, server, or minister of the Eucharist who may be distributing Communion follows the same procedure as the celebrant. The formula for distributing Communion to the faithful is now the old one that Ambrose knew back in the fourth century.[23] In the old Missal the formula was a wish of the priest for the recipient: "May the body of our Lord Jesus Christ preserve your soul for everlasting life. Amen." The new formula is much better, since the recipient is no longer a passive listener to another's wish for a fruitful reception; he now acts as a mature person and confesses his faith in the Lord's body.

Communion in the hand or on the tongue has now become a divisive question in many localities. It is certain that at the Last Supper the Jewish custom was followed: the bread over which the blessing was to be spoken lay on the table or on a cloth or mat, and was taken into the president's hand at the blessing and then broken. That is what Christ did: he took the bread, blessed it, broke it, and distributed it, placing it in the hand of each person at table. If he had acted otherwise, he would have departed from custom, and the evangelists would certainly have reported this departure as something possessing symbolic significance.

Later representations of the Last Supper — for example, in the Syrian Rabbulas codex of 586 or in medieval paintings — prove nothing, of course. Pictures of the reception of the bread in hands covered with a cloth simply show the rite of a given time. Originally they reflect a practice of the imperial court. When a person received something from the emperor, he received it in a veiled hand, just as when he gave an object to the emperor, he gave it with a veiled hand. Such a custom would be impracticable now.

The giving of Communion on the tongue began in the early Middle Ages and was motivated by fear lest crumbs stick to the hand, fall to the ground, and thus be dishonored (possibly this fear was first felt in connection with the Communion of the sick). Communion in the mouth was thus simply a cautionary measure inspired by reverence and was not regarded as inherent in the idea of taking food, except in the case of little children.

Nor may it be claimed that the tongue is a more suitable organ than the hand for receiving Communion. Paul says that each member of the body has its function in the service of the whole and that no member can claim precedence over the others (1 Cor. 12:12-27). James even issues a warning with regard to the tongue, because although "the tongue is a little member," it is also "a fire. . . . an unrighteous world among our members," and "no human being can tame the tongue — a restless evil, full of deadly poison" (3:5-8). But he is also aware that "with it we bless the Lord and Father" (3:9). The same is true of the hand: it can do unjust deeds and strike blows, but it can also toil, caress, and bless.

The objection that the priest's hand is anointed at ordination has va-

---

[23] *De sacramentis*, IV, 5, 25 (*SC* 25bis:116).

lidity only since the Carolingian period; previously his hands were not anointed any more than those of the other faithful. Therefore the only real argument is that Communion on the tongue assures reverence for this special food. The trouble is that set rituals do not guarantee reverence once they have become routine. Gestures expressing reverence have vitality only if they manifest an interior attitude of reverence. There can be a wide range of different gestures, but they must remain conscious and spontaneous. To receive the host in the left hand that is supported by the right, and then to convey it to the mouth with the right hand can be just as much — or just as little — an expression of reverence as reception on the tongue with the Communion plate being held under the chin (as anticipated in *GI*, no. 80c) to keep particles from falling to the ground.

The traditional way of receiving can be kept for the handicapped, the elderly, the bedridden, and so on. Otherwise the freedom of the individual and his responsible choice must be respected. To make the matter a divisive issue among communicants is a direct contradiction of the spirit of the Eucharist. Let each individual make it his business to assure his own interior reverence and reverence of outward action.

"The symbolism of holy Communion is more evident when it is received under both species, since in this form the sign of the Eucharistic banquet is more complete. There is a clearer expression of God's will that the new and eternal covenant be ratified in the blood of the Lord, and of the connection between the Eucharistic banquet and the eschatological banquet in the Father's kingdom" (*GI*, no. 240).

It was only in the high Middle Ages that the reception of the chalice by the faithful ceased to be customary in the Latin Church. It was practiced thenceforth only by deacons at the papal Mass and when members of the Latin Rite participated in the liturgy of the Eastern Church.[24] All the Eastern Churches practice Communion under both species, as do the Churches of the Reformation, although the latter start from different theological presuppositions.

The Constitution on the Sacred Liturgy (no. 55b) foresaw the reception of the chalice on special occasions, but the number of the occasions has now been extended (*GI*, no. 242). Even apart from the danger of spilling the chalice, there are numerous practical misgivings felt, especially by the faithful, and these are not inspired solely by considerations of hygiene. Yet people should not be too quickly deterred from receiving the chalice, for Article 240 of the General Instruction says, as we just saw, that the Eucharistic sign is more fully present in Communion under both species. The meal aspect of the Eucharist is more clearly expressed; the new covenant as sealed in the blood of Christ (Exod. 24:8; Mark 14:24; Mat-

---

[24] Cf. *Code of Canon Law*, canon 866.

thew 26:28; Luke 22:20; 1 Cor. 11:25; Heb. 9:20 and frequently) is more evident; and the link between the chalice and the banquet of the kingdom was emphasized by Christ himself (Matthew 26:29; Mark 14:25; Luke 22:18). Article 240 might also, and above all, have pointed out that Christ expressly willed us to drink of the chalice (John 6:54-56).

At the same time, however, as Article 241 insists, the promotion of the reception of the chalice should not lessen our Catholic belief that "even under a single species Christ is present whole and undivided, and the sacrament is truly received. As far as the fruit of the sacrament is concerned, therefore, those who receive under a single species are deprived of no grace necessary for salvation." Happily, the same Article also says: "At the same time, however, the faithful should be exhorted to participate more fervently in the sacred rite in which the sign of the Eucharistic banquet is more fully visible."

A merely mechanical introduction of Communion in the chalice or a casuistic treatment of its possibility and liceity or even an appearance of treating some individuals as privileged on certain occasions (cf. *GI*, no. 242), without a deeper grasp of the real-symbolic meaning of such reception, would certainly not assure a more fruitful participation by the faithful. The use of a large number of chalices would again strip Communion in the chalice of much of its symbolic power. As far as possible, therefore, there should be but a single "cup of blessing" (1 Cor. 10:16), just as there should be but a single loaf that is shared by all.

"The Lord's blood can be received by drinking directly from the chalice or through a tube or with a spoon or by intinction" (*GI*, no. 200). This instruction is spelled out in greater detail in Articles 244–257.

Reception directly from the chalice was the method used by Christ and the apostolic communities. Despite the problems it entails, it deserves precedence over the other methods, not only because it is named first in the passage just quoted but also because it is simply the normal way in which we today drink a liquid. It has been in use unchanged through the centuries among the Eastern Syrians and the Ethiopians.

Communion through a tube was long practiced in the papal Mass, but the reintroduction of the practice would not be feasible, since we are used to drinking directly from the cup or other container. Moreover, for the time being at least, there would be disagreeable associations with drinking liquid refreshment through a straw.

Distribution by placing a spoonful (with the bread) in the mouth of the recipient is customary especially in the Byzantine Rite. In its origin, as we saw earlier, this custom is connected with the practice of softening the hard leavened bread, especially, it seems, in connection with Communion at Masses of the Presanctified.

The final form, which makes Communion in the hand impossible, is the dipping of the host halfway into the precious blood. The pieces of bread in this case must not be too small. For this method, as with the use of a spoon, a special Communion plate might still be necessary.

Drinking from the chalice is usually accompanied by Communion in the hand. Drinking through a tube will doubtless be the least likely form to become customary. The other two forms are best suited to situations in which people still want to receive the host on their tongues.

d) The Communion song

> While the priest and the faithful are receiving the sacrament, a Communion song is sung. Its purpose is to express the spiritual union of the communicants in a union of song, to show the joy they have in their hearts, and to intensify the brotherly spirit in all as they come forward to receive the body of Christ. The song is to begin when the priest receives Communion, and to continue as long as seems suitable while the faithful are receiving the body of Christ. If there is to be a song after Communion, the Communion song should be ended in good time (*GI*, no. 56i).

This song was originally a processional song, accompanying the advance of the communicants to the altar and back to their places. It gives an interior dimension to the outward action, creates a spiritual union through shared song, and is a sign of festive joy.

As for its content, it may be a whole psalm with a versicle, a single Communion verse, or a popular hymn. The singers may include everyone, or the schola (or cantor) and congregation singing alternately, or the schola alone. In this matter, the feeling of the community for what is suitable can be followed. Not everyone coming to and returning from the altar may want to sing aloud; many will prefer to maintain a recollected silence. The carefully chosen new Communion antiphons should always be brought into the celebration at some point if they do not provide the text for the Communion song itself. They can be introduced in connection with the invitation to Communion, as substitutes for the words, ''Happy they who are called . . . ,'' or as a stimulus to quiet reflection and thanksgiving after Communion (see the next section).

e) The cleansing of the vessels

It should be a basic principle that when the Communion procession and Communion song are finished, there be a suitable period of quiet and silence. Such a period is undoubtedly at least as necessary here as it was at the penitential act, after the reading, after the homily, and so on. Unless there is a conscious effort to develop a piety that is focused on the reception of the Eucharistic Jesus, all the promotion of active participation in the Mass will be meaningless. Therefore, at this point in the Mass any unnecessary bustle in the sanctuary and any activity at the altar that can be postponed should be avoided as much as possible, since it only disturbs and distracts.

After the distribution of the bread (and wine), the priest returns to the altar and consumes the remaining hosts, especially if they are few, and the rest of the precious blood. If the hosts are numerous, he (or the deacon) places them in the tabernacle, whether this be in the sanctuary or in a chapel reserved for Eucharistic adoration (the latter location is preferable according to *GI*, no. 276).

The priest then carefully collects any particles left on the corporal or in the ciborium and puts them in the chalice. Reverence requires this, although reverence is not to be confused with anxiety or scrupulosity. Ever since Berengarius's watering down of the doctrine of the Eucharistic presence in the early Middle Ages, it has been the Church's practice to treat the sacred species with special care. This care is to be a sign of deep faith and profound reverence for the Christ who is still present in the particles of bread and drops of wine. On the other hand, the particles and drops must be such that we can still speak of them as bread and wine — they must not be microscopic! Even the most rigid interpretation of the doctrine of transubstantiation since the Middle Ages and the Council of Trent has maintained that Christ is present in the substance of the bread, while the accidents remain those of the bread. Consequently, to take an example, the prescription that the priest keep the thumb and forefinger of each hand pressed together from the consecration to the purification of the vessels has now been dropped.

We must be careful, of course not to eliminate reverence when we get rid of the "fear of the particles"! The General Instruction tells us: "If a fragment of the host sticks to his fingers, as can happen especially after the breaking of the bread or the distribution of Communion to the faithful, the priest should clean his fingers over the paten or, if necessary, wash them. He should likewise collect any particles lying outside the paten" (no. 237). "The priest or deacon should purify the sacred vessels after Communion or after Mass, at the credence if possible. The chalice is cleansed with wine and water or with water alone; the priest or deacon then drinks the liquid. The paten is usually wiped with the purificator" (no. 238). The cleansing of the vessels at the credence, or side table, is quite proper; we do not clean the dishes and silverware at the dinner table but elsewhere!

The General Instruction allows for another possibility: "The vessels to be cleansed, especially if there are several of them, can be left standing, suitably covered, on a corporal, either on the altar or on the credence, and cleansed after Mass when the congregation has been dismissed" (no. 120). Such a procedure would promote the quiet and silence generally, as well as the recollection of the priest himself, who otherwise would be kept needlessly busy. This recollection is also the aim of the prayer the priest says while purifying the vessels. This prayer has been retained from the old Missal and asks that the priest may receive with a pure heart the food he has taken into his body and that the temporal food may be for him a healing source of eternal life.

All in all, then, the ritual of cleansing the vessels should be as brief and inconspicuous as is consistent with reverence.

f) Meditation and hymn of thanksgiving

It used to be customary for the communicants, often few in number, to remain in the church after Mass for a private thanksgiving, while the bulk of the congregation exited in more or less haste and with little attention to the music being provided by the organ. Nowadays it is usual for everyone to leave the church right after the dismissal; in other words, the people take the dismissal literally and leave. Yet it would be a great loss if the good old practice of private prayer were to die out completely, especially now that many more people are receiving Communion. It is always a good thing for liturgical action and liturgical contemplation to be closely linked so that they interpenetrate and feed each other.

The new rubric at this point in the Mass represents, consequently, a real progress: "Then the priest can return to his seat. A suitable period of holy silence may be observed, or a psalm or hymn of praise may be sung." All those responsible for the liturgy should make it their business to turn this possibility into a salutary practice, since experience has shown its undoubted value. The length of the silence must vary, of course, according to the type of congregation and the situation, but it should be long enough in any case for the faithful to enter into real prayer.

There is a widespread desire for such a period of prayerful silence, as questionnaires have shown. One of the chief objections to the new liturgy is that all the activity and constant directives from priest or commentator make it impossible to pray. There is always something going on! The period immediately after Communion is undoubtedly the best time for giving prayer and adoration their due in the Mass. On the other hand, the time allowed should not be too long, lest those who really have important things to do (mothers with small children, for example) become restless and start whispering or coughing nervously. The feeling that the Mass was being arbitrarily lengthened would then defeat the aim of the silence.

A few words by the celebrant to stimulate prayer and meditation can doubtless be profitable; he might use the Communion antiphon of the day if it has not already been sung. But the atmosphere must be calm and relaxed; there must be no new urging to "do something." The period of meditation after Communion will also be a help to fostering private adoration outside of Mass.

The rubric and the General Instruction (no. 56j) suggest that a hymn of praise or thanksgiving may be sung. This can be in place of or in addition to the period of silence; the choice must take into account the individual case and situation. Silence is certainly more important than song, especially when there has already been a good deal of singing during the Mass. At this point, hymns may well be chosen whose subjective character would, in other circumstances, make them less suitable as replacements for a liturgical hymn or some part of the Ordinary of the Mass.

5. THE CONCLUDING PRAYER

"Standing at his seat or at the altar, the priest faces the congregation and says 'Let us pray'; he then recites the postcommunion prayer. The prayer may be preceded by a short interval of silence, unless a period of silence has been observed immediately after Communion. At the end of the prayer the congregation responds with the acclamation 'Amen'" (*GI*, no. 122).

The altar is generally a better and more meaningful place from which to read the concluding prayer. Orations are always the conclusion to an entire liturgical act or to some essential part of the service; but the place where the Eucharist has been celebrated is the altar. The Communion, too, is directly linked to the altar, even if it usually involves the priest moving some distance from it. It is fitting, therefore, that the Eucharistic action be concluded at the altar.

On the other hand, the prayer is also the conclusion of a period of silent prayer which the participants have observed at their various places. It is legitimate, therefore, for the celebrant to offer the concluding prayer at the place where he has been sitting, especially since in this case the silent adoration replaces the usual pause for prayer after the invitation "Let us pray."

The concluding prayer is an official prayer of the celebrant, and therefore follows the stylistic laws governing presidential prayers: invitation to prayer, orant posture, and acclamatory Amen. The point of the concluding prayer is given in the General Instruction: "In the prayer after Communion the priest asks that the mystery which has been celebrated may bear fruit" (no. 56k). The range of motifs for prayer is relatively narrow. Usually the prayer combines thanksgiving with a petition that the sacrament may be fruitful in daily works of love or that it may be a pledge of eternal life and bring us to our fulfillment.

4 THE CONCLUSION

The rite of dismissal has always been surprisingly short and concise. The reason why it was never properly developed may be that frequent Communion ceased rather early in the Church's history and the faithful left the church in large numbers before the Communion of the priest.

1. THE ANNOUNCEMENTS

The time after the concluding prayer and before the blessing and dismissal is psychologically the best for short announcements; it is certainly better than connecting them with the homily, where they can only be a distraction.

The announcements should be short and of concern to everyone. Extended communications should be inserted in the church bulletin or placed on a bulletin board in the vestibule of the church. Such longer announcements would include the list of Mass intentions for the week, banns of marriage, times and places for the meetings of parish organizations, etc. This is the kind of information people do not easily retain from hearing it. In the time for announcements before the dismissal, the priest might well mention baptisms and deaths so that the community may be stimulated to take part or condole, etc.

2. THE FINAL BLESSING

The blessing is introduced by a greeting, which corresponds to the one given at the beginning of the Mass. The custom is a self-evident one, since people greet one another when they arrive and when they depart, and thus manifest the ties of brotherhood that bind them. At the beginning of Mass, several forms of greeting were provided, but at the end the usual one is simply: "The Lord be with you — And with your spirit." There is no need here of paraphrasing it or adding personal wishes to it (wishes for the coming week, etc.). What the priest might well do, however, is to add special wishes for the community (for the elderly or those sick at home, for example) to the preceding announcements.

The priest's blessing within the Mass is a relatively recent addition, originating at the end of the Middle Ages. Previously, the priest used to bless individuals who requested it as he made his way to the sacristy; he often blessed them with the chalice or the paten or especially the corporal, which he applied to diseased or painful organs (to the eyes, to the cheek of someone with a toothache, etc.). This older kind of blessing during the departure from the sanctuary is now given only by bishops, though often in a very stylized form ("once to the left, once to the right").

The fact that the priest's blessing within the Mass was a relatively late addition explains why until 1967 the dismissal preceded the blessing. Of course, if the faithful had hastened to do what they were being bidden to do (in Latin, luckily), the priest would have found himself blessing their departing backs! The reversal of the order was long overdue.

The formula of blessing is deprecative: "May almighty God bless you, the Father, and the Son, and the Holy Spirit." As he pronounces the names of the Blessed Trinity, the priest makes a large sign of the cross with his right hand; the people bless themselves as he does so, and then say their acclamatory "Amen." "On certain days and occasions this formula of blessing may, in accordance with the rubrics, be preceded by another and more solemn formula or by a prayer over the people" (GI, no. 124). Such formulas of blessing are an ancient tradition, especially for the dismissal of the non-communicants before the greeting of peace. On the weekdays of Lent they took the form of a "prayer over the people" after the postcommunion prayer.

The new Missal contains a large number of tripartite blessings for feasts and festive seasons, but also for the rest of the liturgical year. These can be used not only at the end of Mass but also at liturgies of the word, at the end of an Hour of the Office, or to conclude the administration of a sacrament. The deacon (or the priest himself) signals the beginning of the blessing: "Bow your heads and pray for God's blessing." The priest then extends his hands over the people and says or sings the tripartite blessing, after which he also pronounces the usual final blessing. After each of the three parts of the solemn blessing the people answer "Amen." These expanded blessings are undoubtedly an important gain for the reformed Mass, since they specify and interpret the general formula of final blessing.

In addition to these tripartite blessings, the prayers of blessing said over the people have been reintroduced; they used to be a regular part of the liturgy on the weekdays of Lent. They can now be used throughout the liturgical year and constitute a rich treasury of prayer. The celebrant can select the prayer to fit the situation; he really should make a deliberate choice and not settle for just any of the prayers. These prayers will usually be recited, not sung, and will thus be less festive than the final blessing, for which the Missal provides musical notation. In saying the prayer over the people, the priest likewise extends his hands over the people instead of adopting the orant posture, as he used to for the prayers over the people in Lent. In style, however, these prayers are official prayers, and the people respond to them with an "Amen." At the end of the prayer the regular final blessing is given, and to this, too, the congregation answers "Amen."

3. THE DISMISSAL

"Immediately after the blessing the priest joins his hands and says 'Go, the Mass is ended,' and all respond 'Thanks be to God'" (*GI*, no. 124).

This formula of dismissal is now used in all Masses, since the earlier "Let us bless the Lord" in Masses without a Gloria, and the "May they rest in peace" in Masses for the dead have now been eliminated. Gone, too, is the old concluding prayer *Placeat tibi, sancta Trinitas* ("May you be pleased, O Holy Trinity") which was originally a private prayer that the priest said on his way from altar to sacristy. Only because in the course of time the priest gave his blessing at the end of Mass (after the dismissal) instead of on his way to the sacristy did the *Placeat* likewise become part of the Mass. The "Last Gospel" (John 1:1-14) is no longer read; this was never a form of proclamation, but was regarded as a prayer of blessing. These reforms are among the ones requested by the Fathers of Vatican II (cf. *CL*, no. 50).

The Latin Missal uses for the dismissal the traditional *Ite, missa est*, to which the response is *Deo gratias*. The word *missa*, from which the entire Eucharistic liturgy eventually took its name, is a late Latin form of *missio*, that is, "dismissal" (cf. *collecta* from *collectio, secreta* from *secretio*, etc.). The words "Go in peace," which are found in all three forms of dismissal provided in the English Missal, are scriptural (cf., e.g., Mark 5:34; etc.), and are similar to the words of dismissal in the Byzantine Liturgy: "Let us go in peace."

If another liturgical action, for example a procession, follows immediately upon the Mass, the concluding rite of blessing and dismissal will naturally be omitted.

4. THE KISSING OF THE ALTAR AND THE EXIT

"The priest kisses the altar as he did at the beginning of the Mass" (Rubric).

The reform of the liturgy has led to the end of the Mass being a mirror image of its beginning. At the beginning the priest silently greets Christ, who is symbolized by the altar, as the master of the house; he then addresses a wish for blessing to the community and begins the service. At the end he says farewell to the people with a blessing, dismisses them, and finally again greets Christ as symbolized by the altar. Such an ordering of beginning and end is quite natural for a gathering and even for a dialogue. A letter usually shows the same structure, since it has an address and a final greeting; in antiquity these parts of a letter were usually more cere- monious than with us. To these parts of a letter Paul expressly adds formulas of blessing that give a solemn framework to the entire composi- tion.

The kissing of the altar at the end of the celebration is an ancient liturgical tradition that is followed in most Rites. Its meaning had become obscured in the Latin Rite because from the late Middle Ages on the various blessings given by the priest as he left the sanctuary were changed into a concluding blessing for all and simply attached to the older conclu- sion of the Mass (consisting of "The Lord be with you," the postcommun- ion prayer, and the kissing of the altar). But once the blessing was given a second "The Lord be with you," the kissing of the altar came to be interpreted, not as a gesture of farewell to the altar, but as part of the *Dominus vobiscum* greeting! This could happen because it had long been the custom for the priest to kiss the altar before every *Dominus vobiscum* so that his wish for the people might come, as it were, from the altar, that is, from Christ himself.

The many kissings of the altar that were thus connected with the re- peated *Dominus vobiscum* have been eliminated in the reform, because such repetitions, as we all know from experience, lessen rather than in- tensify the force of the gesture. When, following the logic of the rites, the authorities put the blessing before the dismissal, the kiss given to the altar continued to be connected with the *Dominus vobiscum*. Now at last the proper order has been fully restored: farewell greeting to the congrega- tion, blessing, dismissal of the congregation, kissing of the altar by the priest (and by the deacon, if there is one), and the exit of the celebrant with his assistants.

The altar is kissed in silence, because the action is expressive enough in itself. The East Syrian Liturgy does have a prayer that brings out the spirit and meaning of the kiss: "Abide in peace, holy altar of God. I do not know whether I shall be allowed to approach you again. May the Lord grant me to see you again in the church of heaven!"

"The priest, together with the servers, makes the proper sign of reverence and leaves [the sanctuary]" (*GI*, no. 125). This sign of reverence is usually a deep bow, but a genuflection if the tabernacle is located on the altar.

The exit is simpler than the entrance, for at the latter the cross and the liturgical books were carried in the procession. On solemn occasions, however, there is no problem about making the exit correspond to the entrance. In many places it has become customary for the community, or part of it, to gather for a while in the parish hall or in some other place. Such a custom makes it even clearer that the Mass is the center of the community's life.

Chart I

	Sequence of actions in the Mass	Significance of the actions
Beginning of the Mass		The Lord is present among those who are gathered in his name (Matthew 18:20)
	Entrance and entrance song	Formation of the community and preparation for the celebration.
	Kissing of the altar	In kissing the altar the priest kisses Christ, the true Lord and Priest of the assembly, and by his greeting strengthens the spirit of love and peace in the community.
	Sign of cross, liturgical greeting, introduction to the celebration	The community knows it is a community of sinners and asks God's mercy.
	Penitential act, Kyrie	
	(Gloria)	As community of the redeemed it praises the Triune God.
	Prayer of the day	The community recalls the presence of the mystery of salvation proper to the day or feast.
Liturgy of the word		The Lord is present to his Church in his word
	First reading and responsorial psalm	The Lord comes in his word.
	(Second reading) verse/Alleluia	The community receives him with ready faith and reflects on the proclamation.
	Gospel	The proclaimer actuates the word in the concrete here and now.
	Homily	
	(Creed)	The community responds (in the profession of faith and)
	Intercessions	in priestly intercession for the salvation of the world.
		The Lord is sacramentally present to his Church in the form of bread and wine
	Preparation of the gifts	The gifts presented symbolize the community's will to give itself, for the gifts are both God's gift and fruit of man's labor.
	Procession with the gifts	
	Presentation of the gifts at the altar	
	Private prayer of priest; washing of hands	Self-giving requires humility and purity,
	Prayer over the gifts	so that the gifts may become the body and blood of Christ.

Liturgy of the Eucharist (real sacrificial memorial)	*Eucharistic Prayer* Dialogue with preface and Sanctus Consecretory epiclesis Account of institution Anamnesis and prayer of offering Communion epiclesis Intercessions Concluding doxology	God is to be praised as Creator of the world and Lord of salvation history. In the power of the Holy Spirit Christ's body given and blood poured out are present as a sacrifice in the bread and wine. Christ takes the sacrificing Church into his own once-for-all sacrifice, and intends to give himself to her in the sacred meal by the power of the Spirit. In this expiatory sacrifice the Church prays for the salvation of all men, for she knows she is linked to both the living and the dead, and she climaxes her thanksgiving with praise of the Triune God.
	Communion Our Father Prayer for peace Breaking of the bread Reception of Communion Concluding prayer	In this prayer at table the community asks for the Eucharistic bread and for freedom from sin; it renews its spirit of love and peace, breaks the one bread (1 Cor. 10:17) in order to participate in the body of Christ, nourishes itself with the flesh and blood of Christ, and asks that this Communion may bear fruit in daily life and in eternity.
Conclusion	The announcements The final blessing The dismissal	refer to the concrete life of the community. is the seal upon our fruitful participation in the celebration. sends the community forth once again to its service of the world in everyday life.

Chart II

Structure of the Roman Canon (Eucharistic Prayer I)

	Content and Function	Texts
E¹	Praise in dialogue: Preface and Sanctus	Dominus vobiscum to Sanctus
D¹	Transition and First Prayer for Acceptance	Te igitur
C¹	First Intercessions: for Church, Pope, Bishop for the Living First List of Saints	In primis Memento Domine famulorum Communicantes
B¹	First Formula of Offering First (Consecratory) Epiclesis	Hanc igitur Quam oblationem
A	Double Consecration: Bread Wine (Exclamation and Acclamation) Anamnesis	Qui pridie Simili modo (Mysterium fidei . . .) Unde et memores
B²	Second formula of offering Second (Communion) Epiclesis	Supra quae Supplices te rogamus
C²	Second Intercessions: for the Deceased for the Participants Second List of Saints	Memento etiam Nobis quoque peccatoribus et societatem donare digneris
D²	Concluding Blessing	Per quem haec omnia
E²	Praise of the final doxology	Per ipsum et cum ipso

Chart III

Structure of Eucharistic Prayers II–IV

I	II	III	IV
Dialogue	same in all Eucharistic Prayers		
Preface	Linked to the body of the Eucharistic Prayer but variable	Varying with feast or season	Linked and invariable
Sanctus	same in all Eucharistic Prayers		
Transition	"Lord, you are holy indeed"	"Father, you are holy indeed"	Continuation of praise of God's saving deeds
Consecratory epiclesis	"Let your Spirit come upon these gifts"	"We ask you to make them holy by the power of your Spirit"	"Father, may this Holy Spirit sanctify these offerings"
Introduction to of the account institution	"Before he was given up to death"	"On the night he was betrayed"	"When the time came for him to be glorified"
Account of institution	same in all Eucharistic Prayers: Take . . . eat . . . drink		
Acclamation	same choice in all the Eucharistic Prayers		
Anamnesis	"In memory of his death and resurrection"	"Father, calling to mind the death"	"Father, we now celebrate this memorial"

Communion epiclesis	"May all of us who share in the body and blood"	"Grant that we, who are nourished by his body and blood"	"By your Holy Spirit, gather all"
Intercessions	For Church, pope, bishops, dead, community	For Church, pope, bishops, people, entire world, dead	For pope, bishops, clergy, participants, entire people, all men, the deceased
Transition to doxology	"Through your Son, Jesus Christ"	"Through Christ our Lord, from whom all good things come"	"Through Christ our Lord, through whom you give us everything that is good"
Doxology		same in all Eucharistic Prayers	
Acclamation		same in all Eucharistic Prayers	

BIBLIOGRAPHY

The source and basis for any liturgical undertakings in the community must be the Constitution on the Sacred Liturgy of the Second Vatican Council and the General Instruction that accompanies the new Roman Missal. The Constitution is readily available in various English versions; in this book, the translation in *Vatican II: The Conciliar and Postconciliar Documents*, edited by A. Flannery, O.P., has been used. The Latin text with an English translation and with an introduction and good commentary by J. A. Jungmann is to be had in *Commentary on the Documents of Vatican II*, edited by H. Vorgrimler and translated by L. Adolphus, K. Smyth, and R. Strachan, 1 (New York, 1967), pp. 1–87. for a good commentary on the General Instruction, see *Commentary on the New Order of Mass*, giving the official text with an English translation by the Monks of Mount Angel Abbey, together with a commentary edited by J. Martin Patino (Collegeville, Minn.: The Liturgical Press, 1970).

For a more detailed knowledge of the Mass, the reader must turn to the unmatched standard work of J. A. Jungmann: *The Mass of the Roman Rite: Its Origins and Development (Missarum Solemnia)*, translated by F. A. Brunner (2 vols.; New York, 1951–55). The most recent German edition, the fifth, was published in 1962; the book is thus preconciliar, and a new edition of it is needed, but it is hardly likely that anyone will be willing to tackle it. Jungmann himself has given a description of the reforms in his *Messe im Gottesvolk: Ein nachkonziliarischer Durchblick durch Missarum Solemnia* (Freiburg–Basel–Vienna, 1970). This book has not been translated into English, but one of Jungmann's books that has thus far ap-

218

peared only in English covers pretty much the same ground: *The Mass: An Historical, Theological, and Pastoral Survey*, translated by J. Fernandes, edited by M. E. Evans (Collegeville, Minn.: The Liturgical Press, 1976).

Jungmann was undoubtedly one of the great experts on the Roman liturgy. Anything he wrote deserves study and will be of help, especially *Public Worship: A Survey*, translated by Clifford Howell (Collegeville, Minn.: The Liturgical Press, 1958), and *The Early Liturgy to the Time of Gregory the Great*, translated by F. A. Brunner (Notre Dame, Ind., 1959).

For a history of the Mass against a broader historico-cultural background, see T. Klauser, *A Short History of the Western Liturgy: An Account and Some Reflections*, translated by J. Halliburton (New York, 1969). This book is concise, well organized, and important especially for its rich bibliography, which is not simply a mechanical listing but represents a selection of high quality. See also Marion J. Hatchett, *Sanctifying Life, Time and Space: An Introduction to Liturgical Study* (New York, 1976).

A somewhat older book but one that contains a great deal of important information on the history of the liturgy is A. Baumstark's *Comparative Liturgy*, revised by B. Botte and translated by F. L. Cross (Westminster, Md., 1958). The first German edition was published in 1923. Botte's French version, from which the English was translated, dates from 1953 and represents an expansion and to some extent a new edition.

The period of liturgical decadence has been described, on the basis of an extensive knowledge of the sources, by A. Franz, *Die Messe im deutschen Mittelalter: Beiträge zur Geschichte der Liturgie und der religiösen Volkslebens* (Freiburg, 1902; reprinted, Darmstadt, 1963). The book contains important insights and is indispensable to the medievalist.

Among the manuals of liturgical studies, we may mention William J. O'Shea's *The Worship of the Church: A Companion to Liturgical Studies* (Westminster, Md., 1957), and John H. Miller's *Fundamentals of the Liturgy* (Notre Dame, Ind., 1960).

A multi-volume translation, under the editorship of A. Flannery and V. Ryan, has been undertaken of the major French work: A.-G. Martimort (ed.), *L'Eglise en prière: Introduction à la liturgie* (1st ed.: Tournai, 1961). Vol. 1 appears as *The Church at Prayer: Introduction to the Liturgy* (New York, 1968). Vol. 2, *The Eucharist* (New York, 1973) contains extensive sections on the Mass by N. M. Denis-Boulet (pp. 1–193).

For a study of the institution of the Eucharist, see J. Delorme (ed.), *The Eucharist in the New Testament* (Baltimore, Md., 1964).

The texts for a more detailed study of the Eucharistic prayers are available in A. Hänggi and I. Pahl (eds.), *Prex Eucharistica: Textus e liturgiis antiquioribus selecti* (Spicilegium Friburgense 12; Fribourg, 1968). The book is a practical and reliable collection of all the sources, Eastern and

Western, including the Jewish models. Convenient English translations of much of this is found in: *Prayers of the Eucharist: Early and Reformed*, texts translated and edited by R. C. D. Jasper and G. J. Cuming (London, 1975); B. Thompson, *Liturgies of the Western Church* (Cleveland, 1961); L. Bouyer, *Eucharist. Theology and Spirituality of the Eucharistic Prayer* (University of Notre Dame, 1968); T. Guzie, *Jesus and the Eucharist* (New York, 1974).

Texts concerned with the practical aspects of liturgical celebration include: J. D. Crichton, *Christian Celebration: The Mass* (London: Geoffrey Chapman, 1971); Robert W. Hovda, *Strong, Loving and Wise: Presiding in Liturgy* (Washington, D.C.: The Liturgical Conference, 1976); Melissa Kay (ed.), *It Is Your Mystery: A Guide to the Communion Rite* (Washington, D.C.: The Liturgical Conference, 1977); Virginia Sloyan (ed.), *Touchstones for Liturgical Ministers* (The Liturgical Conference and the Federation of Diocesan Liturgical Commissions, 1978).

Also to be recommended are the various specialized surveys and articles by reliable experts in encyclopedias and dictionaries such as *The Oxford Dictionary of the Christian Church* (now published in paperback), *Interpreter's Dictionary of the Bible, Sacramentum Mundi: An Encyclopedia of Theology*, and *A Dictionary of Liturgy and Worship* (ed. by J. G. Davies).

For questions regarding the main locale for the celebration of Mass, see *Environment and Art in Catholic Worship* (Washington, D.C.: Bishops' Committee on the Liturgy, National Conference of Catholic Bishops, 1978); Fédéric Debuyst, *Modern Architecture and Christian Celebration* (New York, 1978); and E. A. Sövik, *Architecture for Worship* (Minneapolis, 1973).

Among the available periodicals dealing with the liturgy, the following are recommended: *Worship* (Collegeville, Minn.: The Liturgical Press) and *Living Worship* (Washington, D.C.: The Liturgical Conference).

INDEX OF THE MORE IMPORTANT SUBJECTS
AND NAMES

Quietness, 76, 105

Reader, xxv, 33, 36, 105
Reading, 28, 30, 31, 32, 34, 36, 60, 76, 77, 87, 141, 142. *See also* Pericopes, list of
Real presence, 22, 84
Relative clauses, 46, 130
Relics, veneration of, 42, 73, 81, 92, 109–10
Rendering present, 18–19, 37, 40. *See also* Zikkaron
Representation in expiation, 8. *See also* Martyrdom, theology of; Sacrifice of expiation
Responsorial psalm, 141–42, 143
Responsorial singing, 107
Return of Christ, xvi, xvii, 182
Reverence, 202, 205
Reverence attestations of, 61, 108–9, 144, 160, 201
Ritual, xxiii, 62, 69, 85, 95
Ritualism, 93
Rome, Roman Liturgy, 44, 51–54, 55, 59, 60, 65, 69–70, 84–89, 128–31, 138, 150, 163, 170–80, 183, 196–97
Romanticism, 91
Rubricism, 62, 89, 90, 94
Rubrics, xxiii, 62, 77, 85, 95, 103
Rupert of Deutz, 73

Sacramentality, xv–xvii, xxi, xxii, xxiii, xxvi, 3, 19, 40, 73, 114. *See also* Presence, sacramental
Sacramentaries, 59, 62, 161, 174. *See also* Libelli sacramentorum
Sacramentary, Gelasian, 59–60, 66, 77, 192
Sacramentary, Gregorian, 60, 67, 123
Sacramentary, Leonine (or of Verona), 59, 167
Sacraments, xxiii, xxiv, 11, 23, 84, 97, 113, 135
Sacred Heart devotion, 88
Sacrifice. *See* Eucharist as sacrifice
Sacrifice of expiation, xxi, 4, 6–11, 37, 176
Sacrifice, preparation for the, 109, 157–68. *See also* Gifts, preparation of
Sacristy, 105

Sailer, J. M., 92
Saints, feasts of; veneration of, 60, 73, 81, 86, 88, 138
Saints, lists of in Eucharistic Prayer, 173, 176, 177, 181, 182
Salvific will of God, 51, 96, 187
Sancta, 196
Sanctuary, choir, 47, 71, 88, 105
Sanctus, 53, 61, 169, 171, 172, 179–80, 185, 186, 188
Saving action of God, xvi, 94, 131, 142, 156, 178, 186
Schola, xxv, 34, 61, 77, 92, 107, 120, 123, 125, 142, 165
Schott, A., 172
Screen, 71, 88
Scripture, private reading of, xviii
Schürmann, H., 11, 12
Secret. *See* Gifts, prayer over
Self-blessing, 113
Self-giving, 157, 166, 167. *See also* Gifts, preparation of; Sacrifice, preparation for the
Sequence, 86, 143
Sergius I, Pope, 198
Servant of God, 8–10
Servers, xxv, 71, 74, 76, 87, 105, 147, 195
Service, Caritas, xvii, 36, 157
Service, Service of world, xvii
Service, readiness for, 20
Showing of Eucharistic gifts, 199
Sign, xiv–xv, xxiii–xxiv, 17, 19, 93, 97, 113, 195
Sins, confession of, 78, 116, 117, 129. *See also* Confiteor
Sins, forgiveness of, 8, 119–20, 147, 156
Sicard of Cremona, 73
Silence, 34, 108, 117, 129–30, 142, 167, 198, 205–6
Singing, 30, 31, 34, 41, 61, 68, 75, 77, 88, 91, 106–8, 171. *See also* Chant, Gregorian; Hymn
Sitting, 141
Sociology of worship, 58
Solesmes, 91
Sövik, E. A., 220
Spontaneity, xix, 43, 90
Standing, 30, 146. *See also* Bodily posture in prayer
Stational liturgies, 86